TO: MARK   Best wishes

2017

The Illustrated
DELAWARE
RIVER

The History of a Great American River

Hal Taylor

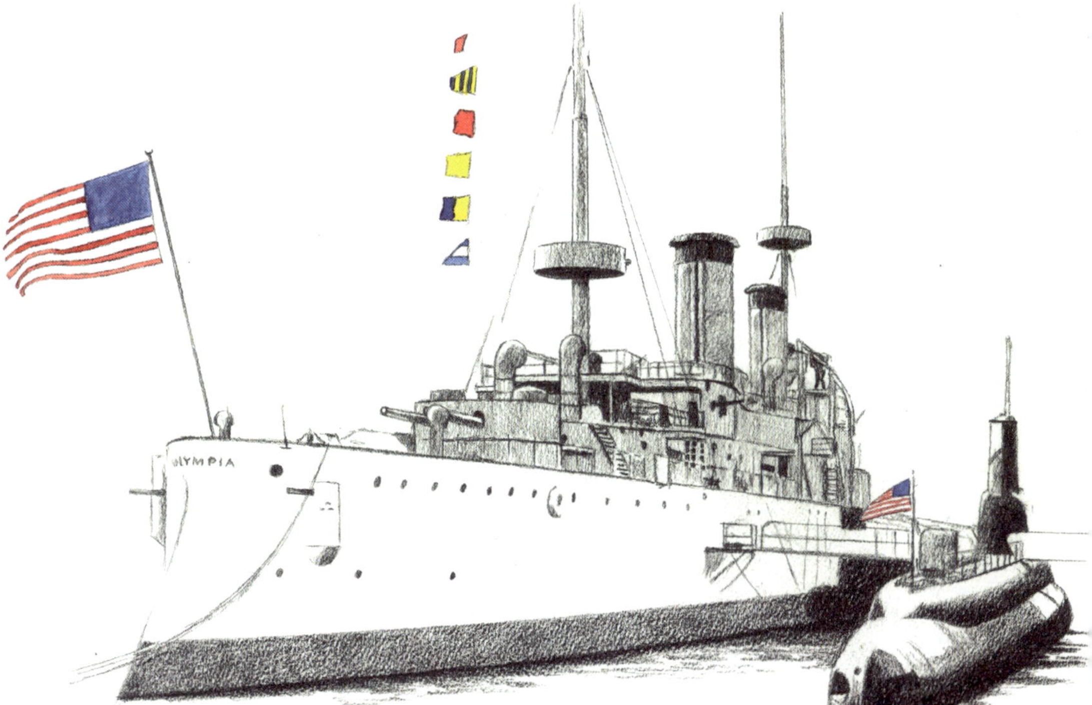

4880 Lower Valley Road • Atglen, PA 19310

Other Schiffer Books on Related Subjects:

A Tale of Two Rivers, Ronald F. Lasko, 978-0-7643-4440-4

My Virginia Rivers, Will Daniel, 978-0-7643-4325-4

Copyright © 2015 by Hal Taylor

Library of Congress Control Number: 2015946027

All rights reserved. No part of this work may be reproduced or used in any form or by any means—graphic, electronic, or mechanical, including photocopying or information storage and retrieval systems—without written permission from the publisher.

The scanning, uploading, and distribution of this book or any part thereof via the Internet or via any other means without the permission of the publisher is illegal and punishable by law. Please purchase only authorized editions and do not participate in or encourage the electronic piracy of copyrighted materials.
"Schiffer," "Schiffer Publishing, Ltd. & Design," and the "Design of pen and inkwell" are registered trademarks of Schiffer Publishing, Ltd.

Cover designed by Brenda McCallum
Type set in Minion Pro

ISBN: 978-0-7643-4932-4
Printed in China

Published by Schiffer Publishing, Ltd.
4880 Lower Valley Road
Atglen, PA 19310
Phone: (610) 593-1777; Fax: (610) 593-2002
E-mail: Info@schifferbooks.com

For our complete selection of fine books on this and related subjects, please visit our website at www.schifferbooks.com. You may also write for a free catalog.

This book may be purchased from the publisher. Please try your bookstore first.

We are always looking for people to write books on new and related subjects. If you have an idea for a book, please contact us at proposals@schifferbooks.com.

Schiffer Publishing's titles are available at special discounts for bulk purchases for sales promotions or premiums. Special editions, including personalized covers, corporate imprints, and excerpts can be created in large quantities for special needs. For more information, contact the publisher.

Contents

Preface 4
Acknowledgments 6
Introduction 7

Chapters
1. Roots 9
2. The Valley of the Swans 17
3. The Jersey Cape 23
4. Consider the Oyster 32
5. We'll Leave the Light on
   For You 38
6. Fortescue 50
7. The Green Mile 57
8. The War of the Forts 67
9. Greenwich 75
10. Salem 84
11. Rat Call 93
12. Fort Mott 99
13. Finn's Point 105
14. New Castle 110
15. Wilmington 115
16. Mercer & Mifflin 124
17. Camden 131
18. Penn 141
19. Brotherly Love 149
20. Burlington 161
21. The Bend in the River 171
22. The Crossing 179
23. The Canals 189
24. Fish & Floods 198
25. The Windmills of
    Your Mind 207
26. The Forks 213
27. The Gap 221
28. The Dammed 229
29. Tri-States 235
30. The Source 245

Notes 255
Bibliography 270
Index 272

Preface

In the 1980s, my wife and I rented a little house on the Delaware Bay in Southern New Jersey, in a little community called Gandy's Beach. It was a shack, and living there was a lot like camping at the beach. The plumbing was unreliable, as were the few appliances, and there was always sand on the floor. We cleaned crabs in the living room.

We used it on weekends and any other time my wife and I could get a few days off from work. The community was so friendly and safe that we could turn the kids out to play in the morning—as my mother used to say, "Go out and get the stink blown off ya." They would collect shells and driftwood, flip over stranded horseshoe crabs, examine local wildlife, get invited into Painter John's or Fisherman Joe's for popsicles and ice cream, or wind up going for a joyride in someone's boat. They loved every minute of it.

I worked as a freelance graphic artist and couldn't take a normal vacation, but I did have a flexible schedule, so I got down there as often as I could. I would travel to Florence, New Jersey, to pick up assignments, drive to my home studio, work for a couple of days, then head back to Florence to drop off the finished products. Florence is an old river town near Trenton, and there was a small public park at the river's edge. I would think, "This is the same water that makes its way down to the bay, lapping the shoreline at Gandy's Beach." As soon as I could, I would do the same thing, following the the river down to the beach house.

The river has always symbolized travel. And I'm not too stationary, either. I would often explore the back roads of Cumberland and Salem Counties on the way to Gandy's. Back then it truly was "the sticks." The area supports many small farms, and many tiny roadside stands offered just-picked veggies, fruit, and flowers. This downright cheap produce was paid for using an honor box—usually an old jar or coffee can. Life proceeded at a very slow pace, like how I imagined the rural South. Except this was South Jersey (much of which is, however, below the Mason-Dixon Line).

One of my favorite spots to visit was the old fishing village of Bivalve, a conglomeration of decay clinging to the banks of the Maurice River, once the epicenter of the Delaware Bay oyster industry. I found the decrepit buildings and old boats and rusting machinery a bit sad and lonesome—and completely fascinating.

My travels took me farther and farther from Gandy's Beach but always hugged the bay as I looked for history and forgotten treasures. Another hidden

Preface

gem was the Greenwich Boat Works, where a yard of ancient abandoned fishing boats sat rotting, propped up by cut-off pilings; a ghost fleet waiting for non-existent buyers. Many of them were oyster boats built during the salad days of the late nineteenth and twentieth centuries. Hard-worked vessels, many showed years of patching with mismatched wood planking or metal sheeting hammered on the hulls in an attempt to coax out another season of oystering. Some were beyond repair, pocked with gaping holes and sagging keels. New oyster boats are not built here anymore.

We eventually lost the Gandy's house when the owners decided to sell and a bidding war ensued that we could not compete in. But it was just as well, as the kids were growing older and their love affair with the beach was fading.

I kept exploring, though. The farther I traveled, the more absorbed I became in the river's history. It seemed every back road I traveled, every corner I turned, some morsel of the past would reluctantly call attention to itself. Like a long abandoned lighthouse or a remote road that abruptly ended at Finn's Point National Cemetery, where Confederate prisoners captured at the battle of Gettysburg are buried. And though I had lived in Southern New Jersey my entire life, I never had a clue that it had once been part of Nieu Nederland, the Dutch claim to North America. I found a large rock on the lawn of a school in Elsinboro Township inscribed with a dedication to Swedish soldiers who had manned a nearby fort over 350 years ago. I also learned much more about the American Revolution and its causes than I ever had in school.

I would share my meanderings with friends and acquaintances, a few of whom would raise a smug eyebrow and say, "Huh, you didn't know about that?" But many others had never heard of the discoveries I described. I began to think that I should share my enthusiasm with like-minded folks and others who had never considered their local history—before much of it disappears.

And so this book emerged. A historical travelogue, it starts not where the river begins physically, but at its end. It is not meant to be a definitive history of the river and its people, but a primer—a starting point from which to begin your own exploration. It'll keep you busy for quite a while.

I added illustrations to help readers envision the people, objects, places, and events, and to nudge the narrative along. In addition to my own drawings, the book features artwork by Brother E. Clayton West, who introduced us to Gandy's Beach, and David M. Boone, the premier marine artist of the Delaware River.

Acknowledgments

Many thanks to Sharon Vinz of The Library Company of Burlington; Prof. Robert Nichols of Richard Stockton University; Skylar Harris of the New Jersey Historical Commission; Robert Rando; marine artist extraordinaire David M. Boone; Brother E. Clayton West; John Gilligan; Rachel Cobb; Julita and Janeen at Copy Plus; my good friend Rick, who is always up for a road trip; our Angel of Mercy Ally, and friends who helped me in ways they don't even realize.

To my wife Chris, who has been my patron,
business manager, drinking buddy,
financier, worthy adversary, and best friend.

Introduction

I was born in a city on the Delaware River in New Jersey. Originally known as Cooper's Landing, it is now called Camden. Cooper Hospital is where the event took place, where I was delivered by Dr. Cooper. The hospital is not far from the Cooper River, which empties into the Delaware.

Hessian soldiers landed there in 1777 from across the Delaware in Philadelphia, marched to Haddonfield, and headed down The King's Highway. They were on their way to attack rebel forces at Fort Mercer where they were soundly defeated. The fort was on the property of James and Ann Whitall—a 400-acre farm called Red Bank. Ann became known as the "Heroine of Red Bank" for caring for the wounded soldiers. Her maiden name was Cooper. Her brother, John Cooper, served in the Continental Congress of 1776.

Walt Whitman lived the later years of his life in Camden, where he finished his final edition of *Leaves of Grass*—just a few blocks from the street called Cooper.

The Illustrated Delaware River

The Delaware River Watershed

1
Roots

Occasionally, on weekend mornings, I like to jump in my car and head out on the road. I work at home and may never leave my house for weeks at a time except for errands. Usually I have no idea where I'm going, but more often than not I wind up somewhere along the Delaware River. My good friend Rick says I'm one of those people who can enjoy going for a long ride to a place that has absolutely nothing. Rick never leaves his house, either, but he's happy with that.

THERE'S SOMETHING about a large body of water that stirs me, and probably most people, especially if there's some ship traffic. I wonder where the vessels are going and where they've been. The water stirs the same curiosity. There's a history to the river.

In 1624, Captain Cornelius Jacobsen Mey sailed the *Nieu Nederlandt* seventy-five miles up the Delaware River and landed several families and single men on Matennecunk Island, in the middle of the river. (It is now known as Burlington Island, owned by the city of Burlington, New Jersey). These were the first Europeans to settle in what would become New Jersey. They were Walloons, French-speaking people from the future country of Belgium. They were enticed by the Dutch West India Company to participate in establishing a permanent colony in the New World in exchange for land. In their wake would come Dutch, African slaves, Germans, free blacks, Swedes, Finns, English Quakers, Irish, Scots, Welsh, West Indians, Italians—they all arrived via the great highway that is the Delaware River.

The American colonies declared their independence from Britain near its banks, and it was crossed and re-crossed many times by troops in the war that followed, including Washington's famous campaign on a snowy December night in 1776. The first brick house in the US was built near its banks, as was the first log cabin and the first public school in the American

Colonies. The *American Weekly Mercury*, the first newspaper in the Middle Colonies, was published along the river. The first successful trial run of a steamboat took place on its waters in 1787. And Lena Blackburne Baseball Rubbing Mud, collected from a secret location along its banks, is used to rough up baseballs for the Major and Minor Leagues.

Born as run-off from the receding Wisconsin Glacier 10,000–15,000 years ago, the Delaware rises from the western slopes of the Catskill Mountains. Its headwaters are actually two branches, the East Delaware and West Delaware, that converge in eastern New York State and become a natural boundary between New York, Pennsylvania, New Jersey, and Delaware over a run of more than 330 miles.

The river has always been a highway. The Indians plied it for centuries in dugout canoes; the early Dutch explorers felt right at home on it. They came from a water-bound country. They knew how it behaved and exactly what to look for. It was much more comfortable for them to take a long voyage by boat than to trek overland to the same location, a much shorter but more dangerous trip through virgin forests teeming with wild animals, occasional hostile natives, insects, and poisonous plants. But sail power had its hazards too: the river and bay are littered with wrecks. As more towns and industries developed along the Delaware, the traffic increased with imports, exports, immigrants, and eventually pleasure travelers. Sail gave way to steam power, and steam to diesel. Ships no longer had to wait for tides, currents, or weather conditions, and traffic increased even more. Eventually, trains, trucks, and aircraft took over much of the work of the water. To this day, major and minor roadways continue to follow the course of the river, laid down decades ago to provide access to the towns and cities that sprang up along its banks. Despite ground and air transport, heavy maritime traffic continues on the Delaware—it is one of the busiest waterways in the US, second only to the Mississippi—and the longest un-dammed river east of the Mississippi. Any day of the week, you can stand along its banks and watch oil tankers, barges pushed by tugboats, barges pulled by tugboats, and of course the ubiquitous container ships carrying God knows what to who knows where.

The river takes its name from English nobleman Thomas West, the Third (or Twelfth, if you're able to decipher the mysterious British titling system) Baron

Eagle Point Tug. Courtesy of David M. Boone, www.tugboatpainter.net

De La Warr (or Warre), who sailed for Queen, country, and the London Virginia Company to North America and landed in the Virginia colonies on June 10, 1610 (my birthday, although not that year). He had been petitioned to persuade the Jamestown settlers not to give up on their nearly disastrous attempts to establish a colony and go home to England. The colonists had arrived in the middle of a drought in 1607 and were ill-equipped to live in a land that could be abundant in good times but completely wretched in bad times. Even the native Powhatan called it "the starving time." These settlers were businessmen and English dandies who naively expected to step off their ship and literally find gold and other valuables waiting for them. Almost none of them possessed adequate survival skills, and as a result, one in five died.

Help was on the way, however, in the person of Captain Samuel Argall, an English explorer and adventurer who had been appointed to find a northerly route to the New World to avoid harassment from the Spanish—which he did. Until this time, the customary route was to sail south toward

the Caribbean, and then catch the trade winds to the coast of North America. When he arrived at Jamestown, Argall unloaded his life-saving cargo of supplies and was soon ordered to head out for more. On the way, however, he was blown off course in a storm and found himself in a very large bay, unaware that Henry Hudson had been there a year before, almost to the day. Where Hudson had not given any name to the bay, Argall took the opportunity to name it in honor of his employer, the Baron De La Warr.

Upon arrival, West immediately initiated the first Anglo-Powhatan War, raiding villages, burning cornfields, and stealing provisions, and for his accomplishments, he was appointed governor-for-life. Leaving his deputy Samuel Argall in charge, he returned to England to write humbly about his experiences: "The Relation of the Right Honourable the Lord De-La-Warre, of the Colonie, Planted in Virginia." To investigate charges that Argall was becoming a bit of a tyrant, he set sail for Virginia again in 1618, but died en route and was supposedly buried in the Azores. So the entire river, state, valley, and any number of other entities have been named for Thomas West, Baron De La Warr, even though he probably never saw any of it. Even the natives were called the Delaware, although they called themselves by their own name—Lenni Lenape, which means original people. They had lived in the area for thousands of years, nearly as long as the river itself, which they called Lenape Wihittuck— Rapid Stream of the Lenape.

They were part of the larger Algonquian nation, divided into three main groups: the Munsi (People of the Stony Country) in the north, Unami (People Down River) in the central regions, and Unilachtigo (People Who Live Near the Ocean) of the southern and coastal regions. It was an area roughly the equivalent of the Delaware River watershed itself. There were even more sub-tribes, some of which we'll meet later. The more aggressive Iriquois tauntingly referred to the Lenape as "old women" because of their generally peaceful demeanor and their willingness to act as arbitrators between warring tribes. Their lifestyle was also based on agriculture, particularly in the southern regions where they grew beans, maize, and squash.

The Lenni Lenape's first known encounter with Europeans occurred in 1524, when they met Italian navigator Giovanni da Verrazano, who was exploring the New Jersey coastline. He described the natives in glowing terms as being "most beautiful and having the most civil customs." Strangely, Verrazano somehow missed finding the Delaware Bay. But Henry Hudson did not. An English navigator and explorer hired by the Dutch, Hudson entered the bay in 1609 on his ship, *Half Moon*, while searching for the ever-elusive Northwest Passage, spent the night, and announced this was not it.

The Lenape next met explorers and traders from the Netherlands who named the Delaware the Zuydt (South) River, in contrast to the Noort (North) River, which eventually became the illustrious Hudson.

The Dutch were followed by the Swedes and Finns and then English Quakers, who negotiated treaties through William Penn, founder of Pennsylvania. One of the most important treaties was agreed upon in the little village of Shackamaxon (now known as Fishtown) along the banks of the Delaware in 1682, and signed by Penn and the Lenape chief Tamamend ("The Affable"). It promised that the two peoples would "live in love as long as the sun gave light." The event has become cultural legend thanks to paintings by Benjamin West, Quaker artist Edward Hicks (famously renowned for producing his composition *The Peaceable Kingdom* sixty-one times), and other painters throughout Europe, as well as a reference by Voltaire. But the attempt at peaceful coexistence didn't last long. In 1737, Penn's sons, John and Thomas, perpetrated one of the earliest land swindles in the country by producing a bogus document called the Walking Purchase. It was an incomplete, unsigned draft of a deed in which the Lenape reportedly promised to sell a tract of land beginning at the junction of the Delaware and Lehigh Rivers and extending as far west as a man could walk in a day and a half. Unknown to the Lenape, the Penns took great care to hack clear paths through the forests and then hired the three fastest runners in the colonies to traverse the paths as far as they could go in the time allotted. The result was that the Lenape lost a parcel of land roughly the size of Rhode Island: 1,220 square miles. They complained bitterly to the King of England, but it fell on deaf ears. Normally a peaceful people, the Lenape violently tried to reclaim their lands with encouragement from the French during the French and Indian Wars. The hostilities continued through the Revolutionary War, but by the late 1700s, they had been pushed out of the Delaware Valley.

In 1853 a tribal representative lamented: "We are driven back until we can retreat no further. Our hatchets are broken. Our bows are snapped. Our fires are nearly gone out. A little longer and the white man will cease to pursue us for we shall cease to exist."

From a population of approximately 20,000 in 1600, their numbers had dwindled to around 4,000 by 1700. Over the next several hundred years, the Lenape were forced ever westward through West Virginia, Ohio, Indiana, Ontario, Michigan, Missouri, Arkansas, Louisiana, Texas, Wisconsin, Kansas, and finally onto a reservation in Oklahoma where their current population has recovered to about 16,000.

Their lyrical language remains throughout the Delaware Valley, giving us place names such as Allegheny, Lehigh, Kittatinny, Lackawanna, Navasink, Pocono, Manayunk, Wissahickon, and of course Mauch Chunk.

A mind-bogglingly immense display of objects and artifacts created or used by the Lenape, including arrow- and spearheads, pottery, tools, and clothing can be seen at the Cumberland County Prehistorical Museum in Greenwich, New Jersey: http://www.cchistsoc.org/prehistorical-museum.html.

THE ILLUSTRATED DELAWARE RIVER

The Zwaanendael Museum

2

The Valley of the Swans

The mouth of the Delaware Bay, as seen on a map, looks like the profile of a large extinct fish with big teeth—or maybe a snapping turtle. The teeth are two capes—Cape May to the north with the big overbite, and Cape Henlopen to the south with the undersized mandible. This lower jaw was the site of one of the first European colonies in America.

Lewes, Delaware, proudly calls itself "the first town in the first state." But its first European name was Zwaanendael—Dutch for the Valley of the Swans.

In 1629, agents of the Dutch West India Company arrived at Cape Henlopen to "purchase" land from the local Indians for Samuel Godyn, a wealthy merchant who had been awarded rights for settlement. (An early Dutch map labels the Delaware Bay as Godyn's Bay). He arranged for "patroons," people who would be given various amounts of land in exchange for investments. (A prime result of this system was Rensselaerswyck Manor on the Hudson River in New York State. Though established by Kiliaen van Rensselaer, he never set foot on the property, which eventually became Albany). Godyn also enlisted David Pietersz de Vries to be the general administrator, who in turn hired Peter Heyes as a ship captain, and Gillis Hossitt to be in command of the settlement.

From the town of Hoorn in the Netherlands, the expedition arrived to set up shop on the banks of Blommaert's Kill (Lewes Creek) near Cape Henlopen in spring 1631. Their ship was called the *Walvis* (Whale), which was appropriate since one of their quests was to establish a whaling station. They were also to take up trade with the Indians, farm tobacco and grains, and in general look for any opportunities the land and sea would provide to establish a physical claim to the land. They built fortifications and sowed seeds, and by July had crops growing. They were even able to construct a house from bricks that were part of the *Walvis* cargo. This was all brought about at the behest of the Dutch West India Company, whose name you'll hear frequently throughout this book. The Dutch were the premier entrepreneurs of seventeenth-century Europe, and the New World was where they invested much of their expertise and efforts, especially the region they christened New Netherland. Its boundaries were the body of water they called the South River (the Delaware) and the Connecticut River in the north with vast areas of what was to become New York, New Jersey, Pennsylvania, and Delaware in between.

Detained in Holland during this first expedition, within a year, de Vries received the disturbing news that all the members of the new colony, "two and thirty men," had been massacred and all their buildings and defenses burned to the ground. In December 1632, de Vries sailed into the South River with a new group of colonists and supplies to discover for himself what had happened. After surveying the carnage, he was able to communicate with the local Siconese Indian tribe and found that a dispute had occurred over the theft of a tin Dutch coat of arms that had been placed on a pole. The thief, an Indian chief who was fascinated by the tin, stole the piece with the intention of making pipes from it. He was killed by his own people, who then returned with his severed head to the colonists to let them know that justice had been served. But, perhaps from a lack of communication or a clash of cultures, the Dutch improperly intoned, "Well you didn't have to kill him! We just wanted to tell him not to do it again!" This didn't sit well with the Indians, who felt their intentions had been insulted. The Indians exacted a disproportionate revenge. They came back to Zwaanendael with furs for bartering, which turned out to be a ruse. They killed the trader who was stationed in their lone building and a worker who was lying ill, and put twenty-five arrows into a mastif guard dog whom they had long feared. They then surprised the rest of the men who were working in the fields, slaughtering every one.

There was not much de Vries could do about it; the local tribes were scattered widely and he was vastly undermanned. After a long, unsuccessful trip up the Delaware to replenish dwindling food supplies, de Vries returned to the colonists he had left behind at the abandoned village. He then set sail for the Virginia colonies and returned with enough supplies for the voyage back to Holland. It would have been foolish to try to recolonize Zwannendael, especially since investors would have been wary after such a disastrous beginning. The project was abandoned and was not revisited for many years.

The Dutch returned to the region in the 1650s to reestablish trade with the Indians, this time creating a permanent settlement renamed Hoerenkill. In 1663 they were joined by a Mennonite contigent, also from Holland. But misfortune lingered like a thick fog. In 1664, the English took control of New Netherland, and once again, the Dutch lost their colonial foothold on the Delaware. As if not enough abuse had been heaped on them, Lord Baltimore's soldiers raided the village in 1673. Baltimore claimed that the territory was part of Maryland. William Penn then arrived in 1682 and further complicated the issue, arguing that this same real estate was part of the Pennsylvania territory that had been given to him by Charles II. It was not until both Baltimore and Penn were long gone that the matter was finally settled by surveyors Charles Mason and Jeremiah Dixon.

IN THE MEANTIME, Penn renamed the village Lewes and the county Sussex, after their respective counterparts in England. But the abuse continued. Unwanted visits from pirates in 1690 and 1698 forced the passage of a law requiring Lewes citizens to own a musket and ammunition for protection. There were also continued raids by privateers, and bombardment by British warships during the War of 1812, which resulted in the death of a chicken and a pig having its leg broken. And, of course, Lewes is included in umpteen different East Coast locations where Captain Kidd reportedly buried treasure.

Despite its inauspicious beginnings and continued woes, Lewes was able to rely on the sea for much of its subsistence. Menhaden, an extremely oily fish, was not fit for consumption but had a variety of other uses, such as fertilizer, which the Native Americans used for years before the Europeans arrived. Colonial settlers used its oil to fuel lamps. Starting in the twentieth century, Lewes built menhaden processing plants, and by the 1930s the Consolidated Fisheries Company had the largest facility in the country. Menhaden was also used in paint production and animal feed. The aroma, a by-product of the processing, made the locals joke that it "smelled like money." But by the 1960s, the area had become

Menhaden, known locally as Bunker

overfished and the boom times were over. With the more recent discovery of the health benefits of Omega-3 fatty acids, menhaden has become sought-after again, though not in Lewes. Some menhaden is still fished locally, however, as bait for commercial crabbers.

Lewes is still an East Coast port of call with an excellent harbor sheltering a large recreational and commercial fishing fleet.

The Dutch Colonial period is remembered fondly in the town of Lewes. Its centerpiece is the Zwaanendael Museum (http://history.delaware.gov/museums/zm/zm_main.shtml), an ornate, faithfully reconstructed replica of the town hall of Hoorn, Holland. Built in 1931 to commemorate the 300th anniversary of the original colony, it contains many artifacts, mostly of the nautical variety gathered from local shipwrecks. One of the finest exhibits anywhere features His Majesty's sloop of war *DeBraak*, an eighteenth-century British warship raised from the Delaware Bay in 1986. It is the only ship of its type recovered anywhere in the world. The copper-sheathed hull of the ship, or what remains of it, is in nearby Cape Henlopen State Park awaiting permanent preservation, but many of it's original contents are on display in the museum. Built in Holland in 1795, the *DeBraak* found it's way into the British Navy, where it was re-fitted to their needs. It found it's way to the bottom of the Delaware Bay in 1798 when a sudden storm slammed the ship onto its side, taking forty-seven men down with it.

The British tried for months to raise the ship, but it stayed put for the next 186 years until a salvage company using side-scanning sonar located the wreck and began bringing up an amazing collection of artifacts. There were the usual cannons and ammunition, muskets, and other weaponry, but also more mundane objects that provide an unusual glimpse into everyday ship-board life in the eighteenth century: toothbrushes, footwear, pottery, a wool hat, and even a bottle bearing the title "ketchup." So remarkable is the collection that movie director Peter Weir studied it to achieve authenticity for his 2003 movie *Master and Commander*.

Despite all this priceless history, what really excites visitors from local schools is enclosed in a glass case on the second floor of the museum—the famous Fiji Mermaid, a copy of the bogus creature that P. T. Barnum shamelessly exhibited in New York City in the 1840s. Described as the preserved corpse of a mermaid caught in the South Pacific, it's the hideous, withered little head and body of a monkey with a vaguely fish-like tail. The children love it.

Lewes is well-known today as the southern terminal of the Cape May–Lewes Ferry, which saves travelers heading north or south along the coast a ton of time. The closest alternate crossing of the Delaware River is nearly eighty miles to the north at the Delaware Memorial Bridge. The ferry cruise is especially pleasant in the summer months when dolphins are often spotted swimming and feeding in the bay. The ferry carries many walk-on passengers who travel just for the sheer joy of a boat ride. But not many passengers pause to explore Lewes; most are on their way to southern beaches and the Chesapeake Bay, which is unfortunate since Lewes is a beautiful old town, full of history and recreational activities. I'm betting, though, that a lot of residents and visitors prefer it that way—especially the Delaware River pilots, some of whom live in Lewes.

These are people whose families have made their living on the river for generations. It is the pilots' job to guide commercial vessels over 100 feet long up and down the shipping channel to ports along the river from the Atlantic Ocean all the way north to Trenton. They also board outgoing ships from Philadelphia, Camden, Wilmington, and Delaware City and are responsible for leading ships in and out of the eastern portion of the Chesapeake and Delaware Canal. The Delaware Bay and River Pilots

A Delaware Bay Pilot Boat

Association is based at the ferry terminal at Lewes. From there, the pilots board launch boats and are shuttled out to waiting incoming ships. They'll then climb a thirty-foot, perpetually wet rope ladder, sometimes in nasty weather and almost always at night, and make their way to the bridge, where they'll take over the helm to guide the ship upstream for the next six to nine hours. The pilots usually average two ships on round trips each week, spending about fifty hours on the job.

The job requires extensive training and apprenticeship, and the final exam is little changed from Mark Twain's days as a river pilot. On a blank piece of paper they must draw the river from Cape May to Trenton to scale from memory, including every lighthouse, buoy, bridge, pipeline, wreck, shoreline, and depth marker.

So the next time you take the ferry, leave some time to explore Lewes. Park your car; it's a great walking town. Or just park yourself on a bench and take in a breath of historic air.

3
THE JERSEY CAPE

On the day that Henry Hudson eased his ship *Halve Maen* (Half Moon) gingerly into the shoal-strewn Delaware Bay in 1609, he could not have dreamed he was sailing past what would one day become one of the premier vacation resorts on the Atlantic Seaboard. Playboys and presidents would relax and spend oodles of money in refined elegance. It would become one of the greatest collections of Victorian architecture in the country, earning National Historic Landmark status.

Hudson, an English navigator and explorer, was not concerned with the possibilities of land development. He had convinced the Dutch East India Company that he could find a passage to the Orient that would ensure a direct and lucrative trade route to the spice islands.

This would happen over and over again during the next 300 years, with many failed expeditions and many lives lost trying to locate an elusive "Northwest passage." Hudson himself would eventually become one of the casualties on a later expedition when his crew mutinied and set him adrift in what would become known as Hudson's Bay. Roald Amundsen discovered a northern route to the Pacific Ocean in 1906, but it proved impractical for commercial navigation.

The directors of the VOC (de Verenigde Oostindische Compagnie) had ordered Hudson to find a northeastern route, but Hudson ignored them, setting a course for Newfoundland. He hugged the coast southward as far as the Chesapeake Bay, then abruptly turned around and headed north, concerned that the English at the Jamestown colony might not appreciate an exploratory visit on the part of the Dutch. August 28, 1609, found Hudson in the mouth of the Delaware Bay, where he spent the night grounded on a sandbar. The next morning, a nasty storm blew in and battered the *Half Moon*, but also dragged it from the sand and back out toward the Atlantic. Convinced that this could not be the elusive route to Cathay, Hudson continued north. Hugging the coast again, he came to another large bay that also proved a false passage across the continent. It would eventually become known as New York Harbor.

Almost on the heels of Hudson's departure, another English navigator, Samuel Argall, stopped by the bay for a brief visit. He was actually on a foraging expedition for the starving Jamestown colonists. Believing he was at the northern edge of the English-invested Virginia territory, he named the bay and river for his superior—Thomas West, Baron De La Warre, the new governor of Virginia. But the name was not to stick—just yet.

Six years later, another European navigator, a Dutchman, entered the Delaware Bay, this time with the intent of surveying the area and establishing trade with the Indians. He was employed by the New Netherland Company, which in turn was under control of the Dutch West India Company (not to be confused with the VOC). His name was Cornelius Jacobsen Mey. The area appealed to Mey, reminding him of Holland. He named the northern cape of the bay Mey and the southern cape after Hindloopen in his native land. Mey would later bring the first immigrant families to what would become New Amsterdam, and for about a year he was its director. His name was eventually anglicized and it is because of him that we now have Cape May, Cape May County, Cape May Point, Cape May Court House, and so on.

THE UNIVERSAL appeal of sun, sand, and surf was not lost on the first vacationers to the Jersey Cape: the Tuckahoe and Kechemeche tribes of the Lenni Lenape nation who spent summers hunting and fishing—and got there without using the Garden State Parkway. They walked, of course, creating their own paths, some of which eventually became modern roads that are still used—and used extensively, as any weekender can tell you. Route 618, also called Indian Trail Road, was once known as the King Nummy Trail after a legendary local chieftain.

The Indians lived on the cape during the summer growing season. The women cultivated beans, squash, and corn, and the men brought home deer and small game and fish, clams, oysters, and mussels that could be harvested with relative ease along the shorelines. Most would consider it a primitive but idyllic life, and no doubt it was, for many began to live there permanently. Gradually, however, the Indians began to get visitors, much like a modern beach house owner who soon discovers many more friends than he knew he had.

The Dutch had big plans for the shores of the Delaware: a colony at Cape Henlopen, fortified outposts for trading with the Indians at Burlington Island far up-river, Fort Nassau in present-day Gloucester, and a proposed whaling station for Cape May. Peter Minuit, the director-general of the New Netherland colony, ordered the purchase of land for the station to be built on the cape, thus creating the first patent for European property ownership on Cape May. The Indians were taken aback by the action, as no one had ever bought land from them before. To them it meant nothing more than an agreement to share the land in exchange for some useful household items. The tract of land amounted to about sixteen square miles. But the whaling factory never materialized along with the dreams of a Dutch colonial empire in North America. The West India Company became disorganized, Charles II was restored to the throne of England, and in 1664 the British quietly but firmly seized control of New Netherland.

NOT MUCH is known about European settlement on the cape in the first half of the seventeenth century. There is mention of a group of New Haven Puritans in the 1640s who made their way down-river from temporary settlements at Varken's Kill near Salem, but no physical evidence exists. Sometime in the 1680s, settlers began to arrive from the New England colonies with the intent of establishing a whaling industry. (It's been said that there are more Mayflower descendants in Cape May than anywhere else except Plymouth.) The idea of whaling off the coast of New Jersey may seem far-fetched today. However, whales were much more prevalent in the seventeenth century. Instead of the New England style of whaling in ships, the Cape May fishermen waited for the whales to come to them. Lookouts were posted on the shore, and when a spout was sighted, small boats were launched through the surf. With a great deal of effort and even more luck, a whale would be harpooned and towed back to shore to be processed—a dangerous job, but the rewards seemed to outweigh the hazards. Whaling off Cape May continued for many years, but eventually the whale population was depleted or moved to safer waters, and the colonists turned to farming, fishing, shipbuilding, and other means of livelihood.

During the American Revolution, Cape May County became a base of operations for privateers. They were ship owners who had permission from the Continental Congress to plunder British shipping, and they became so good at it that raiding was a major enterprise during the war. The Cape May sea captains even formed partnerships with major Philadelphia merchant houses whose profits would help finance the fledgling county's war efforts.

It has been suggested that Cape May, originally known as Cape Island, was already becoming a haven for seashore visitors as early as 1766. But after the Revolution, with increased road construction and infrastructure, Cape May had clearly become a popular summer vacation spot, making it the oldest resort in the country. The owner of an unlicensed house of entertainment was indicted in 1799 for causing a public nuisance, a sure sign of vacation behavior.

A survivor of the 1878 fire, circa 1848

For the next fifty years, visitors from New Jersey, Pennsylvania, Delaware, Maryland, Virginia, and New York flooded the cape every year to escape the summer heat. A regular steamboat service developed between Philadelphia, Delaware, and Cape May in the 1820s. The voyage would take approximately six hours, during which the passengers would be entertained by a full orchestra. They would bring their meals packed in shoe boxes, prompting the term "shoebee," which came to mean anyone making a day trip to the shore. Construction workers were kept busy building hotels and rooming houses to accommodate the flood of vacationers, including the Mount Vernon, at its time the largest hotel in the world.

After many years of tangled New Jersey and regional politics, a rail line was built linking Cape May to Philadelphia, via Millville. And in August 1863, the first cars made the trip in three hours and thirty minutes. Previously, if a traveler chose to take an overland route to the resort, they could expect to spend at least two days in bone-jarring transit on bumpy and either muddy or dusty roads. The railroad also began to bring in VIPs, such as department store tycoon John Wanamaker. The new, moneyed visitors organized a yacht club in 1874, welcoming visiting President U. S. Grant. Cape May has hosted eleven presidents, including Franklin Pierce, Andrew Jackson, James Buchanan, Woodrow Wilson, Gerald Ford, and Ronald Reagan. William Henry Harrison made Congress Hall the Summer White House during 1882 and 1883 while John Philip Sousa and the Marine Corps Band performed on the hotel's lawn, inspiring Sousa to later pen the "Congress Hall March." Other politicians visited, too, such as former presidential candidate Henry Clay, who traveled from Kentucky for a look-see at Yankee "watering places" and was greeted by other distinguished guests, like Horace Greeley.

Congress Hall, originally constructed in 1816

But all this prosperity went up in smoke—literally. In 1878 the largest fire in Cape May

County history burned some forty acres, destroying many of the large hotels and numerous cottages, including Congress Hall. Fire-fighting equipment was shipped by rail from Camden, but it was a case of too little too late.

The property owners were resilient, however, and immediately began to rebuild. What rose from the ashes is now one of the most impressive collections of Victorian architecture in the country, second only to San Francisco. Ornate was the latest statement, prompting the name Painted Ladies to describe the array of new gingerbread-covered confections. Even Congress Hall was rebuilt, this time of brick. Speculators from Philadelphia and New York poured millions of dollars into the town. The Cape May Real Estate Company made this promise in 1903: "In full view of the ocean, within a few steps of its sand-tiled floor, on which sweep gentle billows and foam-capped breakers, and with invigorating or cooling breezes from the Mighty Deep—truly, here will care be banished and pleasure be unrestrained."

Many of these homes and hotels have been converted into lavish B&Bs, most of which still maintain authentic period furnishings. I'm partial to the Windward House on Jackson Street. Directly across the street is the Mad Batter, a restaurant dating back to "hippy days" when the menu was charmingly eclectic and the service was maddeningly inefficient. I visited recently and happily discovered that a confused waitstaff was still in place. There is no shortage of eateries in Cape May, and many are outstanding.

The seaside town turned out to be a strategic military location during both World Wars. The US Navy built two bases in Cape May during World War I and took over the Hotel Cape May to use as a hospital and training facility. During the next war, the Army Corps of Engineers built a canal across the entire cape to protect Delaware River shipping from the threat of U-Boat attacks. And on May 14, 1945, one of these German submarines was indeed sighted off Cape May. It was the U-858 surrendering to the US Navy. The war with Germany was over. The U-boat was taken to Fort Miles, Delaware; her crew was dispatched to Fort DuPont, Delaware, as POWs, and eventually shipped back to Germany. It was rumored that U-858 was one of six submarines carrying guided missiles to be launched against specific American cities. The alleged missiles were not on board, however, when she was surrendered.

An artillery bunker with two six-inch guns was installed near Cape May Point, along with two sister installations across the bay at Fort Miles. They were supported by fire control towers, which were used to spot targets. The bunker originally sat 900 feet from the ocean, but due to erosion is now directly on the beach. This immense pile of concrete sits on a jungle of wooden pilings, and no one knows when it will eventually collapse. The canal is still very much in use as part of the Intracoastal Waterway and also contains the northern terminal of the Cape May-Lewes Ferry near the bay end. After World War II, the Navy transferred ownership of its bases to the Coast Guard, which promptly enlarged them. There has been a Coast Guard presence in Cape May since 1924, when it was kept busy chasing rum runners during Prohibition. Today Cape May is the nation's only Coast Guard Recruit Training Center.

The Center is situated on Cape May Harbor, which is also home to a commercial fishing fleet, the second largest fishing port on the East Coast. Typically, the ships come in with hauls of scallops, squid, flounder, lobster, fluke, and round fish such as bluefish and weakfish. A large variety of this catch can be purchased at the Lobster House seafood store at Fisherman's Wharf, which at one time was known as Shellenger's Landing. It doesn't get much fresher. Such a romantic and picturesque experience—buying fish practically right off the boat—belies the reality that commercial fishing is one of the most hazardous professions in the world. A fishermen's memorial at the end of Missouri Avenue can attest to the mortalities: seventy-five names including the most recent victims who died in March of 2009 on the scallop boat *Lady Mary*. But for many, it's a family affair; saltwater runs through their veins.

At the tip of the Cape May peninsula, looking out over "the Ripps," where the Delaware Bay meets the Atlantic Ocean, is Sunset Beach, where a sharp eye might spot a "Cape May Diamond." These are translucent pebbles of pure quartz crystal washed down the Delaware and polished naturally over many years by sand and water turbulence. They were highly prized by the Kechemeche, who believed they possessed great power. The pebbles would be used as wampum and jewelry and given as gifts to their closest friends. These little gems can be purchased, but it's much more interesting and rewarding to find your own. They're free! Sunset beach

The concrete ship Atlantus before running aground in 1926

is also the landing site of the steamboats that brought vacationers to Cape Island in the early nineteenth century. And who can leave Cape May without taking a peak at the concrete ship *Atlantus*, broken in pieces and lying just off shore? You're probably thinking, "Concrete ship? Isn't that an oxymoron, like a lead balloon?" The ship was part of an experimental fleet built during World War I when steel was scarce. In service for just a few years, the *Atlantus* was retired to a salvage yard in Virginia. She was purchased in 1926 to be used as part of a dock for the proposed Cape May Ferry. That same year, she was towed to Cape May but ran aground when her moorings broke during a storm, and there she has lain ever since, gradually crumbling into the sea. The ferry would have to wait until 1964 to become a reality.

A little farther north from Sunset Beach, up Sunset Boulevard, is Cape May Point State Park and the Cape May Light House. It's also a prime gathering spot for watching migrating birds. It is said that over 45,000 raptors can be spotted during peak season, and the variety is astonishing. Northern harriers, bald eagles, American kestrels, sharp-shinned hawks, peregrine falcons, and more can be seen in the fall. There are even volunteer "spotters" stationed on the platforms. I visited unwittingly during one crisp autumn day, and though many bird people with telescopic lenses and binoculars were ooohing and aahing, I didn't see a damn thing. Trying to make amusing conversation, I asked one middle-aged woman in bird-watching gear if she had spotted any penguins. She fixed me in a raptor-like stare, as if I were potential prey.

Birders can be humorless people.

4
Consider the Oyster

The oyster is an interesting and delicious animal. A town in New Jersey is named after it: Bivalve—the epicenter of the world's oyster industry from the mid-nineteenth to the mid-twentieth centuries. It's situated at the mouth of the Maurice River, just a short ride across the marshes from Port Norris in Commercial Township. At it's peak, around 1930, the oyster crop of New Jersey was valued at $5 million annually, representing a catch of approximately 3,600,000 bushels, or roughly 400,000,000 individual shellfish. In 1886, eighty railroad cars of oysters were shipped daily from Bivalve. Delaware, too, had entire towns grow up around oystering: Bowers Beach, Leipsic, Little Creek. Port Norris could claim more millionaires per square mile than any other town in New Jersey. The industry provided employment for as many as 4,000 oystermen and related industries like shipping, ship building, sail making, blacksmithing, boat repair, and more.

Back then, oyster saloons were as plentiful as pizza shops, and much like today's food trucks, oyster sellers hawked their wares on the streets of Philadelphia, Trenton, and New York. The oysters were packed live in barrels of brine and shipped nationwide. Old oyster shell bits can still be found in Upperville, Virginia, and other Civil War battle sites where soldiers slurped down the bivalves between exchanges of gunfire. People would buy barrels for home consumption and keep the oysters alive by feeding them dried oatmeal. Eventually, shucked oysters were also available in cans, and with railroad service arriving, an even larger market was created. To make them even more enjoyable, the oyster cracker was introduced in 1847. Originally intended to be used in oyster stew, it became an essential condiment in seafood restaurants everywhere. Who hasn't slathered a big spoonful of horseradish on an oyster cracker, popped it in their mouth, and waited for the top of their head to explode? And judging from large piles of shells or middens left from pre-historic times, the indigenous people were enjoying the shellfish eons before any Europeans arrived.

The crustaceans were harvested almost daily by a huge fleet of sail-powered oyster schooners and sloops. Over 600 oyster boats were built between 1846 and 1930 in towns along the Delaware Bay, such as Bridgeton, Greenwich, Cedarville, Dividing Creek, Dorchester, Leesburg, and Mauricetown. Very few boats are left today, and those that are require a good deal of maintenance. Oystering was originally done by sail, but after World War II, dredging under mechanized power was allowed, so most of the oystermen cut their masts and installed engines. They're a leaky fleet, named after families that have lived in the region for many generations: Robbins, Lore, Sockwell, Reed, and many more. New Jersey's tall ship, the *A.J. Meerwald*, is named for one such family and was rescued from the mud through the efforts of Megan

Wren, a native of Money Island in Downe Township. Wren began the Delaware Bay Schooner Project in 1988 to restore the decrepit schooner. With the help of many volunteers, including boat builders forced to learn as they went along, the *Meerwald* (originally built in 1928) was relaunched in 1998. The Schooner Project is now the Bayshore Center at Bivalve and the *A. J. Meerwald* has become a floating classroom. Her home port is Bivalve, but she also docks in Cape May, Burlington, and occasionally in Philadelphia. Just about all crew and maintenance work is done by volunteers, and I'm proud to say I was one of them for a brief time. I toted equipment, filled oil jugs for the *Meerwald*'s engine, and painted the address of the organization's headquarters on fifty-gallon plastic trash cans. While I was there, the Bayshore Discovery Project had also acquired another old schooner named *Cashier* for $1. At the time, it was the oldest continuously used fishing boat in the world, dating to 1846. Its paint was an inch thick in some places. Sadly, the paint was the only thing holding the Cashier together. She is now slowly rotting in the mud at the restored wharves of Bivalve.

BIVALVE IS ALSO home to the Bivalve Packing Company, and it was there that I watched another local oyster schooner —the Ada C. Lore—being rebuilt practically from scratch using reclaimed lumber from an old New England barn. I would stop by the shipyard occasionally to check on the boat's progress, and I once had the opportunity to ask a few questions of the part-time boat builders. How did they know where to begin? What plans were they working from? They just chuckled and scratched their heads. They were honestly working from instinct, I believe. Of course, they had rudimentary boat-building and carpentry skills, but the real knowledge was in their blood.

The construction continued for several years, and finally one beautiful August day, it was ready for launch. Practically the whole town of Port Norris turned out for the spectacle; it was like a holiday, and it took all day. A large crane capable of lifting fifty tons was hired, along with a semi-trailer to haul the boat from its construction site to the nearby Port Norris Marina. There was one small problem, though. In ordering the trailer, someone had misplaced a zero and the trailer that arrived could haul only 10,000 pounds when a 100,000-pound trailer was needed. A heated discussion

The Ada C. Lore

ensued. The crane was already there, it would take another day to switch trailers, and they would have to pay another day's crane rental. Nobody was really sure how much the *Ada C. Lore* weighed, but an estimate came in at about 25,000 pounds. They finally decided to load her on the trailer and see what happened. These were either very stupid or very brave souls to risk several years' worth of work on someone's math error. But people who make a living on the water are used to risks. The crane was put into position, a huge harness was slung under the boat, and she was carefully lifted onto the waiting trailer and chocked and shimmed into place. The back of the trailer sank to about two inches from the ground and the rear tires were visibly splayed. But very slowly the *Ada C. Lore* started on her journey to the water. Everyone held their breath when a tight turn was negotiated, but the only mishaps were a telephone pole bent to a twenty-degree angle and a stop sign destroyed.

It was nearly twilight when the schooner arrived at her launch site, with the crane following and setting up at the new location. The boat was harnessed again, lifted off the trailer, and swung out over the water. In the best maritime tradition, the owner, who was by now nearly emotionally drained, smashed a bottle of cheap bubbly on her bow and she was lowered into the muddy Maurice River amid much celebration.

OYSTERS IN THE Delaware Bay estuary were concentrated in the upper and lower bay. Seed beds in the upper bay have a lower salinity level, causing the spats to grow more slowly. They were eventually transplanted to growing areas farther down the bay where oyster "farmers" distributed old oyster shells and other hard materials for the seed oysters to attach to and grow to market size. It was hard but profitable work, keeping a chain of people busy from sailors to shuckers. But with the newly allowed use of engine power after World War II, the oystermen became a little too successful, and production began to fail. Then in 1957, disaster struck.

The oysters were dying. Within two years production dropped by ninety to ninety-five percent. Dr. L.A. Stauber of Rutgers University discovered the cause: MSX (multinucleated sphere X), a protozoan parasite that thrived on oysters in the high salinity of the lower growing beds. The exact cause of the infestation is still under debate, but as a result, the oyster industry collapsed utterly and completely. The once-thriving seafaring communities in New Jersey and Delaware were practically turned into ghost towns. To make matters worse, the oysters were just starting to develop a slight resistance when another disease, Dermo (yet another parasite) struck in 1990. The loss was a detriment not only to the food business, but to the bay itself. Oysters act as siphons, cleaning millions of gallons of water; they also stabilize sediment and help provide fish habitats.

The oyster industry's collapse devastated the working population. Cumberland County is now the poorest in New Jersey. The sales tax is just three percent—half that of the rest of the state. Knowing there was plenty of cheap labor available, New Jersey began building prisons in the county. And that is what the inhabitants of Cumberland County do: work in the prisons, glass factories in Millville, or scrape a living from the bay by crabbing or oystering.

An Old Salt

Today there is optimism that the industry can make a comeback, although nowhere near that of its heyday. That optimism comes from the fact that the Delaware's waters have been cleaned up considerably. We once again have Cape May Salts, a gourmet oyster grown and harvested near the cape and sold throughout the Delaware Valley and beyond, mostly in high-end restaurants such as the Plaza Hotel in New York, and even in Boston raw bars, where they go for over $3 apiece. They do have a unique, delicious, salty taste prized by oyster connoisseurs. They are also getting raves from foodies and from the slow food movement, which praises the sustainable methods used to grow them, thanks to the efforts of the Delaware Bay Oyster Restoration Project (www.delawareestuary.org/science_projects_oyster_restoration.asp). Cleaned clamshells are "planted" in the bay, making an excellent surface for oyster sprat to attach to. They are then transplanted farther north in the bay, where there are fewer predators, and grown to harvesting size. This method is gaining measured success and with proper funding can bring oystering back to a healthy industry. Stats indicate a significant growth in harvesting since 2005.

5
WE'LL LEAVE THE LIGHT ON FOR YOU

Of all the sights along the Delaware, the channel lights—tiny Victorian houses sitting on pedestals in the middle of the bay—are probably the most charming. Many people, even locals, don't know they exist, let alone what unique architectural wonders they are. Originally they were operated manually by lighthouse keepers, therefore the need for housing, and what interesting housing it is. Most have superstructures fashioned from cast-iron molds in multiple stories with mansard roofs, gables, decks, and interior wooden paneling—all the comforts of a real house, but on a smaller scale. They were tended by civilian keepers, but in the 1930s the Coast Guard was given responsibility. Most would have a crew of three or four who would typically rotate two weeks on and one week off. This was not a cush assignment, though. The houses were cramped, cold in the winter, and hot in the summer and the work was boring and lonely at times—obviously there was nowhere to take a stroll. It was much like being on a ship that didn't go anywhere.

In the early 1970s, the lighthouses became powered by submarine cables running from the shore, eliminating the need for keepers. Most of the bay lights can only be seen up close from a boat, except for the East Point Light in Heislerville. The Rear Range lights are also accessible by land and are similar to those at Finn's Point and Tinicum. The good news is that there are cruises to visit the off-shore lights organized by the Delaware Bay Lighthouse Keepers & Friends Association (www.delawarebaylightkeeper-friend.org), who will show you an excellent time and give you a lot of history. I have gone on several of them, and on one cruise there was a former Coast Guard member who had actually been stationed on the lights before they were automated. Right out of a Popeye cartoon, complete with sailor's cap, he entertained us with stories about life on the lights, like the time he requisitioned a lawn mower for one of the lights. Another tale was told of two keepers stranded for three months on the Fourteen Foot Bank Lighthouse when ice choked the bay. One of the keepers, Chester P. Joseph, remarked, "I don't believe I ever was as tired of looking at another person in my life."

Today, through the use of GPS and other modern navigational aids, many of the lighthouses are nothing more than historic eye candy. But in the nineteenth century, they were some of the most important structures in the country. Oceans and rivers were the highways of industry and commerce. Philadelphia, in particular, had become one of the leading industrial centers of the US, and it was crucial for raw materials and finished products to arrive and depart safely on the Delaware River. Many wrecked ships in the river and bay attest to this traffic. The early shipping channel was not very wide or deep and wound its way through shoals and other obstacles, most of them discovered by accident. Eventually, the channel was dredged and marked. Some of the earliest attempts at warning beacons involved lightships, but bad weather could pull them off location and winter ice floes could make it impossible for them to remain on duty. Permanent lighthouses, though more costly, proved the solution.

As of this writing, the Ship John, Miah Maull, and Brandywine lights have been declared "excess" by the US Coast Guard. They can be had for free! But only to an individual or organization willing to foot the bill for upkeep. The following pages contain illustrations of the lighthouses with encapsulated histories. There is much more detailed information available online or in your local library.

Ship John Shoal

Located 2.8 miles south of the mouth of the Cohansey River.

Latitude: 39.30528
Longitude: -75.3767

Declared excess by the US Coast Guard, its future is uncertain.

With its Second Empire Victorian styling, the Ship John Light is considered by many to be the jewel of the Delaware Bay lighthouses. It takes its name from a ship called—wait for it—*John*. On its way to Philadelphia from Hamburg, Germany, the ship grounded on a shoal near the mouth of the Cohansey Creek in December, 1797. The German passengers and much of the cargo were rescued and taken to Greenwich, New Jersey, where the figurehead and bell from the ship still survive. The ship did not, however, and a temporary wooden lighthouse was erected to mark the shoal, only to be destroyed by ice.

A steel caisson was constructed in 1874, but the finished light would have to wait while the beautiful cast iron superstructure was displayed at the 1876 Centennial Exhibition in Philadelphia, complete with a keeper tending a working light. In the interim, a lightship was stationed alongside. The light housed a Coast Guard crew until it was automated in 1973. Four years later, the Fresnel lens was removed and replaced with a solar-powered beacon.

Elbow of Cross Ledge

The Elbow has had a hard life. It started in 1907 when a temporary platform used by workmen to sink the base of the lighthouse was swept away during a storm, drowning one workman and stranding another. The light was completed in 1910 with living quarters constructed of brick. The crew often slept in life jackets due to the lighthouse being struck repeatedly by ships that strayed from the channel.

In 1951 the light was seriously damaged by a severe storm, and after that the Coast Guard pulled the crew and ran a power cable from nearby Fortescue. A second cable was then run between the Elbow and the Miah Maull light, whose crew controlled the Elbow's beacon. Finally, in 1953 a ship running through a thick fog plowed into the Elbow, toppling the upper two-thirds and damaging the base. It cost $100,000 to demolish what was left of the superstructure and replace it with a steel skeleton tower. But the troubles continue. Fisherman have broken the submarine power cable numerous times, despite posted warnings. Regardless, it still remains a popular fishin' hole.

Located approximately 26 miles up the Delaware Bay from Cape May and five miles offshore from Fortescue.

Latitude: 39.182226

Longitude: -75.268443

Still in use as an important navigational aid.

Miah Maull Shoal

Located near the center of Delaware Bay, 8 miles south of Fortescue, 18.5 miles northwest of Cape May.

Latitude: 39.126647

Longitude: -75.208682

Delclared excess by the US Coast Guard, its future is uncertain.

This vividly colored lighthouse was named for Nehemiah Maull, a Delaware River pilot who drowned in 1780. He was bound for England on a ship whose captain was unfamiliar with the bay and wrecked on a shoal. The shoal was named Nehemiah Maull; later the name was shortened to Miah Maull.

In 1904 the Lighthouse Service erected a shoal warning light. It was completed in 1913, much to the delight of many a river pilot. The Coast Guard took responsibility for the light in 1939 with three crewmen stationed in rotating shifts of two weeks on and one week off. It was indeed a small house with bedrooms, kitchen, living room, and even a real bathroom, instead of using an outhouse. It was also equipped with a foghorn, which would have been maddeningly loud for the crew, particularly when used for days at a time. The last crew member was removed in 1973 when the light was automated.

East Point Lighthouse

One of the most photographed lighthouses in New Jersey, the East Point Light was originally known as the Maurice River Lighthouse. At the mouth of the Maurice River, it was an early navigational guide for the huge oyster industry that thrived there, and for the glass manufacturing center up the river in Millville. Built in 1849, it is the second oldest lighthouse in New Jersey and was manned continuously until 1911. It was then fitted with an acetylene light that could operate for weeks on fuel supplied by tanks in the lighthouse.

The light was extinguished during World War II and then discontinued altogether. The New Jersey Division of Fish, Game, and Wildlife eventually wound up with it. But they allowed it to deteriorate and eventually vandals set it on fire, causing extensive damage. The Maurice River Historical Society saved the day, raising the funds to partially restore it and convincing the Coast Guard to reactive the light. Restoration is ongoing and when complete will display the fourth order Fresnel lens from the Miah Maull Light.

Located at the mouth of the Maurice River near Heislerville in Cumberland County, New Jersey.

Latitude: 39.19587

Longitude: -75.0273

The light is an active navigational aid.

Fourteen-Foot Bank

Located 12 miles off Bowers Beach, Delaware.

Latitude: 39.048249

Longitude: -75.182205

Private residence.

This lighthouse got its name from the depth of water over the Joe Flogger Shoal that it sits on. A pithy name, it's a pithy they didn't use it for the lighthouse (sorry). It was the first time the pneumatic-caisson method of setting the base was used for a lighthouse in the US. A large wooden structure was dug into the seabed, filled with concrete, and then the cast iron base was erected on top. Later a metal Classical Revival-style superstructure was placed on the base—a miniature house complete with gables and an outside privy.

The light was activated in 1887 and automated in 1973. Aside from being a navigational aid, it also contained sophisticated monitoring equipment used by the University of Delaware's College of Marine Studies. But now it houses something else—a brewery. The lighthouse was sold in 2007 to a private owner who plans on making enough beer to cover the cost of maintaining the structure, which will also be used as a summer residence. He has installed a desalination system and claims he will make the first beer brewed from seawater.

Brandywine Shoal

The first lighthouse at this location used screw-pile technology—screw blades were attached to iron pilings and twisted into the sea floor. It was the first use of this technology in the US. First lit in 1850, the nine piles used to support the structure were not adequate to resist moving ice, and over time sixty-eight more piles were placed around the light. But more is not always better, and in 1914 a new lighthouse sitting on a reinforced concrete base was constructed next to the old one.

The third-order Fresnel lens used in the old structure was installed in the new one. Automated in 1974, the Brandywine was the last lighthouse on the bay to have a crew.

The Fresnel lens is now on display at the Tuckerton Seaport Museum in Tuckerton, New Jersey (www.tuckertonseaport.org).

Located on the Delaware Bay about 8.5 miles northwest of Cape May.

Latitude: 39.986232

Longitude: -75.113185

Declared excess by the US Coast Guard, its future is uncertain.

Harbor of Refuge

Located at the eastern end of the outer breakwater in the harbor at Lewes, Delaware.

Latitude: 38.81465

Longitude: -75.09244

Still in use as an important navigational aid.

Between Cape Charles, Virginia; and Sandy Hook, New Jersey, there is no natural safe harbor for ships to escape stormy weather. Thus, the Delaware Breakwater was built after appropriations were made by Congress in 1828. This proved to be too shallow, however, for advancing ship technology and the Harbor of Refuge Breakwater was added in 1901. The lighthouse that indicates the southern end is actually the third light to be built there since 1902. The two others were not stormworthy. The current light, built of cast iron, was lit in 1926 using a fourth-order Fresnel lens and is now illuminated by solar power. It also contains a solar-powered fog horn.

The Harbor of Refuge Lighthouse is now under the care of the Delaware River and Bay Lighthouse Foundation, which has secured funds for ongoing repairs not only to the light but also to the breakwater. The Foundation offers tours each summer.

Delaware Breakwater East End

This is the lighthouse that signals the opening to the east end of the Delaware Breakwater. It was built to replace the Cape Henlopen Beacon, discontinued in 1884. A cast iron tower lined with brick, it became operational in 1855. It also contained a fog horn that was typically in operation an average of 400 to 500 hours per year. But in 1904 and continuing into 1905, it blared for an astounding 645 hours with nowhere for the keepers to escape the noise.

The light was automated in 1950 with a power cable running from the shore, and finally in 1996 the Coast Guard declared it excess property. It was turned over to the General Services Administration for disposal, but the state of Delaware expressed interest and was granted ownership. Through a partnership between the Delaware River & Bay Authority and the Delaware River & Bay Lighthouse Foundation, a group of volunteers was able to ready the old light for public tours, which are periodic throughout the summer months.

The Delaware River & Bay Authority operates the Cape May–Lewes Ferry that docks nearby.

Located at the east end of the inner breakwater in the harbor at Lewes, Delaware.

Latitude: 38.79724

Longitude: -75.10002

No longer in use.

Cape May Lighthouse

Located at the southernmost point of New Jersey.

Latitude: 38.93302

Longitude: -74.9604

Still in use as an important navigational aid.

Just a few steps (199) will take you to the top of this 170-foot lighthouse with a view of the Atlantic Ocean, Delaware Bay, and on a good day, Cape Henlopen across the bay. This is the third lighthouse to be built at Cape May Point; the other two are currently underwater. The first was erected in 1823 about 1,750 feet from the current light. Erosion forced its demise. The second was built in 1847 about 600 feet closer, but poor construction soon rendered it obsolete and the sea also claimed it. The third and latest lighthouse was lit for the first time on Halloween, 1859, using its first-order Fresnel lens.

The Cape May Lighthouse was automated in 1933, but Harry H. Palmer, the keeper for forty years, continued to look after the place with his family in his retirement. Once a keeper, always a keeper.

The light is now part of Cape May Point State Park, a favorite spot to observe migratory birds along the Atlantic Flyway, especially in the Fall.

But wait—there's more! The New Jersey Lighthouse Challenge—to visit as many lighthouses as possible over a two-day period—takes place every October (www.njlhs.org). The challenge covers the Delaware Bay lights, including the Tinicum Rear Range in Paulsboro, Finn's Point Rear Range in Pennsville, East Point Light in Heislerville, Cape May Lighthouse, and the Cape May County Museum, which houses the original first-order Fresnel lens from the Cape May Lighthouse.

My friend Rick accompanied me on one challenge in which we started at Tinicum and called it a day at Hereford Inlet. It poured buckets the whole time, but being road-tested veterans, it didn't bother us in the least. We had to make a lot of pit stops, though. Maybe it was all that water. By the time we got to Heislerville, the road to East Point was flooded and we had to wait for the tide to go out so the volunteers could get through to open the facility. When we found our way to the Cape May County Museum, a story was circulating that a party had done the entire challenge and was finished by three o'clock in the afternoon. It's not the Indianapolis 500! What was the point?

Rounding Cape May Point and heading up the coast, you will visit the Hereford Inlet Light in North Wildwood, Absecon Light in Atlantic City, and the Tuckerton Seaport, where there is a reconstruction of the Tucker's Beach Lighthouse, which serves as an excellent maritime museum. The original lighthouse fell into the Atlantic Ocean in 1927 and there is an amazing sequence of photographs on display that documents its final moments.

Then on to the Barnegat Lighthouse (designed by Gettyburg hero George Meade), north to Sea Girt (similar to Hereford Inlet Light), the Twin Lights of Navasink—the highest spot of America's coastline between Maine and Texas—and finally Sandy Hook, the US's oldest working lighthouse, first lit in 1764.

It's a grueling but satisfying road trip, and for a small donation you will be rewarded with some type of memento that changes year to year.

6

Fortescue

Visiting Fortescue today, you would never guess that it once had a "reputation." After passing through a long stretch of pastoral marshland in Downe Township, Cumberland County, New Jersey, you'll come to a small bridge over an inlet that meanders out to the Delaware Bay. You'll see Higbee's Marina on the right, occupied by a few fishing boats; gulls whirling about, squawking at each other mostly; and a small number of boaters wandering around or shooting the breeze. It's a sleepy scene, to be sure.

Higbee's is the last refuge of a fleet of party boats that used to carry hundreds of recreational fishermen out for a day on the water—every day. During the gravy days, visitors would stream into the bayside town for a chance to do some serious fishing in "The Weakfish Capitol of the World!"

Fishing was not the only recreation in Fortescue. During the 1930s, this seemingly innocuous little village was a mecca for rum runners, speakeasies, and dance halls that stayed open until the wee hours. Places like the Green Door and the Gray Goose were raided regularly by ABC (Alcohol Beverage Control) agents, adding to the excitement of visitors and vacationers from all over the Eastern Seaboard. (More often than not, the officers in charge of the raids were just looking for free drinks.) And it seems they actually had peep holes in their doors, just like the familiar cliches. Fortescue was just far enough off the beaten path of the oceanside resorts to make it an ideal spot for off-loading illegal liquor. A mother ship carrying the booze would anchor at "Rum Row" just outside the three-mile limit near the mouth of the Delaware Bay, and smaller, speedy smuggling boats would pick up the illicit cargo in the middle of the night. Boats like the *Robbi*, *Goose*, *Osenosisakak*, and *Kashagawigamog* would play cat and mouse games with the Coast Guard on a regular basis.

In August of 1933, a Coast Guard cutter from Cape May began chasing a suspected runner off Fortescue. The pursuit lasted for fifteen miles before the cutter finally fired on the fifty-foot boat, causing an explosion that sank it. The bootleggers dove overboard and were hauled aboard the cutter and taken to Camden to await a hearing. Events like this were typical during Prohibition.

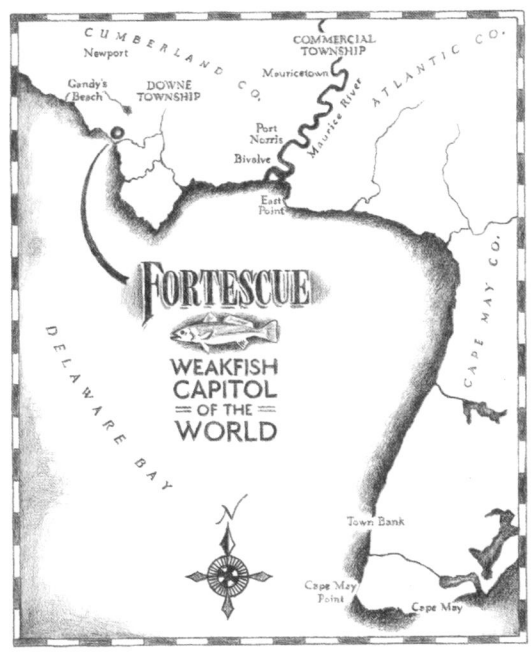

Fortescue's story goes back much farther than the 1930s, however—back to the early eighteenth century, when Lord John Fortescue's wife Mary came into possession of about 10,000 acres of bayside property in Cumberland County. The Fortescues were from Cullington, England, but it's not clear if they ever visited their New Jersey property. There were plans for development, but instead the land was sold in 1776 to one William Smith for a meager five shillings. He decided to retain the sellers' name, perhaps for status, or perhaps because Fortescue sounded tonier than Smith.

A fishing community began to take shape at the mouth of the newly named Fortescue Creek, and in 1824 a large hotel was built to house and feed visiting sportsmen from Philadelphia. They would come by steamboat, which was much easier than traveling an old teeth-rattling "corduroy road" through the wetlands that disappeared during flood tides. (This was also the type of road much favored by both armies during the Civil War due to the abundance of natural materials—logs.) The Garrisons, one of the first families in the area, built and maintained the only hotel on the island. They named it the Fortescue House, which incidentally also offered the only restaurant in town. Unfortunately, as seemed to happen regularly in the nineteenth century, the hotel burned to the ground in 1892.

Without accommodations, fishermen stopped visiting and the town went into decline. But in 1901, one of the Garrison clan named Herbert began selling building lots, and before long one of the oldest fishing villages on the bay was again prospering. Adding to the splendor, a bridge was built over Fortescue Creek in 1904, and a taxi service shuttled visitors from the nearby Newport trolley terminal. Hunting was as popular as fishing. Muskrats were plentiful then and are still hunted for fur and food, along with ducks and other water fowl. (I have never had the opportunity to try muskrat. If it was offered to me, I would have to think about it for a long time, hopefully buying myself enough time to change the subject.

COMMERCIAL FISHERMEN also found Fortescue to their liking. Many would live in houseboats along the bay, following the runs of migrating fish while they built their own boats. The bay has always provided an incredible abundance of seafood, including shellfish such as clams, crabs, and oysters, as well as bluefish, shad, flounder, striped bass, sea bass, drum fish, and croakers. But what really brought Fortescue to prominence as a fisherman's paradise was the astounding amount of sea trout, better known as weakfish, prompting its grandiose nickname.

As the town began to develop a fishing reputation, more than a dozen marinas were established where party boats or rowboats could be hired—with or without motors. On busy summer days, more than 100 boats would be rowed, towed, or driven out into the bay for a full day of fishing.

In 1929, during the height of the Delaware Bay oyster industry, a boat race was held for commercial oyster dredges, beautiful boats that carried upwards of 4,000 square feet of sail. In what would be the only schooner race ever on the bay, the *J & E Riggin* emerged as the winner. Two years before the race, the legendary boat was built for Captain Charles Riggin

at Stowman's Shipyard in Dorchester, New Jersey, on the Maurice River. The captain named the boat after his two sons, Jacob and Edward. She is still working today, though not as an oyster dredge. She has been restored as a cruise ship, operating on Penobscot Bay in Maine, and designated a National Historic Landmark by the National Park Service. About the same time as the Delaware Bay race, another race between two schooners—the *Eloise Moore* and the *Samuel Jacoby*—was run between Bivalve and Philadelphia. Eloise Moore was the winner, but neither boat fared as well as the *J & E Riggin*. Their remains are lying in the mud at Bivalve and Money Island.

Fishing and hunting were not the only draw. Soon people began buying property to build summer homes. With the vacationers came hotels and eateries. A nearly mile-long boardwalk was constructed to ease visitors to the establishments. Seafood was high on most menus, which featured not only freshly caught fish but also the highly prized Delaware Bay oysters, duck, and yes, even those muskrats. The Garrison family continued its heritage as restaurateurs and innkeepers by building the Garrison House and Garrison Lodge. Among the many fine hotels and restaurants, the only one remaining today is the Hotel Charlesworth, built in 1925 by Ruella Charlesworth. There is also Higbee's Restaurant at the marina, but one would have to classify that as a luncheonette. This is where the local crowd comes for breakfast, lunch, and a heaping side order of hot gossip, served up by Betty Higbee, the First Lady of Fortescue, who still does the cooking. It's a funky and fun place, full of old postcards, antique oyster cans, fishing tackle, and all sorts of memorabilia. Her family owns the restaurant, marina, and the *Miss Fortescue*, one of the last remaining "headboats," which means anyone can go on board to fish when the boat is available (www.missfortescue.net).

DURING WORLD WAR II, and continuing for about twenty years after, members of the Philadelphia Sketch Club (www.sketchclub.org) visited Fortescue at the invitation of Herbert and Preston Foster, who owned side-by-side summer homes known as the Salt Box and the Seahorse Cottage. The club is the oldest artists' organization in the nation, founded in 1860 by a group of students at the Philadelphia Academy of the Fine Arts—"bohemians," as they called themselves. I have had my work displayed at the Sketch Club, but despite that indiscretion, they remain one of the class acts in the American art world. During the construction of the academy's new facilities in the 1870s, the club invited the school to use its building, where Thomas Eakins conducted life drawing classes and was made an honorary member.

The club has an equally distinguished list of other members that included illustrators, painters, watercolorists, and sculptors of the likes of N. C. Wyeth, Howard Chandler Christy, Henry Pitz, Joseph Pennell, Thomas P. Anshutz, Benton Spruance, and Edward Redfield, among many others, including cartoonist Pete Boyle. As a child, I remember watching a local TV show he hosted called "Lunch With Uncle Pete." I would eat my lunch every day in front of the Philco while "Uncle Pete" would show off his drawing skills and run old animated cartoon clips. He was also the father of actor Peter Boyle, who appeared as the monster in *Young Frankenstein*. He screams out "Puttin' onna Riiiiz!" which was being sung by Gene Wilder as he was presenting his creation to a group of doctors and physicians. It puts me on the floor every time I see it.

After spending a week in Fortescue painting and drawing, the visiting members of the Sketch Club would sell or give away their work to local cottagers. It would be interesting to find out how many of those pieces still exist. At least some of the work made it back to Philadelphia and was exhibited at the Sketch Club galleries in 1950.

SOME OF THE WORKS have no doubt been lost to the musings of Mother Nature. Situated on a large body of water, Fortescue is constantly at her mercy. Anyone who has spent any time on the bay will soon develop a healthy respect for its many moods. You can be enjoying a perfectly lovely day, and in what seems like just moments, the weather can turn ferociously stormy.

Fortesue was changed forever in the devastating flood of 1950. Homes and businesses were scattered like children's toys around the island. Rental boats were smashed against summer cottages. The National Guard was called in to evacuate the flood victims to Newport, where they were cared for by the Red Cross.

The devastation was repeated in 1980. And that's just the destruction caused by water. In addition to the burning of the Old Fortescue House in

1892, there have been numerous other fires—in the 1890s, 1928, 1943, and "the big one" in 1963 when embers from a smoldering barge raced down New Jersey Avenue, laying waste to half the town. The year 2007 saw another potentially disastrous fire fanned by high winds. Fortunately, only two cottages were lost. Damage from Superstorm Sandy could have been worse, but compared to previous storms, Fortescue was relatively unscathed. The bay actually offered some protection in this case.

Betty Higbee's son Jim, who captains the fifty-five-foot Miss Fortescue, has lately been running the boat at a loss, and he knows the times are changing. Fishing is not what it used to be since the weakfish began to disappear in the late 1980s. The Miss Fortescue is one of only three headboats left of about thirty-five that used to sail daily out of the marinas. Fortescue has always been a fishing village and most of the long-time residents would like to see it stay that way. But tough economic times may force some changes. Waterfront property is much more valuable for residential use than recreational or commercial fishing. Fortescue may find itself turning into a resort, but not just yet.

Stray crabber buoys under a house on New Jersey Avenue

A man in his mid-fifties, Jim Higbee plans to keep on keeping on as long as he can. You can't get that bay water out of your veins. Maybe that tenacity is paying off: lately the weakfish are returning, although there is now a legal limit of one. But the oyster industry is on the rebound and there are still plenty of flounder, bluefish, croakers, stripers, drum fish, and crabs.

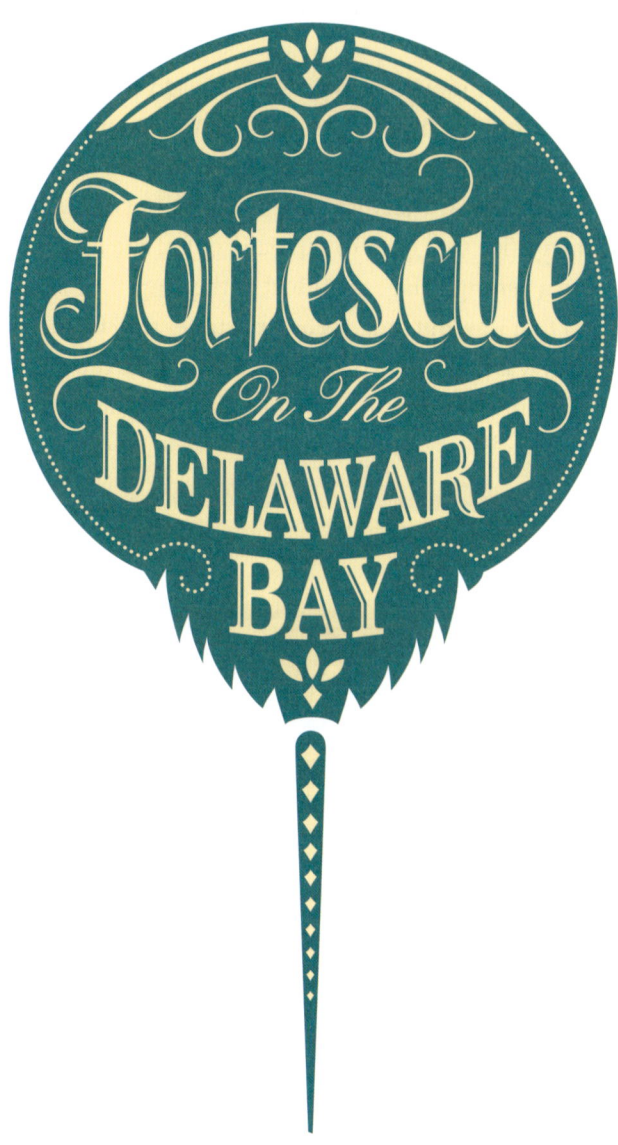

7
THE GREEN MILE

WHEN THE WIND IS FROM THE NORTH, NO FISH COMES FORTH.
WHEN THE WIND IS FROM THE EAST, THE FISH BITE LEAST,
WHEN THE WIND IS FROM THE SOUTH, NO FISH WILL COME OUT,
BUT, WHEN THE WIND IS FROM THE WEST, THE FISHING IS BEST.

From The Book of Wedges by Painter John

The first time I went to Gandy's Beach, I thought I was leaving the planet. It was about three a.m. after a night of doing what young people do on a Saturday night. We drove down a narrow, winding road through seemingly endless marshes under a pitch-black sky. I was convinced we were far from civilization. But we weren't that far, really—about fifteen miles south of Millville, New Jersey, famous as a glass manufacturing center for many years. My wife and I were taken there by my friend Clayton and his wife Jean. Jean's family had a small cottage that they bought in the 1960s for what seems now like a laughably small amount of money. Just about a mile in length with close to sixty homes, Gandy's Beach sits right on the Delaware Bay with one road leading in and out.

Gandy's Beach is named for Miles Gandy, whose family originally owned the land. They were farmers who harvested salt hay and other produce. Gandy is a common name in these parts, producing, aside from farmers, many people who make their living from the water. Miles had the idea for a waterfront community and started selling lots in 1939. Each lot cost $100. Today, some of those waterfront properties are priced at more than $200,000.

That would have been beyond comprehension when the area was first established as Downe Township in 1772. It was named for Elizabeth Downes, wife of then New Jersey Governor William Franklin, illegitimate son of Benjamin Franklin. Over time, the "s" was dropped from the township name.

Jean's cottage was basically a one-room shack with a carport. The interior was paneled in beautifully patinaed knotty pine, re-purposed from packing crates. You cannot buy stuff like that today. There was an old electric stove that looked like the front end of a vintage Studebaker, a fridge, a few cabinets, and a kitchen table, and that was about it. Sleeping was done in a small loft above the kitchen area. This was luxury compared to many of the buildings on the beach—mostly fisherman's shacks for men who spent their days on the water and their nights passed out on a cot. That first night we were there, electrical storms danced over the bay, giving us a spectacular light show. I

Drawing courtesy of Brother E. Clayton West

don't remember much else about our first visit—it's like that old adage about Woodstock: if you can remember being there, you probably weren't. But I know this: we returned many times.

My son took his first steps and peed in the toilet for the first time there; I caught my first fish and ate my first blue crabs there—Clayton's mom would deride anyone for not sucking the meat out of the tiny legs, while Clayton would grumble that you could starve to death eating these things.

Eventually, Jean's family enlarged their cottage, making it nearly twice as large as before, but not before the house had to be moved due to a nor'easter in 1980. The storm removed more than a few homes. Some structures just collapsed into the bay, and one house was blown off its pilings and into the marsh across the island. Bill Bowen, a long time resident of Gandy's and the neighboring community of Money Island, told me that the table was still set in the house when they went to retrieve it; not a plate or glass was out of place. There were houses with lawns on the bay side of the road that disappeared during the storm.

Eventually, everyone who could rebuild or repaired their homes, and even though it looked a bit different, the place still had the same relaxed, laid-back feel. After Clayton and Jean's marriage took a tumble, we could not stay away from Gandy's and found a rental apartment that suited us well for a couple of summers until the owners sold the property and the new owners kept the apartment for family.

But we found a house that the owners almost never used and were able to negotiate a rental from them. We treated it as our own, rearranging the humble decor and even making numerous plumbing repairs, which I didn't mind since the rent was ridiculously cheap. It was like camping out in a house. As a bonus, the old Studebaker stove from Jean's house somehow found its way there. The cottage also contained a tiny, ancient refrigerator with a freezer about the size of a brick, and it usually froze our food as hard as one, while the fridge temperature was just shy of tepid. Every day I would make a run to Gandy's Beach marina to buy ice for beer and food. (Am I crazy, or does beer taste colder and better from a cooler?) As it happened, our house sat next to Painter John's. It was his second Gandy's house; his first was lost in the storm, scattered over the floor of the Delaware Bay.

We had known Painter John Gilligan since our first visits to the beach. He loved children and always had a freezer full of popsicles for any kid he saw wandering down the road, whether he knew them or not. But his most outstanding asset was storytelling. In the evenings, when everyone was properly lubricated, he would grab an unsuspecting child, swing him onto his lap, and bellow, "Let me tell you about Jack and the Beanstalk!" He would then launch into a wild epic loosely based on the children's fable and punctuated with local surroundings and residents. The adults loved the stories as much as the children. There were plenty of other tales, too: Like the time he bought a boat in Westville and as he was sailing it down the bay, it sank with a full case of Piels Beer. And every full moon, the boat would rise up from the bottom of the river with the case of Piels still on it. There was also a tale about a giant horseshoe crab named Molasses that would appear every full moon, and a story of Grandpop Gilligan, who sailed with Captain Horatio Hornblower in search of gold "gablooms." My kids called him Uncle Paint. He was a gentle man with a big beard, a huge heart, and a magnetic personality. He was an excellent fisherman, never wore shoes, and had feet like a hobbit. He could never say no to anybody and had his own sense of time, or rather lack of it. This was a man who hung a bug-zapper in his living room and always had a refrigerator full of Schaefer beer, a headache in a can.

I was having a few beers with Uncle Paint one day and talk turned to Delaware Bay oysters. I said I had never had one, and John, being the man that he was, said he would see what he could do about that. A couple of days later, over to our house came Paint with a paper shopping bag full of oysters. He didn't say how he had come by them, but I thanked him profusely and offered payment, which of course he refused. I admitted I had no idea how to open them, so he suggested I go talk to Roger. Roger and his wife Gail owned the Money Island Marina, which was just on the other side of Nantuxent Creek, about a quarter of a mile from Gandy's. So I drove over to see Roger with my bag of oysters. I explained how Painter John had given me these lovely oysters but I didn't have a clue how to open them. Roger, who had a great sense of humor and also drank a bit, gave me an arched eyebrow and told me he was the one who had procured the oysters. So I also thanked Roger, again offered payment, and again was refused. He disappeared into the marina office for a moment and returned with an old screwdriver with which he showed me how to shuck the oysters. We shared a couple, and they were outstanding!

I returned to the house and spent the rest of the day nearly opening several arteries as well as the oysters, but managed to shuck them all and enjoy them with some neighbors and lots of beer. (There is actually a tool for shucking oysters, and I suggest you use it instead of a screwdriver.)

The next day I drove back to Money Island to return the makeshift oyster knife, but Roger was out fishing. Gail was there, however, and I gave her the tool and explained how Roger had procured the oysters and showed me how to open them. Again I received an indignant raised eyebrow. Gail told me *she* was the one who had gotten the shellfish from one of the oyster boats tied up at the commercial dock near the marina. So I resolved the issue by presenting her with a large bottle of wine. She seemed satisfied. They were a fun couple, but too much drinking got them into trouble, and they wound up going their separate ways.

My friend Rick came to visit us at Gandy's several times, and during one visit we took a small road trip along the bay. Traveling the back roads of Cumberland County (the poorest county in New Jersey) is like going back in time. There is never any congestion; generally you have the road to yourself.

There is the occasional lone dwelling, and small collections of homes and businesses pop up out of nowhere. There is not much opportunity for employment down here; most people either worked at Wheaton Glass, which has closed down, or at one of the prisons the state has placed here because it is remote. There are also a few crabbers and oystermen, but those are mostly part-time occupations these days.

We came upon a yard sale, and of course had to check it out. In a cardboard box were several strings of old Christmas lights like the kind used in *National Lampoon's Christmas Vacation*. I bought the whole box and brought them back to the beach. We plugged them in for a test run and there was a lot of electrical arcing. But Rick is good at repairing that sort of thing, and before long they were usable with minimal danger of fire. We strung them around the front porch and for many nights created a gaudy display. Our lights could be seen far out in the bay, and we later heard that the Coast Guard was warning boaters not to use our house as a navigational aid.

Autumn is probably the best season at the beach. We would sit and watch a parade of Monarch butterflies shimmer along the coastline and then turn to cross the bay for their long journey to Mexico. But a lot of other bugs are gone, too, like the greenheads—vicious, biting creatures that arrive in early summer and thankfully die off in late August. That's why I call Gandy's the Green Mile. I think that's very witty, but nobody else does.

When we first started visiting Gandy's, it was not unusual on a Spring morning to find literally thousands of horseshoe crabs crowded on the beach, piled on top of each other, some almost buried in the sand. Many would be stranded upside-down, thrashing their long, pointed tails to try to right themselves. My kids loved to wander the beach, turning the horseshoes over and sometimes putting them back in the water. They had come there to spawn, producing millions of little aqua-colored eggs that covered the

Drawing courtesy of Brother E. Clayton West

beach. Those eggs would produce more horsehoe crabs, of course, but they also provided high-protein fuel for the rufa red knot, a remarkable bird that logs more miles per year than any species on the planet. Every Spring, they fly from the southern tip of South America to the northern reaches of the Arctic, a journey of nearly 10,000 miles. Their migration is only possible because of the egg buffet on the Delaware Bay. But like many things relating to the natural world these days, the latest news is not good. The horseshoe crab population is in decline, which in turn decreases the rufa red knot population. Both species are currently being studied; hopefully, the symbiotic relationship can be stabilized with scientific help.

THERE WAS A good deal of beach at Gandy's when we first started visiting. The kids would play there, climbing over the remains of concrete septic tanks left from the houses destroyed during the 1980 storm. In fact, you could walk pretty much the whole length of the village at low tide. The beach is nearly gone now, mainly due to erosion. A double bulkhead restrains Cove Road from falling into the bay. And Superstorm Sandy's visit in October 2012 hasn't improved the situation. The road was washed out again, at least twenty-five homes were damaged, some severely, and I know of one house that disappeared, leaving nothing behind but a few pilings poking out of the bay. There may soon come a time when all of Grandy's Beach will disappear.

There are a number of other bayside fishing communities like Gandy's that haven't changed for years and years. They don't advertise for the tourist dollar—most residents don't want tourism. There are few restaurants or attractions other than fishing and crabbing. In most cases, you have to travel closer to civilization just to find a convenience store. And that's the beauty of it.

One example is Money Island—mysteriously named because a visit will convince you "there ain't no money here!" But legend persists that Captain Kidd buried treasure there. Bill Bowen also suggests that years ago a hermit named Money was the sole resident. Oyster boats still dock here to unload their catches. (Maybe that's where the real money is.) Just north of Money Island is Bay Point, home to a small marina and signs warning sightseers and visitors that it's a private community.

And then there's Sea Breeze up the bay on Cohansey Cove, near the mouth of the Cohansey River. It once had a watering hole called Sea Breeze Tavern where visitors could arrive by boat. Painter John had stories about that place, too. Unfortunately, about all that's left are stories. The tavern, built after the repeal of Prohibition, was destroyed by Hurricane Gloria in

A lone survivor at Sea Breeze

1985. Before that, the Seabreeze Hotel, dating to 1887, was destroyed by fire. And the forty-room Warner House once welcomed vacationers arriving from Philadelphia aboard the steamboat *John A. Warner*. In 2008, the remaining few property owners asked the New Jersey Department of Environmental Protection to buy their properties, as they were in danger of being lost to erosion. The state did so, and for a time Seabreeze was a shorefront ghost town. In 2012, all but a few of the homes were bulldozed. It will now be given back to nature.

THE ILLUSTRATED DELAWARE RIVER

8

THE WAR OF THE FORTS

Fort Nassau, Fort Casimir, Fort Christina, and Fort Elfsborg are not exactly household names, not even to Delaware Valley natives. That's because they don't exist anymore, and haven't for more than 350 years. Fort Nassau is thought to have been in Gloucester, New Jersey, it's exact location a matter of speculation. Fort Casimir was along the riverfront at what was is now New Castle, Delaware. Fort Christina was an early outpost that grew to become Wilmington, Delaware. And Fort Elfsborg was in Elsinboro Township, near Salem, New Jersey, a victim of changing river patterns and erosion. It's exact location is also a matter of debate. These forts were built at a time when the entire river basin was a wilderness inhabited only by wildlife and indigenous peoples.

THEIR STORY BEGINS with the Dutch. Although Englishman Henry Hudson "discovered" the Delaware Bay in 1609, he didn't stay long. He concentrated his explorations in New York Bay and the Noort Rivier (North River, now the Hudson). Holland claimed much of the northeastern seaboard as New Netherland, extending from southeastern Cape Cod to as far south as the Delmarva Peninsula. This was an infringement on lands previously claimed by England, but at the time they were not in a position to stop it. Early explorations had proposed locating the capital of New Netherland along the Suyd Rivier (Dutch for South River, now the Delaware), but that idea was scrapped due to mosquito infestations in the summer and choking ice in the winter. So New Amsterdam (New York) became the nerve center of the new Dutch colonies, but the Delaware River continued to hold possibilities for exploitation. The Dutch West India Company made modest attempts at establishing settlements, but none proved fruitful. That is, until 1624 when navigator and explorer Cornelius Jacobsz Mey dropped off a small group of colonists at what is now known as Burlington Island, in the Delaware River

The Kalmar Nyckel

just off present day Burlington City, the first European settlement in New Jersey. Two years later Mey built Fort Nassau at the confluence of several tributaries of the Delaware in present-day Gloucester, New Jersey, to be used as a trading outpost. The disaster at Zwannandael, covered in chapter two, was a major setback that took the Dutch years to recover from.

THE SWEDES had always gotten along well with the Dutch. Dutch was widely spoken in Sweden, Swedish students went to school in Holland to study commerce, and Dutchmen served in the Swedish army and commanded Swedish ships. Both were major powers in Europe. Sweden was, in fact, a military empire that controlled Finland, part of Norway, Lithuania, Latvia, and Estonia, plus significant parts of Russia, Poland, and Germany. But the Dutch had the West India Company, an incredibly efficient government-sanctioned monopoly that traded with North and South America and the western coast of Africa. It was even permitted to fly its own flag and hijack Spanish vessels, relieving them of cargoes of gold and silver. One of the founders of the company, Willem Usselinx, became disgruntled when he felt he was being under-compensated for his efforts. He requested an audience with Gustavus Adolphus II, the King of Sweden, and planted a bug in his ear about starting a competitive trading company. Never mind that the Dutch, English, French, Portuguese, and Spanish had already laid claim to everything in the lands across the Atlantic. The king, who at this time was busy fighting the Thirty Years War, had not given much thought to world trade. However he became convinced that it was a splendid idea and gave his blessing. But things went sour. Not enough money could be raised, the king was killed in battle, and Usselinx went back to Holland. Still, the idea lingered. Since the king's only heir to the throne was his six-year-old daughter, Christina, the country was now run by Count Axel Oxenstierna. The count restored the late king's interest in a world trading company and recruited the services of Dutch merchant Samuel Blommaert, another former West India Company director. He was willing to help the Swedes with advice and his pocketbook. Along with Blommaert came Peter Minuit, who by this time had also had a falling-out with the DWIC. His vast knowledge of New Netherland and long experience in the Indian trade was a tremendous asset to the venture. Together they formed the New Sweden Company, raised capital from Dutch and Swedish investors, and acquired two ships, the *Kalmar Nyckel* (Key of Kalmar) and the *Fogel Grip* (Griffen Bird).

Peter Minuit

Minuit (pronounced Min-wee), who spoke German and Dutch but whose family was originally from France, had trained as a diamond-cutter in Utrecht, Netherlands. Finding that profession too boring, he volunteered his services to the West India Company and sailed to the little outpost on the Hudson River known as New Amsterdam, the administrative center of the newly formed colony of New Netherland. The Dutch government tried to rule its untried colony from Europe, but they had little understanding of the problems of establishing a virgin province, and their efforts proved rather clumsy. However, it was not long before Minuit impressed his fellow settlers with his leadership skills, and they elected him their on-site commander.

One of Minuit's first acts was to purchase the island where the colonists had settled, called Manhattan. It was purchased for sixty guilders' worth of goods, or what amounted to $24 in 1626.

The small, free-market colony began to prosper, but adversity soon appeared in the form of its first minister, the Reverend Jonas Michaelius. The moodiest, most miserable, and bitter "man of God" most had ever encountered, he immediately took a disliking to Minuit, writing to West India Company directors that Minuit was cheating them. The directors, always referred to as "Their High Mightinesses," called Minuit and his accuser to Holland to address the matter in person. Unbelievably, the directors gave Minuit a formal dismissal, claiming that he had not recruited enough settlers to people New Netherland. After this humiliation the outraged Minuit teamed up with Willem Usselinx, and together they dreamed up a plan for their own colony to be settled under the name of Sweden.

In November of 1637 they set sail from Gothenburg, Sweden, with mostly Dutch sailors, Swedish and Finnish soldiers, and a smattering of Germans—about 60 or 70 men in all. After storms, layovers for repairs, and a side trip to the Caribbean, they entered the Delaware Bay in March of 1638. Unknown to anyone in the expedition, Peter Minuit carried secret instructions.

They were to sail into the Dutch-named Minquas Kill, a tributary of the Delaware about forty miles up-river. This spot was chosen to avoid detection by any ships traveling to or from Fort Nassau. Minuit was then to make sure there were no Europeans living on the Minquas Kill. If the land was unoccupied, he was instructed to request of the natives "that the land be made over to the crown of Sweden, everything in the presence of the officers; and let them, in the interest of trade, subscribe to the purchase of the land possession of the savages." They would be free to build a fort and establish Swedish ownership before the Dutch knew they were there.

Minuit fired the Kalmar Nyckel's cannon, which brought both Minquas and Lenape tribes to the ship. Five native chieftains were brought on board and made their marks on officially drawn documents that they couldn't possibly understand, gifts were lavishly distributed, and the deal was done. The region would now be called New Sweden. There was no haggling, no title searches, no closing fees, no taxes. However, the intent of the transaction was misinterpreted by both parties. The Indians could not conceive of anyone owning the land. Their closest notion was to share it, which was, of course, in direct conflict with European real estate fundamentals. This would come back to bite the Swedes on their pantalooned behinds.

The fort-building began. In the early colonial context, a fort was not a large medieval fortress built of stone, with drawbridges, moats, and the like. These early structures were made from whatever materials were handy, and since they were in a heavily wooded area, logs were the ideal choice. Minuit named it Fort Christina in honor of the now twelve-year-old future Queen of Sweden. They also built something else never seen before in the New World—a log cabin. This quintessential symbol of Americana was actually a Scandinavian import. With all this construction taking place, it didn't take long for the garrison at Fort Nassau to discover what the Swedes were up to. They sent Minuit a stern warning that he was infringing on Dutch West India Company trading grounds, which he promptly ignored.

Minuit returned to Sweden on the *Kalmar Nyckel*, leaving about twenty-five men behind to trade with the Indians, clear the land, and plant crops. First, however, he sailed to the Leeward Islands in the Caribbean to exchange what liquor and wine he had left for a cargo of tobacco, which had become extremely lucrative in Europe. After loading, Minuit was invited to visit the *Flying Stag*, a Dutch merchantman. While on board, a hurricane struck and forced a number of ships out into the open sea to ride out the storm. The *Kalmar Nyckel* made it through the storm undamaged, but the *Flying Stag* and Peter Minuit never returned.

The *Nyckel* sailed back to Sweden with the news about Minuit and also the unfortunate news that the expedition's expenses had exceeded its profits. Although the Dutch investors were sorely disappointed, the Swedish backers saw promise and immediately mounted plans for the expansion of New Sweden. This voyage would involve whole families. But trained craftspeople, which were needed most, were unwilling to give up their comfortable lives in Sweden and Finland to travel to an unknown land filled with "savages and wild beasts." The solution was to draft deserters from the Swedish army and Finns convicted of petty crimes, and allow them to bring their families, pay them a small stipend, and promise that they could return in two years. Under the command of Peter Hollander Ridder, yet another Dutchman, the *Kalmar Nyckel* arrived at Fort Christina in April of 1640 and discharged her cargo of new colonists and supplies. Ridder immediately began acquiring more land from the natives, extending the New Sweden territory along the western side of the Delaware from present day Lewes, Delaware, north to the Schuylkill River and along the eastern side in present-day New Jersey, from Salem to Cape May. The Dutch again sent threats, and they were ignored, despite their complaints to the Swedish government.

> "No governor of Delaware
> Before or since,
> Has weighed as much
> As Johan Printz."

A hefty 400 pounds, Johan Printz (known behind his back as "Round John") was selected to become New Sweden's next leader. He was a man with a distinguished military career and an even more distinguished physique. Even the Indians called him "Big Belly." Headstrong, overbearing, arrogant, but a capable administrator, he was the first native-born Swede to govern the new colony. His objectives were to corner the fur trade with the natives; produce wool for export; find out whether metals or minerals were available for mining; establish a salt works, fishery, or whaling industry; and, almost comically, see if the ham-handed Swedes and Finns could create a silk industry to compete with Japan. Under his direction, the New Sweden colony grew slowly. To further solidify Swedish holdings, Printz decided to move the "capital" of New Sweden to Tinicum Island, north of Fort Christina, at the mouth of the Schuykill River. He built an elaborate, two-story governor's manse with fireplaces made of imported Swedish brick, which he modestly named Printzhoff. For added security, he had another fort called New Gothenburg constructed on the island. In the Swedes first incursion onto the east side of the Delaware, he also ordered the building of Fort Elfsborg, near today's Salem River, equipped with enough fire power to forestall any enemy ships sailing up the river.

When this news reached the Dutch, they were absolutely steamed and sent the new director-general of New Netherland, Peter Stuyvesant, to do something about it. He traveled overland to Fort Nassau, where he had prearranged a rendezvous with eleven Dutch ships, the largest European flotilla yet seen on the Delaware. After dismantling the fort, he proceeded with its armament and supplies to a place about six miles south of Fort Christina called Santhoeck. Here he constructed Fort Casimir with a storehouse, barracks, and several houses, all made of logs and contained within palisades. Stuyvesant had effectively outflanked the Swedes and gained control of the river with no loss of blood on either side. The conflict had become a war of forts, essentially a Scandinavian pillow fight.

Both sides claimed the land they controlled had been purchased from the Indians, who were certainly not to blame, since they were merely accepting gifts for the use of the land. They couldn't tell the difference between a Dutchman, Swede, or Finn, nor did they care.

This chess match over disputed territories continued with the arrival of Johan Rising (Ree-sing). He replaced Johan Printz as governor, who by this time had over-stayed his welcome in New Sweden and was heading for home by way of New Amsterdam. Pleased with his triumph, Stuyvesant left a small contingent of soldiers at the new fort and also returned to New Amsterdam. When Rising arrived in the Delaware in May of 1654, he was already well aware that Fort Casimir had been built. Approaching it cautiously, he fired a couple of warning shots. When none were returned, a boatload of musketeers was sent ashore to investigate and found the fort defended by only nine men who had no gunpowder. The fort was surrendered on May 21—Trinity Sunday—and renamed Fort Trefaldighet (Fort Trinity).

Needless to say, this was not the end of the festivities. When the peg-legged Peter Stuyvesant received the news about this latest incident, he was furious. A man with a legendary temper, he vowed, with full support from the DWIC, to drive the Swedes and Finns out of New Sweden forever. Gathering an attack force of ships in New Amsterdam harbor, he sailed up the Delaware to Fort Trinity and established a beachhead near the fort. Overwhelmed by the show of force, Sven Skute, the officer in charge of the fort, quickly capitulated. The Hollanders then moved on to Fort Christina, preparing for a siege. After several days of negotiations, Governor Rising turned over control of New Sweden to Stuyvesant on September 15, 1655, and that was effectively the end of New Sweden. It was another bloodless coup, the only casualty being a Swedish soldier shot in the leg for trying to desert.

Stuyvesant generously allowed Swedish and Finnish settlers to remain and get on with their lives, or leave if they wished. About 250–300 decided to stay and lived peacefully under Dutch rule until the English forcibly took control of New Netherland in 1664. Even then, the English considered the Scandinavian settlers harmless and they continued their rural lifestyles, gradually becoming absorbed into the growing British colonies.

9

This charming folk art graphic was re-created from a hand-painted sign done by Rich DeMarco. It's located along the Greenwich-Bridgeton Road.

If you want to avoid offending someone from the small waterfront community of Greenwich, New Jersey, do not pronounce the name of their town "Gren-itch." Pronounce it "Green-witch." This is not because the local population are a bunch of yokels who can't speak the Queen's English; it's a matter of great pride and pedigree going back several hundred years. During the revolution, the townsfolk railed against anything English—including the name of their town.

There is some dispute over the name's origin. Some claim it comes directly from Greenwich on the Thames, while others believe it is a derivation of Old Greenwich in Connecticut. Going back further still, the town's original name was Cohansey, after the river where it is located, which takes it's name from the Lenape. And if you haven't had enough, Cohansey can be spelled about nine different ways.

There are other river towns with English origins and strict adherences to their individuality. Mauricetown comes to mind, an old fishing and oystering village on the Maurice River, northeast of Port Norris. In terms of pronunciation, "Morristown" is correct; "Morees-town" will be met with hostility.

Greenwich, in Cumberland County, takes it's name from William Augustus, Duke of Cumberland. The son of George II, he was responsible for crushing the Jacobite Rebellion and Bonny Prince Charlie's aspirations to the throne in 1746.

The town straddles two bends of the Cohansey River, which winds its way to the upper reaches of the Delaware Bay. It is a small, tightly-knit, peace-loving community of about 800 residents. There have been no murders there in over 300 years, possibly because of the Quaker influence. Called the Williamsburg of New Jersey, it should be the other way around: Greenwich was established fifteen years before Williamsburg. It has also never been restored like the colonial showplace in Virginia—what you see has been there from it's earliest days. Change occurs slowly; people who have lived here for perhaps twenty years are still referred to as outsiders. The town has deep roots.

Long before Peter Minuit, Captain Mey, or even Henry Hudson saw the Delaware, the Lenni Lenape were living here. And not living too badly either, judging from the contents of the Cumberland County Prehistorical Museum in Greenwich. The museum is filled with thousands of stone arrowheads, spearheads, clubs, tools, pottery, and other artifacts. The Indians thrived on an abundance of game, fish, and shellfish. In addition, they grew maize, beans, and squash. Still, it was a Stone Age existence, as there was no fabric for clothing and no metal for knives or other tools. They simply used what was available—stone, clay, and bone. Understanding this makes it easier to grasp how the Lenape were so accepting of the early European settlers. These foreigners brought gifts that were beyond comprehension, such as bolts of cloth, knives, and iron cooking pots. The early Dutch explorers established healthy trade relationships with the Indians that lasted for years with each new wave of settlers.

In 1675, Major John Fenwick, who had once fought in Cromwell's army and had since become a Quaker, landed at what is now Salem and founded the first permanent English-speaking colony along the Delaware. From there he focused on establishing a twin colony in the area around the Cohansey and

The Old Stone Tavern, circa 1728

proposed sixteen-acre "manor lots." He died before his plan could come to fruition, but his executors were able to follow the directions he carefully described in his will. After the rules set down by the crown, the main street was to be 100 feet wide starting at a landing on the Cohansey River and extending north for one mile. To this day it is still called Ye Greate Street and lined with stately trees and homes from the colonial era.

Fenwick, and many of the early English settlers who were Quakers, found themselves persecuted not only for refusing the Church of England but also by Puritans who were fond of cutting off their ears and boring holes in their tongues. But the Quakers would not allow intolerance in the colonies, so Baptists lived next to Presbyterians, who lived next to Episcopalians. Scattered throughout were the Quakers, formally referred to as "The Society of Friends."

AROUND 1695, cargo from foreign ports began to be unloaded at a small wharf on the Cohansey. Merchants from Philadelphia and Burlington came to buy the goods, which they then transported on wagons or floated up-river on barges. In 1701, Greenwich was designated an official port of entry for what was then known as West Jersey. Along with the cargo came thirsty seamen, and more than a few taverns sprang up to accommodate them. Just about all survive, but are now private homes.

It was at the port of Greenwich in 1774 that a brig named the *Greyhound* landed with a cargo of tea from the East India Company in London. It was consigned to merchants in Philadelphia, but never arrived. The captain of the brig took on a river pilot at Lewes, Delaware, who informed him that his load of heavily taxed English tea would probably not be welcomed there. Earlier, the *Polly*, also loaded with tea, had been refused entry at Philadelphia, where she had been threatened by a mob of angry patriots. Not wanting to put his cargo or vessel in danger, the *Greyhound*'s skipper, J. Allen, contacted Daniel Bowen, a local Tory, and secured permission to store the tea in Bowen's cellar while waiting for further instructions. Secrets are hard to keep in small towns, and before long everyone knew of the tea's whereabouts.

Separation from England was nearly a forgone conclusion at this time, and the tea's presence merely added to the indignation of patriotic community members. In a repeat scene played out just a year before in Boston, the young patriots of Greenwich dressed as Indians, complete with war paint, broke into Bowen's cellar, and carted the hidden tea out into the town square. A huge bonfire was made using the tea for fuel and before long, many villagers were cheering loudly. The "Indians" galloped out of town when it was over, whooping and hollering, their identities no secret to anyone. When the owners of the tea, John Duffield and Stacy Hepburn of Philadelphia, heard of the incident, they demanded restitution. Greenwich Sheriff Jonathan Elmer was ordered to make arrests and collect a jury. The jury included members of the tea burners families and sympathizers, and since two of the "Indians" were his brothers, Ebenezer and Timothy, the verdict read "no cause for action." Governor William Franklin, a supporter of the crown, was not pleased with the outcome and appointed Daniel Bowen to replace Elmer as sheriff. A new jury was assembled and a second trial took place, but the outcome was the same. The two unfortunate Philadelphia merchants finally gave up.

Many of the tea burners went on to distinguished careers after serving in the Continental Army. Andrew Hunter Jr. became a professor at Princeton; Richard Howell served as a New Jersey governor; Thomas Ewing became a surgeon; and another governor, Joseph Bloomfield, had a city named after him.

In 1908, at Market Square in Greenwich, a handsome memorial was erected to honor the participants in the "tea party," their names engraved on a granite slab. It is still there, as though it happened yesterday. Greenwich and Boston were not the only hosts of tea parties: two months before the Greenwich party, patriots in Annapolis, Maryland, forced a ship owner to burn his own vessel, which contained tea and other imported English goods.

PHILIP VICKERS Fithian was another tea burner who, while not as famous, left a legacy as a chronicler of human nature and physical and social customs. He attended Princeton University when it was known as the College of New Jersey, became a Presbyterian minister, traveled throughout the colonies, and even witnessed Revolutionary War battles first-hand as a chaplain. He kept exhaustive journals that described everything from window pane sizes and quantity to the treatment of slaves. Two of his journals were published 124 years after his death at age twenty-seven. Rich DeMarco, a devotee of Fithian and curator of the Cumberland County Prehistorical Museum in Greenwich, believes he could have become one of America's best-known authors had he lived longer. His most well-known writing describes his time spent as a tutor at Nomini Hall, Westmoreland County, Virginia, where he came in contact with the aristocracy of the Old Dominion: Lee, Washington, Custis, Fairfax, Stratford, and more. It was also during this time that he began a series of love letters to his childhood sweetheart, Elizabeth Beatty, whom he affectionately called Laura.

His observations were so precise that they were used for reference when some of the buildings at Williamsburg were restored. Nomini Hall was described as "76 feet long East to West and 14 feet wide North to South, two stories high, the pitch of the lower story being seventeen feet." He continues: "On the south side or front in the upper story are 4 windows, each having 24 lights of glass. In the lower story are 2 windows each having 42 lights of glass and 2 doors each having 16 lights."

At the end of his tutoring assignment, Fithian happened to pass through Annapolis on his journey home. While there, he witnessed the burning of a ship called *Peggy Stewart*, which was carrying seventeen chests of English tea. This may or may not have inspired him to help instigate the Greenwich tea party.

Although history books claim that no image of Fithian exists today, they are wrong. A print of a charcoal portrait of him hangs in an exposed closet on the second floor of the Gibbon House in Greenwich. The artist and location of the original is a mystery. The house was built by one of its earliest residents in 1730. It is also the home of the Cumberland County Historical Society (www.cchistsoc.org). The building has been immaculately preserved by its owners over the years and is now a superb museum exhibiting period furniture, clothing, utensils, tools, and other items from the colonial era. There is also quite an impressive display of Civil War artifacts, many of them found in the attic, including a large marching drum that some young man must have struggled to carry and beat while marching into battle.

In the kitchen sits a seventeenth-century chair said to have come over on the *Mayflower*. This is a common claim made about furniture and ancestors, but in this case it just might be true. The chair was sent to the Winterthur Museum in Delaware, a former DuPont family estate that contains some of the most extraordinary collections of Early American furniture in the country. Their expert curators examined the Greenwich chair, determined its age and origin, and concluded that it could very well have made it to the shores of Cape Cod with the Pilgrims.

Another remarkable piece of American history is a figurehead rescued from the ship *John* that wrecked at the mouth of the Cohansey in 1797. This brought about the eventual building of a lighthouse at the same shoal, named after the ship, though not for another 79 years.

Perhaps the most interesting piece of early history sits not in the house, but in the back yard. The Swedish Granary was originally located on a nearby farm and donated to the historical society. Thought to have been built around 1660 by Swedes or, more likely, Finns, this ancient structure used for drying grain is one of the oldest log buildings in the nation.

SHIP BUILDING was a key industry in Greenwich from colonial times until the decline of the Delaware Bay oystering business. Between 1852 and 1929 at least 38 ships, mostly schooners, were built there. Some may still be in Greenwich— not on the river but at the Greenwich Boat Works, a full-service marina where a yard is littered with old boats for sale. Most are small pleasure craft, but quite a few old commercial fishing vessels were once among them, beaten and battered with rusty fittings and gaping holes in their wooden hulls. Some oyster boats still in service don't look much better. They are on land for repairs nearly as much as they are on the water. There is still one intriguing old boat there called *New Buccaneer*—a large, old cabin cruiser ninety or so feet long, its hull planking attached with thousands of stainless steel screws. With most of its superstructure removed, it has seen better days, and what days they must have been! The Greenwich Boat Works owner told me it was owned by the US Coast Guard and used as a rescue vessel. It has been slowly rotting for over twenty-five years. I was a bit disappointed that it looks more like a pleasure craft. I could just picture a stereotypical playboy like George Hamilton on the bridge, a hot momma on each arm, sipping a Harvey Wallbanger.

There once was a restaurant at the Boat Works called the Ship John Inn—a rather swanky affair for an area not known for fine eating establishments.

My wife and I dined there on one of our wedding anniversaries. We had seen an ad in a local newspaper promising dinner and a boat ride to see the Ship John Lighthouse at twilight. We arrived at the restaurant just in time to see sailboats coming up the Cohansey to tie up for the night, each one performing a perfect tack as they swung around a bend in the river. After a fine dinner, the restaurant owner took us and a few other diners out in her Chris Craft cabin cruiser to visit the lighthouse just as the sun was setting. It was spectacular. Unfortunately, the restaurant has long since gone dark, but maybe some enterprising soul will take a chance on it again. The location is perfect.

The New Buccaneer at the Greenwich Boat Works

10

Salem

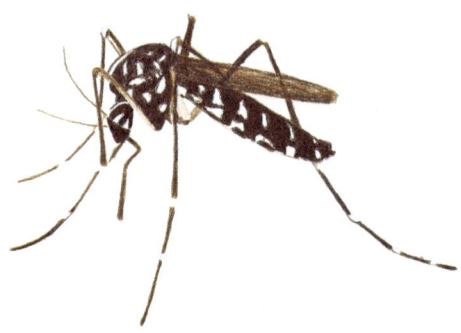

In March of 1654, the Swedish ship *Örn* anchored in the Delaware River near present-day Salem. She was carrying Johan Rising on his way to Fort Christina in Wilmington, Delaware, to become the next governor of New Sweden. On the shore sat Fort Nya Elfsborg, or what was left of it. The fort was deserted and in ruins.

Fort Elfsborg's construction had been ordered in 1643 by Johan Printz, the previous New Sweden governor, to discourage Dutch and English ships from heading up-river to trade with the Indians. Built with 2,700 oak planks, stone, and turf, it was designed with three armed bastions consisting of four iron and four brass cannons that fired twelve-pound balls, and a mortar. It was commanded by Lieutenant Sven Skute, the same man who would surrender Fort Trinity across the river to Peter Stuyvesant twelve years later. Thirteen other soldiers also manned the post. It turned out to be a hell-hole. The fort was built on marshy ground that was home to hordes of mosquitoes. The men affectionately renamed it Myggenborg, or Fort Mosquito. The soldiers could get no rest day or night, and many fell ill from the constant barrage of insect bites. The situation became so unbearable that the fort had to be abandoned.

Along with mosquitoes, there are any number of flying and crawling insects that find habitation along the river—greenhead flies, deer flies, black flies, horse flies, fruit flies, chiggers, ticks, gnats, and millions of other "no-see-ems" that find human blood irresistible.

The precise location of the fort is unknown; no drawings or detailed maps exist to verify the location, but many people love to speculate.

Fort Elfsborg was named after the thirteenth-century fortress offshore from Gothenburg, Sweden. A large stone from that fort now sits on the lawn of a school in Elsinboro Township, just south of Salem. On it is a plaque commemorating the 350th anniversary of those who served there.

It is remarkable that something that existed for a such a short while in history and has been gone for so long is still remembered to such an extent. Even the road to the area is still called Fort Elfsborg Road. Our past means a lot to us.

Near the site of the old fort is the mouth of the Salem River. The Dutch named it Varkens Kill, and its Lenape name is Asamo Hackingskijl. In the seventeenth century this region was claimed simultaneously by England, Holland, and Sweden. To the English it was part of a buffer zone between the overlapping colonies of Plymouth to the north and Virginia to the south. Since the English were not occuping the land at the time, the Dutch helped themselves to it, built a few outposts, and claimed it as New Netherland, to be used for fur trading with the Indians. Then the Swedes raised their flag over the same ground, declaring it New Sweden. All of these interesting ingredients have combined to create a city steeped in history. When some small burg calls itself the "Historic Town of Keisterville," it is kidding itself. Salem is *old*.

SALEM WAS IN an area that came to be known as New Albion, chartered by Sir Edmund Plowden (or Ployden) with the approval of Charles I of England in 1632. Actually, the full proposed name was the Albion Knights for the Conversion of the Twenty-Three Kings. The alleged kings were Indians who would be put to death if they did not convert to the knight's way of thinking. New Albion was to be a quasi-kingdom governed by an elaborate court of deputy governors, supreme councils, chancellors, court barons, captains, and generals; many of the positions were to be held by Plowden's seventeen children. Plowden would never create this kingdom-colony, however, because he was constantly in a state of debt and because the Dutch and Swedes refused to honor his claim.

Meanwhile, the New Haven Colony, an offshoot of the Plymouth colony in Massachusetts, quietly sent a small group of settlers to the Varkens Kill in 1640 to establish an agricultural community. They planned on making tobacco

their primary crop, as it was wildly popular in Europe. This was undoubtedly the first English settlement in New Jersey, although not a permanent one. In the winter of 1642–'43, Dutch soldiers under orders from Governor Kieff, leader of the New Netherland colony, burned their homes and forced them to leave. This may have been the group mentioned earlier who made their way down to Cape May to re-establish themselves, but their story is obscure and steeped in shadows.

In time, the Swedes and Finns would cross the river from Delaware, and they too would farm, as they had in their respective homelands. They would also bring with them their method of temporary shelter—the log cabin. The Dutch had no permanent settlements here, their main endeavor being trade under the auspices of the Dutch West India Company. But in 1655, they put an end to New Sweden, and in 1664 the English put an end to New Netherland. The settlers didn't care what it was called, however, as long as they were left alone.

ON BROAD STREET in today's Salem is an old Friends burial ground, and in the middle of it stands the Salem oak— eighty-five feet high with foliage that covers over a quarter-acre of the cemetery. It is estimated to be between 500 and 700 years old. Major John Fenwick is said to have signed a real estate transaction with a group of Lenni Lenape leaders under its branches in 1675. The price was reported to be four guns with powder and lead, about 336 gallons of rum, eight knives, three pairs of scissors, and some English clothing. (Manhattan was a bargain!)

Fenwick had come from England with nearly his entire family, minus his wife, and a boatload of legal and financial problems. He proposed selling real estate and setting up a haven for those encountering harsh religious persecution, mainly Quakers. The land in question was bequeathed to the Duke of York by his brother, Charles II, after the takeover of the Dutch colony. The duke then turned over the land to John Lord Berkeley and Sir George Carteret to reward their loyalty during the English Civil War. Berkeley then sold his portion to Fenwick on behalf of one Edward Byllynge, a brewer saddled with financial difficulties who was unable to negotiate his own deal. William Penn was then brought into the picture to head a trio of trustees who tried to untangle the Byllynge mess while keeping it a Quaker affair. They divided the newly acquired holdings into fractions until Fenwick wound up with one-tenth of the total property for his services in the transaction, and with this he made plans for his colony. He quickly mortgaged his one-tenth to finance it. He was warned to delay until more elaborate plans involving Penn and others could be instituted, but Fenwick would not wait. He would pay dearly for his impatience. His creditors claimed the mortgage transferred all property rights to them, and Penn himself backed them up. Fenwick felt cheated, but went ahead with his plans anyway.

After landing at Varken's Kill, Fenwick started his colony, meaning to call it Shalom, the Hebrew word for peace, which was somehow anglicized to Salem. Seeking to create a separate crown colony, he appointed himself both Lord Proprietor and Governor, which caught the attention of Lord Edmund Andross, Royal Governor of New York. Andross had Fenwick arrested on charges of impersonating a royal governor and brought to New York in chains. To add to his misery, his own son-in-law sued him in prison and his land surveyors deserted him. Finally, in 1682, Fenwick succumbed to his legal and financial burdens and sold his land holdings to William Penn and others at little or no profit. A year later he was dead, buried in an unmarked grave in an area he had named Fenwick Grove. A monument erected in 1925 along the Salem-Woodstown Road can still be seen today.

A courthouse built on Broad Street in 1692 and replaced in 1735 is still in use today. Only the King William County Courthouse in Virginia is older. In 1774 the Salem Courthouse was the site of a county petition to George III to address colonial grievances and authorize relief to Bostonians, who were suffering under the King's sanctions in reaction to the Boston Tea Party.

It is also the place where Americans found that they would not die from eating "love apples." In 1820 Colonel Robert Gibbon Johnson, a veteran of the Revolutionary War who would later become the first mayor of Salem, stood on the courthouse steps and bit into a juicy tomato in front of a horrified crowd. A doctor stood by in case first aid needed to be administered. When nothing happened to Johnson, the crowd cheered. Colonel Johnson is credited with introducing the eventual multi-million dollar tomato industry into Salem County. This is unconfirmed, of course, but still makes a great little folktale.

Judge William Hancock of the King's Court presided here during the American Revolution. Hancock, like many other early colonists, was a Quaker who took no stand—neither loyalist nor rebel, which makes his story even more unfortunate. During the winter of 1777, Washington sent General "Mad" Anthony Wayne to South Jersey to forage for food and supplies for his starving troops at Valley Forge. In Philadelphia, British General William Howe sent General Charles Mawhood to do the same. However, Mawhood's activities met with stiff resistance from the Salem County militia, which resulted in a battle at Quinton's Bridge, a key link to the bread basket that was Cumberland and Salem Counties. Meanwhile, General Wayne led what came to be known as "the great cow chase" through the streets of Salem and made his way back to Valley Forge with food on the hoof and supplies for the starving army. George Washington later remarked that if it weren't for the arrival of sustenance, the war might have been lost that cold and bleak winter. Out of frustration over the South Jersey colonists' support for the Continental Army, Mawhood issued the order: "Go—spare no one—put all to death—give no quarter." And on the morning of March 21, 1778, 300 British troops commanded by John Graves Simcoe converged on Judge Hancock's house on Alloway Creek and bayoneted everyone inside. Ten were killed and five wounded, including the judge. The British knew there were rebels in the house but had no idea Hancock was there. He died from his wounds several days later.

The Old Salem Courthouse, circa 1735

Judge Hancock built the house in 1734 out of brick made on the premises. His and his wife Sarah's initials are clearly visible on the west side of the house set above a herringbone pattern of glazed bricks in an old English style known as Flemish Bond. The home, a few miles south of Salem, is now a state-operated museum.

On Salem's Market Street, one of the oldest commercial thoroughfares in the US is the home of Abigail Goodwin, a Quaker woman who ran an Underground Railroad station with her sister Elizabeth. They provided lodging, food, clothing, and money to fugitive slaves who had crossed the Delaware on their way north to freedom. She even raised money for abolitionists to purchase slaves in the Carolinas, who would then be brought north and set free. Abigail and her sister secured the freedom of hundreds of former slaves, many of whom chose to remain in Salem, living among the Quakers.

WITH ITS EASY access to the Delaware, Salem developed an early shipping industry, receiving cargo from Philadelphia, Boston, and the Caribbean. It was also the first official port of entry in South Jersey and continued to be an important trade center until the close of the eithteenth century. It grew into a vibrant industrial city in the nineteenth century. It's close proximity to much of New Jersey's farmland led to the development of various machine works that produced canning machinery, mowers, and other agricultural implements. Glass-making also became an important industry; Casper Wistar established the first successful glass factory in America near Salem in 1738. He enticed German glassblowers by offering free passage, land, homes, and a one-third interest in company profits in exchange for their skill and formulas. The town established around the factory became known as Wistarburgh, and the glass became known as Wistarburgh glass. During the nineteenth century, four glassworks were in operation in Salem, including the Salem Glass Works, now the container division of the Anchor Glass Corporation. Glass-making was a huge industry throughout South Jersey due to the abundance of fine sand and silica. Other towns that sprang up around the glass factories included Glassboro

A Wistarburgh bottle

(established by former Wistarburgh employees) and Millville, home of Wheaton Industries for many years. Many others were not as successful and simply disappeared.

More industry is located to the east of Salem in the township of Mannington. This may sound like a typical Anglo name, but is actually derived from the local Indian word Maneto. It was also known as East Fenwick, another homage to Salem's founder, until the early eighteenth century. Mannington Mills, the award-winning flooring manufacturer, has it's corporate headquarters and a manufacturing plant here. In business since 1915 and spanning four generations, it began in Salem as a small vinyl flooring manufacturer and now has plant locations all over the US.

But the largest employer by far is the Salem Nuclear Generating Station, which, along with the Hope Creek Generating Station, provides jobs for 1,500 people. It is considered the second largest nuclear generating facility in the US. Situated on a 740-acre site on the Delaware just south of Salem, the combined stations generate enough electricity for three million homes every day, about half of New Jersey. You know you're within ten miles of Salem when you can see the steam from its cooling tower.

IF A HISTORICAL pedigree was the only prerequisite for success, Salem would be doing fine. Today it's a bit shabby and rough around the edges but is trying desperately to preserve its heritage. Approximately $40 million in private investment has been raised for preservation work involving hundreds of volunteers. There are some gorgeous old buildings originally laid out by old John Fenwick, particularly in the historic downtown area along Market and Broad Streets.Many, including the courthouse, date to the early eighteenth century and are on the Register of Historic Places. The Alexander Grant Mansion (1721) on Market Street houses the Salem County Historical Society (www.salemcountyhistoricalsociety.com), which serves as a museum displaying artifacts dating to the seventeenth century, including Wisterburgh glass and some superb examples of colonial-era furniture. There is also a display celebrating Salem's agricultural roots, including a reconstructed farm kitchen and tools and memorabilia dating far back into the seventeenth century. The collection of locally crafted grandfather clocks is particularly impressive. The building is also home to the Josephine Jaquette Memorial Research Library with collections of deeds, maps, genealogical records, diaries, ship manifests, and periodicals from South Jersey and Pennsylvania. They deserve to be remembered and cared for lovingly. Salem is, after all, one of the oldest towns in New Jersey, if not the nation.

11
Rat Call

Pea Patch Island, situated at a point where the Delaware River expands to become the Delaware Bay, is home to nine different species of herons, egrets, and ibis, and is the largest wading bird rookery north of Florida. It is also home to Fort Delaware, a massive pile of granite and brick built to defend the port cities of the Delaware. More than 12,000 Confederate soldiers lived there during the Civil War, many of whom were captured during the three-day battle of Gettysburg.

THE PRISONERS were housed in barracks a little further north of the fort. This was unique compared to other facilities, like Andersonville in Georgia, where prisoners had to make their own shelter, but it was certainly not a country club. Conditions were deplorable due to the logistical nature of the situation. Funds and resources were directed to troops in the field, especially during 1863 and 1864 when Union forces were in excess of 100,000. One prisoner told of hearing the cry, "Rat call! Rat call!" and seeing a guard throwing rats down to hungry prisoners who scrambled after them. The rats were cleaned, soaked in salt water, and fried. It is doubtful that they tasted like chicken.

In addition to the meager rations, smallpox, cholera, measles, dysentery, and scurvy contributed to many deaths. Imagine facing the rigors of a three-day battle like Gettysburg and then being transported to a prison where conditions were even worse. A slower death than being shot awaited you. Still, Fort Delaware claimed one of the lowest death rates of any US Civil War prisons—ten percent. Early on, the dead were buried on the grounds north of the fort, but due to the proximity to the river and its low water table, they were later exhumed and a permanent cemetery was established at Finn's Point, on the New Jersey side of the river.

Pea Patch Island's strategic position was noted as early as the American Revolution by the Marquis de Lafayette. He proposed a defensive fortification

to protect the major ports of New Castle and Philadelphia. A wood and earthen fortress began in 1817 when the island was wrested from its owner—a Dr. Henry Gale, who used it as a personal game preserve. The US military had offered Gale $30,000 for the island, but he refused. The military eventually got its way by appealing to the Delaware state legislature for the right of eminent domain. Due to the marshy environment, however, construction was halted for years until fire destroyed the unfinished structure in 1831.

The origins of the name Pea Patch Island are a bit cloudy, but local lore has it that a ship carrying a cargo of peas ran aground, spilling its load, which eventually sprouted along the banks.

The present fort was completed in 1859 after nearly ten years of construction and was the largest and most impressive in the country. Some twenty-five million bricks and tons of granite were used to create walls that were thirty feet thick in some places and thirty feet high. Three tiers of guns were installed and a thirty-foot-wide moat surrounded the fort.

Of the engineers involved in the project, none was better known than George B. McClellan, soon to become one of many ill-fated commanders of the Army of the Potomac, removed from his position not once, but twice due to his overly-cautious offensive tactics. He also ran and lost to Abraham Lincoln in the 1864 presidential campaign.

Built for defensive purposes, Fort Delaware never had to use its weapons in battle during the Civil War, as the North controlled most of the Eastern seaboard's port cities. But they did find that it would make a splendid prison once the war was well under way.

The first sizable batch of prisoners were from Stonewall Jackson's army, brought to the fort after the first battle of Kernstown, Virginia, in 1862. This was one of Jackson's rare defeats. The fort had not been constructed as a prison and barracks space was crowded, but in the early days of the war prisoner exchanges were common, so that later in that year, only 123 prisoners were being held. That would change  dramatically after the battles of Vicksburg and Gettysburg in 1863. This was when wooden barracks were built to house the captives, whose numbers kept increasing as the war dragged on, eventually swelling to over 12,000. At one point there were only 300 Union guards to keep watch over this mass of prisoners. And, of course, there were always inmates willing to risk their lives in the icy waters of the Delaware to escape.

The official records of the Union suggest a low number of escapes, but Confederate sources claim hundreds or thousands. The US military reported fifty-four escapes, but an actual number is likely almost twice that.

Swimming to freedom was not a sound idea due to the treacherous currents, but other methods were attempted, such as wearing canteens as flotation gear and fashioning makeshift boats from driftwood or other floatable scraps. There is the story of one winter when Union guards amused themselves by ice skating. For further enjoyment, they had some of the southern prisoners, who weren't used to frigid conditions, give it a try. They strapped skates on one prisoner who proceeded to fall down repeatedly, each spill taking him a little closer to shore until he was able to ditch the skates and run for freedom.

James J. Archer was an inmate there, one of the highest ranking prisoners and the first Confederate general to be taken captive from the Army of Northern Virginia since Lee assumed command. A man with a frail constitution, he was exhausted from the first day of battle at Gettysburg and took cover in a thicket, where he was seized and escorted behind Union lines only to briefly meet an old colleague, Union Maj. General Abner

General James J. Archer, Army of Northern Virginia

Doubleday. This happened frequently during the war; men who had been classmates, had roomed together, had worked together, and had even served together now found themselves on opposite sides of battle. While he was being taken to Fort Delaware, Picketts' famous charge took place, which Archer would have taken part in.

Political prisoners were held at the fort, too, including governor of Texas F. R. Lubbock and Burton H. Harrison, private secretary to Jefferson Davis, who had the distinction of being the last prisoner brought to the fort in 1866. Other notable detainees were Lt. McHenry Howard, grandson of Francis Scott Key, and Capt. Samuel Taylor, grandson of President Zachary Taylor.

THE FORT WAS de-activated after the Civil War, then re-activated during the Spanish-American War with updated weaponry. It was also used in World War I, and after World War II the Pentagon declared it a "surplus site" and abandoned all together. The State of Delaware acquired it in 1947, and the entire island is now known as Fort Delaware State Park.

Today it is accessible only by the Three Forts Ferry that runs seasonally between Delaware City, Pea Patch Island, and Fort Mott. Bring a lunch and wear sensible shoes. Visitors are free to wander through much of the fort, including the lower-level gun casements, which are dark, damp, and a bit creepy, prompting stories of ghostly images. There is also a working blacksmith's shop, laundry, issue room, infirmary, ordnance room, mess hall, kitchen, and a daily firing demonstration of an eight-inch Columbiad cannon. Staffed by a dedicated group of well-informed volunteers and re-enactors dressed in period garb, they even use language and terms specific to the nineteenth century and will discuss their day-to-day topics, such as how much the prisoners complain, "but then, all prisoners complain."

The Illustrated Delaware River

The "Disappearing" Gun Batteries at Fort Mott

12
Fort Mott

As you head down a narrow road in Pennsville Township that winds past a landfill covered with phragmites, a clearing opens up and giant mounds appear as if it were some ancient burial site. These are the gun batteries of Fort Mott, built during the years preceding the Spanish-American War to guard the Delaware River and its ports. The mounds are made of concrete and brick thirty-five feet thick and over 700 feet long, and nearly completely covered with earth and grass so that they blend in with the landscape when viewed from far out on the river. Even the guns were designed to be unseen—"disappearing guns."

The fort is classified as an Endicott Period installation, named for William C. Endicott, Secretary of War under Grover Cleveland from 1890–1910. Cleveland petitioned a military and civilian Board of Fortifications headed by Endicott. He found the US defenses woefully lacking and recommended a whopping $127 million construction program to utilize new heavy ordnance technology. Rather than construct masonry fortresses, like Fort Delaware, a system of concrete emplacements with fewer but

One of the observation towers used to direct fire

larger guns were constructed in various locations around the country, most near ports and coastal areas. One of the first was at Fort Hancock at Sandy Hook, New Jersey, next to the Sandy Hook Lighthouse, the oldest lighthouse still operating in the US. It is now a recreation area, part of the National Park System.

Located north of Salem, Fort Mott was one of three installations built along this part of the river that also included Fort Delaware, which can be seen out on Pea Patch Island, directly in front of the batteries, and Fort DuPont, on the other side of the river. Fort Delaware was already obsolete when Fort Mott and Fort Dupont were constructed, and the later forts suffered the same fate shortly after World War I when Fort Saulsbury was built near Milford, Delaware. In its most active period, Fort Mott contained over thirty buildings, including two large 115-man barracks, officers' housing, a hospital, PX, library, guard house, stable, YMCA, and a school for the soldiers' children. It even had a baseball team. The only remaining buildings are the guardhouse, Post HQ, and the Ordnance Building, which houses the museum. Visitors can wander around, over and inside parts of the fort, taking advantage of a self-guided tour.

A beautiful view of the river stretches out in front of the mounds, peaceful and quiet despite the military presence. It's like the well-groomed estate of a Guilded Age business tycoon. The installation is a park now, tended lovingly by the state of New Jersey with a small playground and picnic tables set in a grove of stately pine trees. The military seems to have a knack for choosing locations that are not only strategic but serene. But at the turn of the nineteenth century, this was a noisy place. Firing practice involved the half-dozen ten-inch and twelve-inch guns installed there. It was not only noisy, but ground-shaking as well. Nearby observation towers were deeply anchored in concrete shock absorbers. These monster guns (for their day) were designed to fire 600- to 1,000-pound shells at targets a good eight miles away. There were also several batteries of smaller rapid-fire guns.

Although shots were never fired in combat, as there were no invasions, there was an incident in August of 1908 involving Fort DuPont across the river in Delaware, a fort nearly identical to Fort Mott in purpose and armament. Fort DuPont's guns were being used for a routine calibration exercise that went terribly wrong. Aimed at a remote target near Salem, on the New Jersey side of the river, two rounds were fired, each weighing 300 pounds and packed with cement rather than live ammo. According to an article in the *Salem Standard and Jerseyman* published several days later, "One projectile struck near Town Bank and tore a hole in the earth about eight feet deep and as many feet square, then bounded to a tomato patch nearby, where it also tore up much dirt. When the missile struck the bank, two children of Norris Pew were crabbing from a boat along shore and they were smeared with mud and their pet dog was hit by a clod of dirt and carried some distance." The other shell "landed in a field at Sinnickson's Landing in Elsinboro Township along Salem Creek. It first struck the water several yards from the landing and ricocheted between the cottages of former councilman John F. Taylor and John Sharp and landed in the rear of a two-story dwelling used as a potato store house. A hole almost large enough to hold a horse and cart was made on the ground. Captain John Foley was sitting on the veranda of his cottage watching the target when the projectile hit the water and he states it sent a stream of water 60 to 75 feet into the air."

The guns are not there anymore, some having been sent as far away as Hawaii and France. A park ranger at the park's museum informed me that the ten-inch guns from Battery Harker had been sent to Canada as part of a lend-lease program in 1941. Officials from Fort Mott tried to have them returned but were told by their Canadian counterparts, "Sure, we'll trade them back for a surplus Apache helicopter." The ranger pointed out the

window and said sarcastically, "Oh yeah, I have a whole yard full of them." Apparently the transaction has yet to take place. A few gun tubes are on display behind the museum, but they were taken from dismantled ships and not from the fort itself.

The fort was named in honor of Major General Gershom Mott, a veteran of the Mexican-American and Civil Wars. He was born in 1822 in Lamberton, New Jersey, a small town on the Delaware near Trenton. (His grandfather was Captain John Mott, who it is said guided Washington on his famous crossing of the Delaware on the way to victory at Trenton). Zebulon Pike, for whom Pike's Peak was named, was also born in Lamberton. (The nineteenth century was alive with colorful first names.)

General Gershom Mott

Mott attained the rank of second lieutenant during the Mexican-American War. During the Civil War he was appointed a lieutenant colonel in the Army of the Potomac and took part in the Battle of Seven Pines, Second Battle of Bull Run, Fredericksburg, Chancellorsville, Spotsylvania, and Petersburg, and was wounded a number of times, including a leg wound suffered three days before the Confederate surrender at Appomattox Court House. Mott was one of the few Union officers to be commended in the debacle that came to be known as the Battle of the Crater. After the war, General Mott was appointed to a number of distinguished positions including New Jersey State Treasurer, commander of the New Jersey National Guard, and warden of the New Jersey State Prison in Trenton.

I have a fascination with traffic on the river, and the fort has a long pier that's great for ship spotting. The Three Forts Ferry docks there during the summer. Occasionally when I find a ship heading south, I'll watch it sail out of sight, then jump in my car and head down to Greenwich. A small road snakes through the marsh and dead-ends at the bay. I only need to wait a bit, and I'll be able to see that same ship come sailing by on its way down to Cape Henlopen.

13

Finn's Point

At the end of a narrow road that passes through the grounds of Fort Mott lies Finn's Point National Cemetery. Surrounded by tall stalks of phragmites, it looks like the last place on earth. For the many interred there, it was. Buried in unmarked graves are 2,436 Confederate prisoners who died at Fort Delaware. Their names, however, are listed on the base of an eighty-five-foot-tall concrete and Pennsylvania granite monument erected in 1910 by the US government.

Near the monument are seven iron tablets inscribed with quatrains of the elegy *Bivouac of the Dead*:

Rest on embalmed and sainted dead
Dear as the blood ye gave.
No impious footstep here shall tread
The herbage of your grave.
On fame's eternal camping ground,
Their silent tents are spread,
And glory guards with solemn round
The bivouac of the dead.
No rumor of the foe's advance
Now sweeps upon the wind,
No troubled thought at midnight haunts
Of loved ones left behind.
No vision of the morrow's strife
The warrior's dream alarms,
No braying horn no screaming fife
At dawn shall call to arms.
The neighboring troop, the flashing blade,
The bugle's stirring blast,

THE CHARGE, THE DREADFUL CANNONADE,
THE DIN AND SHOUT ARE PAST.
YOUR OWN PROUD LAND'S HEROIC SOIL
MIGHT BE YOUR FITTER GRAVE,
SHE CLAIMS FROM WAR HIS RICHEST SPOIL,
THE ASHES OF THE BRAVE.
THE MUFFLED DRUM'S SAD ROLL HAS BEAT
THE SOLDIER'S LAST TATOO.
NO MORE ON LIFE'S PARADE SHALL MEET
THE BRAVE AND FALLEN FEW.

The author of this solemn, heartfelt poem is Theodore O'Hara, but his name is not listed anywhere on the tablets. He was a colonel in the Confederate army and it seemed inappropriate to credit him in a cemetery that was also occupied by Union dead—135 who served as prison guards at Fort Delaware. They, too, are remembered with the Union Guards Monument erected in 1879. The Confederate monument gets most of the attention, as it is quite a curiosity to see Southern soldiers buried in the North, especially in New Jersey. The site was declared a national cemetery in 1875 at the request of Virginia Governor James L. Kemper. He had been a brigade commander under Major Gen. George Pickett and was wounded at Gettysburg on July 3, 1863, during the famous charge that ended the battle.

Those interred at Finn's Point are not limited to Civil War casualties. It also contains the graves of thirteen German POWs who died at Fort Dix, New Jersey,

The Union Guards Monument

during World War II. Unlike their Confederate counterparts, they have individual headstones. Also resting there are members of the US Armed Forces from the Spanish-American War, World Wars I and II, and soldiers who served at nearby Fort Mott when it was active. American service veteran burials are still accepted but are limited to cremated remains.

The cemetery is a peaceful spot, lush, green, and well-kept, but on May 9, 1997, the sleeping dead witnessed a senseless tragedy. The cemetery's caretaker, William R. Reese, was approached by a man who demanded the keys to his truck. When he refused, Reese was shot and killed. Two weeks earlier, Andrew Cunanan from California had gone on a killing spree that started in Minneapolis and continued to Rush City, Minnesota, and on to Chicago. He then somehow found his way to the obscure little cemetery at Finn's Point. Reese's truck was later found in a Miami Beach parking lot one block from the home of Cunanan's last victim, fashion designer Gianni Versace. Eight days later he blew his brains out in a Miami houseboat. His motivation for the murders remains a mystery. The cemetery was placed on the National Register of Historic Places in 1978.

FINN'S POINT takes its name from the earliest European settlers in the area—small groups of Finnish colonists crossing the river from Delaware—in the early seventeenth century. The rich soil along the river appealed to them and is still extensively farmed today.

It's not every town that has a national cemetery, but Finn's Point also has a lighthouse. The Finn's Point Rear Range Lighthouse sits at the foot of Lighthouse Road, which bisects with Fort Mott Road in Pennsville. This tall, black cylinder is the back half of an old two-part navigational system. The front range light was in a now-defunct house-like structure that sat on the banks of the Delaware about a mile and a half in front of the rear-range light. The object was to steer a ship toward the two lights, and when they lined up, top and bottom, the pilot would know he was in the middle of the shipping channel. At over 94 feet tall, the rear-range light is all that's left of the system; the front-range was razed in 1938. The tower was built by the Kellogg Bridge Company in Buffalo, New York, in 1876 and shipped by train in pieces to Salem, where it was hauled by mules to the construction site. Fashioned of ¼-inch-thick wrought iron, it's an eight-foot-diameter black tube supported by a skeletal framework. The lighthouse contains a cast iron spiral stairway leading to the lantern and watch-rooms that the lighthouse keeper would have to climb every six and a half hours to wind the weight, which powered a cylindrical shade that gave the light its on-off sequence.

The Finn's Point lights and the Liston Rear Range Light at Port Penn, Delaware, both built around the same time, were important aids in guiding maritime traffic transitioning from the bay to the river during the late nineteenth and early twentieth centuries. The Finn's Point light was extinguished in 1933 and replaced the following year with an automated system. Then in 1950, the Army Corps of Engineers dredged the river channel and the lights became obsolete, finally going dark a year later. The lighthouse was added to the National Register of Historic Places in 1978 and is only available to tourists on special occasions.

Finn's Point

Finn's Point Rear Range Light

14

New Castle

New Castle, Delaware, is an entire history lesson, completely intact. This is no commercially themed reconstruction, but a real town with real residents who live, work, and play in a national landmark.

It began as a small community that grew around Fort Casimir, built in 1651 at the command of Peter Stuyvesant, the one-legged, ill-tempered governor of New Netherland, whom we met previously. The fort was his attempt to thwart the growth of New Sweden, comprised of Scandinavians who had quietly elbowed their way into Dutch territory in 1638 and were competing heavily for the fur trade with the Indians. It kept the Swedes in check, but support for the fort dwindled, and in 1654, Johan Rising, the new (and last) governor of New Sweden, arrived from Europe and easily took command of the fort, which by this time was garrisoned by only nine men with no powder for their weapons. It was re-christened Fort Trinity to honor the day of the capture.

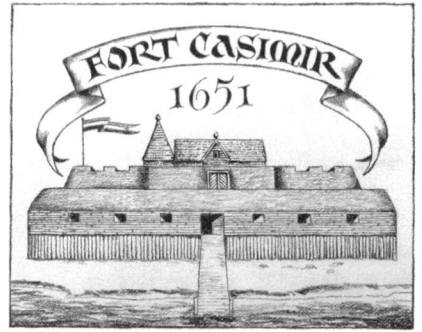

It did not remain in Swedish possession for long. In 1655, Stuyvesant, with a fleet of seven heavily armed ships, sailed from New Amsterdam and quickly regained control of the fort, then captured Fort Christina, the bastion of the Swedish colony, and forced the bloodless capitulation of New Sweden.

There was no confiscation of goods and properties; the Swedes were allowed to stay and live under Dutch rule and keep what they had or return to Scandinavia—the choice was theirs.

Around Fort Trinity, which reverted back to its original name Casimir, the small community continued to grow and was soon named New Amstel after a town near old Amsterdam in Holland. The West India Company saw the potential profits in colonizing the former Swedish holdings and asked for aid from the directors in Amsterdam. It was decided to divide the Dutch colony in two: the northern part including Fort Christina, seven miles to the north, would be called the "Colony of the Company," under the direction of the West India Company. The southern portion, including New Amstel, would be the "Colony of the City," under care of Amsterdam itself. The inhabitants were Swedes and Finns from the now-defunct New Sweden, and of course the Dutch. But other ethnic groups, mostly from Western Europe, were drawn to New Amstel, including French, English, Scots, and Germans.

The Dutch also brought many African slaves with them to round out the labor force. Immigration was encouraged, as it was believed that the area's natural resources could sustain a large money-making operation—all that was needed were people.

Despite the potential for a prosperous Dutch enterprise along the Delaware, the colony suffered many setbacks. Crop failure, disease, disgruntled settlers who moved on to New Amsterdam and other Dutch Settlements, and harassment from their English neighbors in Maryland caused a great deal of ebb and flow in population. Neither the Dutch or Swedish colonies had proper guidance or governors. Those placed in administrative positions were hardly of leadership quality, except for Stuyvesant. Support and supplies were often slow in arriving and sometimes never came at all. Dutch farmers in their homeland were content with their lives and had no desire to uproot their families and set out for an unknown land to start over again. Meanwhile, the English colonies were swelling with new settlers by the hundreds. To them, the Dutch colony of New Netherland was becoming an annoyance, blocking trade routes between the Virginia and New England colonies.

It was at this point, in 1664, that Charles II, King of England, decided to remove the Dutch presence in the New World by granting his brother James, the Duke of York, extensive land holdings that coincided exactly with New Netherland. Colonel Richard Nicolls, a loyal officer of the Duke, sailed into New Amsterdam harbor with four warships carrying 450 soldiers and demanded the immediate surrender of New Netherland. Flustered, Peter Stuyvesant, with no support from the West India Company or Amsterdam, was forced to turn over the city to the English. That city would be ever-after known as New York.

The Dutch House, circa 1690–1710

Shortly thereafter, Sir Robert Carr, a colleague of Nicolls', was dispatched to the Delaware River with two of the four ships and enough men to do the same to New Amstel. This time, however, there was bloodshed. The English ships bombarded Fort Casimir with several broadsides, followed by troops storming the walls. No casualties on the invaders part, but three Dutch soldiers were killed and ten more wounded. This site was also given an English name: New Castle, after New Castle upon Tyne, England's northern fortress throughout the Middle Ages.

Despite a new name and new ownership (and some heavy looting), nothing much really changed for the inhabitants. The Dutch, Swedes, Finns, and others carried on in the same tradition they were accustomed to. But very slowly the area began to become Anglicized as more and more English colonists purchased land and titles. The Scandinavians and Dutch gradually moved west and south.

Not all were tolerant of English domination. There was a short-lived uprising in 1669 caused by one Marcus Jacobson, with the comely nickname "The Long Finn," who spread tales of Swedish warships on their way to resurrect New

Sweden. He was arrested, whipped, branded, and sent to Barbados to be sold as a servant. But while the tales of Swedish ships were pure fantasy, the Dutch were mounting another war with England. And in 1673 a fleet from Holland sailed to Manhattan Island, seized New York, and once again it was in Dutch hands. New Castle (once again New Amstel) and most of New Jersey also reverted to the Dutch. Because it was too difficult to sort out this mixed bag of nationalities—English, Dutch, Swedes, Finns, and others—the rebounded Dutch government guaranteed all the residents along the Delaware their houses, lands, and personal property in exchange for an oath of allegiance to the government of Holland.

But history, like life, is weirder than anything we can make up. Complicated politics in Europe brought the last Dutch-Anglo war to an end, climaxed in February 1674 by the Peace of Westminster. Holland once again gave up their claim to New Netherland, returning it to England. And in the space of 23 years, Fort Casimir had been Dutch, Swedish, Dutch again, English, Dutch and finally English for good.

ON OCTOBER 27, 1682, a gentleman stepped to the dock at New Castle from an English vessel named the Welcome. The next day he was taken to the old fort and given a key. He opened the door to the fort, stepped inside, and locked himself in. When he came out, he was given "1 turf with a twig upon it, a porringer with river water and soil, in part of all." The man's name was William Penn and he had just performed "livery of seisin," a ceremony transferring possession of a great tract of land given to him by King Charles II. Penn's father was a member of Parliament who had gone to Holland in 1660 to bring Charles back to the throne from exile. For this, he was knighted and befriended by the king, who also made him commissioner of the Royal Navy. The king was much more generous with appointments, however, than with payment, and when Penn died in 1670 he was owed a considerable amount of back pay. After ten years, the debt was still owed and young William Penn, his heir, realizing he was not going to see the money, asked for a land grant in America. After negotiations with the Duke of York, the grant was finalized and young William Penn became the proud owner of what was to become Pennsylvania and Delaware. It was the largest land grant ever given to a private citizen. This was to become Penn's "Holy Experiment," as we'll explore later.

After several years of British control, New Castle became a center of commerce, competing with the new city of Philadelphia along the increasingly industrialized Delaware River. It was also a natural port of entry where ships were cleared and could refresh water and supplies after long voyages. Weekly markets and occasional "Grand Fairs" made the town even more vital. You can still visit the "green" with cobblestone streets, the former public square, laid out by Stuyvesant himself.

The town had been the capitol of what were known as the Three Lower Counties because they were considered part of the Pennsylvania territory. But there was a strong desire for the colonists—who could no longer actually be called colonists, as many families had been there for generations—to have their own identity. In September of 1776, the same year the rest of the colonies declared independence from Great Britain, a convention of local leaders met in New Castle and hammered out a new government to be run by the people, making the Three Lower Counties the first state, and naming it Delaware.

Dating from before the revolutionary period, just about all of Olde New Castle displays one example after another of colonial, Dutch, and federal architecture. Entering the town from Route 9 and turning onto Delaware Street, the closer you get to the river, the further back in time you go. You'll really feel like you've entered the Way-back Machine. It's best to park and travel by foot, as many of the main attractions are close at hand, like the Court House, the Amstel House, the Old Dutch House, and the incredibly beautiful Read House & Gardens. You'll discover that Master Read was a signer of the Declaration of Independence. And be sure to stop at Jessup's Tavern and have a beer with Alexander Hamilton in one of the sweetest old river towns on the Delaware.

15

WILMINGTON

There is a Minor League baseball team in Wilmington that calls itself the "Blue Rocks." By all accounts, the name comes from the Brandywine Blue Gneiss granite found all around northern Delaware. But there is another, more romantic, fanciful explanation. In 1638, two ships from Sweden, the *Kalmar Nyckel* and the *Fogel Grip*, landed at a rocky slab along the Christina River. Swedish and Dutch ships of the period were often brightly colored and the *Kalmar Nyckel* was no exception—it was painted royal blue. Some of the paint was scraped off the ship's hull while it maneuvered for a landing, giving the rocks their name. Believe what you will.

There is very little remaining of that rock landing today, much of it having been blasted away to accommodate shipping traffic, but what does remain can be seen at Fort Christina Park on East 7th Street at the Christina River—the oldest section of Wilmington. It's an unexpectedly spacious plot of land surrounded by typical riverside industry—an oil refinery, warehouses, etc. The view across the river is not particularly scenic, either. Overlooking the river, though, is an impressive column made of black Swedish granite. This is the Swedish Tercentenary Monument, presented as a gift to the people of the United States from the people of Sweden, designed and crafted by Swedish sculptor Carl Milles to commemorate the original landing. Atop the column is a stylized vision of the *Kalmar Nyckel*. The park was created by the state of Delaware in 1938 to celebrate the 300th anniversary of the arrival of the colonists. In attendance at the dedication ceremony were Crown Prince Gustav Adolf, Crown Princess Louise, Prince Bertil, and US President Franklin D. Roosevelt. Since then, the 350th and 375th anniversaries have also been attended by Swedish royalty and US dignitaries.

Within hailing distance of the park is the home of the Kalmar Nyckel Foundation, a brand new facility that offers educational programs where students can participate in "hands-on history" discovery sessions. A nearly full-scale portion of the ship has been constructed on the second floor to train volunteers and students in the intricacies of the rigging of a sailing ship. Through the wall-to-ceiling windows of the building is a view of the ship itself, at her berth on the river. A full-scale, highly accurate reproduction of the original, she serves as a floating classroom as well as a unique recreational experience. (Sailing excursions are available from April through November.) The original ship made four Atlantic crossings, the most of any vessel of her day, but the modern ship sails from Wilmington and Lewes, Delaware, to destinations only as far as Virginia and New England.

A portion of the 8 miles of rigging used on the Kalmar Nyckel

Painstaking research and planning for the ship took far longer that the actual construction—from the late 1980s to the 1990s. She was finally launched in 1997, about 200 yards downstream from the site of the original landing at "the Rocks." To learn more about this magnificent floating work of art and maybe book a passage, visit www.kalmarnyckel.org.

By now, you are probably well-acquainted with the historic origins of the New Sweden Colony—how those two ships arrived under the experienced hand of entrepreneur, adventurer, Indian trader, and former governor of New Netherland, Peter Minuit. And how Peter Stuyvesant, his eventual successor, arrived on the Delaware to put an end to the colony in 1655. But instead of taking prisoners or banishing the inhabitants from the country, he kindly and generously allowed them to stay or leave as they wished, "as good and free inhabitants," provided they pledged their loyalty to the Dutch. It was really not much of a choice, the colonists having already put down roots, investing blood and sweat into farms and homesteads. They were scattered over a broad area along the west bank of the river—Upland (Chester), Tinicum, and as far north as the Schuykill River. There was no regular schedule of ship departures or arrivals, either, so those who did leave had to travel to New Amsterdam and then wait for a ship to take them back to Sweden. Most stayed put.

In the early days of the colony, a small village began to appear directly behind Fort Christina. It became known as Christinahamn. This would have been the beginnings of Wilmington, but during the siege that preceded the downfall of the Swedish colony, the Dutch burned the entire village. After the capitulation of New Sweden, the new Dutch regime on the Delaware moved its capital from Fort Christina to Fort Casimir, from which the town of New Amstel and then New Castle would emerge. The triumphant Stuyvesant returned to New Amsterdam after placing a deputy at Fort Christina, which he renamed Fort Altena after a village in the Netherlands. And this, then, was the real origin of what was to become the city of Wilmington.

Nearly ten years would pass and then things would change again—drastically. The English forced the surrender of all Dutch holdings including those on the Delaware. And so began the very slow process of anglicization. Some of the Swedes, Finns, and Dutch who had settled along the Christina River and New Amstel began to migrate to the west and south, while English settlers slowly replaced them, many bringing their slaves along. Meanwhile, the area around the former Fort Christina retained a strong grip on Swedish and Finnish culture. The fort itself was garrisoned by English troops during the takeover and then abandoned. It gradually fell into disrepair and eventually disappeared altogether. Its construction of earth and wood and close proximity to a marshy environment was not conducive to a long existence. There was a limited effort to locate the fort, spurred on by its 375th anniversary, but preliminary tests yielded no results.

NOT LONG AFTER the English gained control of the Dutch colonies, William Penn arrived in New Castle to become the sole proprietor of the Pennsylvania Territory, which included the colonies along the Delaware River. It had been given to him by the Duke of York through King Charles II in payment for debts owed Penn's family. However, the Lower Counties (as they became known) were also claimed by Lord Baltimore, received from a similar debt payment. Baltimore (who already had access to the entire Chesapeake Bay), wanted rights to the waters of the Delaware Bay as well. Penn's dispute

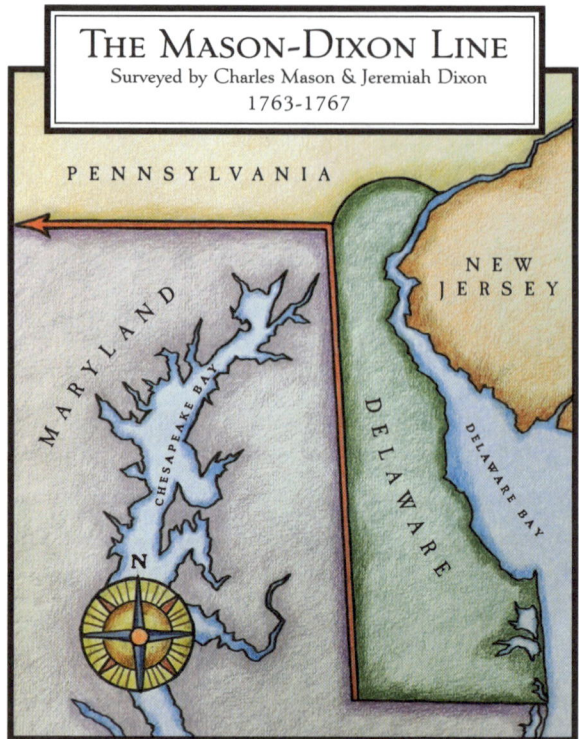

was the obverse—he wanted a port on the Chesapeake. The dispute was so hotly contested that at times it erupted into violence. Until railroads emerged in the nineteenth century, those who controlled the waterways controlled commerce.

It would take until 1763 for Charles Mason and Jeremiah Dixon, two English astronomers, to be brought to America and settle the boundary to everyone's satisfaction. After four years of sightings over difficult terrain, the two were able to finally draw the precise boundaries of the states of Pennsylvania, Delaware, Maryland, and West Virginia (which was still part of Virginia at the time). Using "crownstones" they had brought from England, the surveyors planted one at each mile, with every fifth one displaying an M with Lord Baltimore's family crest on one side and a P with Penn's on the other. A number of these stones are still visible today, although most are on private land.

The line was never intended as a boundary defining the cultural division of the North and South. However, after Pennsylvania abolished slavery, it did serve as the geographical division between slave-holding and free states. Delaware was considered a slave state due to most of it extending south of the line. But it also had a larger percentage of freed slaves than most other states and was one of the first to petition for abolition in it's state assembly. (Minor tidbit of interest: legend has it that the South's fond nickname "Dixie" came from Jeremiah Dixon's last name.)

Most of the land around the Christina River and Fort Altena continued to be owned by just a few Swedes and Finns who had stayed on after the New Sweden absolution. They lived quietly in tightly knit ethnic groups, attending their own churches and still clinging to the old customs and languages. They tended to pass the land along to their families, leaving little opportunity for new settlers. But by the 1730s, nearly 100 years since their ancestors had first arrived from the old country, a rebirth of commercial vitality began to take place. English merchants from Philadelphia invested in the development of a new village on the Christina River about a mile upstream from the Swedes' old settlement. Land near this point had been bought several years earlier by a Swede named Andrew Justison, whose daughter happened to marry one of those English merchants, named Thomas Willing. The two men went into business together, divided a portion of the newly purchased tract into lots, and by 1735 approximately twenty houses had been constructed. Apparently Justison thought enough of his son-in-law to name this new settlement Willingtown.

During this time the major market for farm products of the area was Philadelphia, but now that Willingtown existed, it was closer to the farmlands themselves. There was also easier access to the mills along the Brandywine, which fed into the Christina and then into the Delaware. Willing moved on from his enterprise and turned the reins over to a Philadelphia Quaker named William Shipley along with a number of associates who were described as "some active business characters." A shrewd businessman, Shipley saw the potential for industrial power on the nearby Brandywine and bought nearly the entire existing town. He was much more successful in selling real estate than Justison and Willing were, and before long the number of new properties had doubled, built mostly by Quakers like himself. Shipley then constructed a market house, a brewery, and a commercial wharf, and in 1736 signed, along with a number of other freeholders, a petition addressed to Thomas Penn. They requested the power to regulate their own affairs and businesses and elect their own officials—effectively a town charter. But a quarrel developed when rival purchasing agents began construction on another market house closer to the Christina River. Another petition was sent to Penn to halt construction. Matters became heated when opponents of Shipley took matters into their own hands and tried chopping down his market with axes.

The town petition was still under consideration when Patrick Gordon, the governor of the Lower Counties, passed away. Thomas Penn was not qualified to grant the charter, so it would have to wait until a new governor could be found. The situation was further delayed when Charles, the fifth Lord Baltimore, jumped into the fray, still disputing the Penn claim to the Lower Counties and the Maryland-Pennsylvania line. Eventually George Thomas took the oath as new governor, the charter was granted, and when the dust finally settled, the town was called Wilmington.

Spencer Compton, the Earl of Wilmington and prime minister during the reign of George II, had absolutely nothing to do with the village on the Christina River. But as a friend of Thomas Penn, it was a gesture designed to garner favor in the ongoing Penn-Baltimore squabble.

A new brick market house was built on Second Street, more substantial than the old one, and then a town hall was added on the second floor. This followed the model set by Philadelphia, as well as the town's grid system, undoubtedly influenced by Shipley's earlier association.

Between 1739 and the beginning of the American Revolution, the town's population nearly tripled within one generation. Although still considered a small town by today's standards, Wilmington surpassed New Castle in size and became the largest community in Delaware. It also began to outdistance its neighbor to the south in commerce, as it had both a protected harbor and a tributary stream, used for transporting produce from the nearby farmlands. Wilmington also started to become a major industrial center, thanks to the enormous amount of water power generated by the Brandywine River. Large mills were set up all along the river, processing grain from Pennsylvania, Maryland, and Delaware, and transported by

Conestoga Wagons. These were huge, horse-drawn vehicles invented in Pennsylvania and later used, in slightly smaller versions, by pioneers in the great western migration. Tanning and paper-making also made use of the Brandywine's energy.

But perhaps the biggest industry of all began when Eleuthère Irénée du Pont de Nemours and family immigrated from France to escape the revolution. They settled in Delaware and tried several business ventures that were ultimately unsuccessful. Then in 1802 they set up mills for producing black powder, also commonly referred to as gunpowder. (To view these early beginnings, be sure to visit the Hagley Museum on the beautiful Brandywine River: www.hagley.org) The business  grew rapidly and by the Civil War, DuPont was supplying at least half the powder used by the Union forces. Over the years the company became more and more diverse and successful. It eventually abandoned black powder manufacture but branched out into an almost endless array of chemical-based products produced worldwide that included the development of the world's first synthetic fiber. Its physical influence can be seen almost everywhere throughout Delaware, New Jersey, and eastern Pennsylvania. The DuPont company is now worth more money than most people can fathom. Its corporate headquarters are still in Wilmington.

FROM THE CIVIL WAR onward, the city bloomed in turbulent times due to the production of gunpowder. And other goods were either manufactured or made their way through Wilmington, including ships, railroad cars, chemicals, and leather goods. But following World War II, like so many other industrial hotspots, it cooled down considerably, acquiring big city woes such as unemployment, poverty, and crime. The 1980s saw a big change, however, as the city became a financial mecca due to the Financial Center Development Act. Laws liberalizing banking restrictions led to the construction of gleaming office centers housing institutions like Bank of America, Chase, Citibank, Barclays, and others. Mostly, these are credit card operations.

Curiously, it's difficult to find much street life in this money-driven downtown district, but not so in the surrounding urban sprawl. It has problems typical of any large city: drugs, illegal weapons, murders (twenty-seven homicides reported in 2010), and in 2012 *Parenting* magazine reported Wilmington as the nation's most dangerous city on a per-capita basis.

Much of the city is in a depressed state. On my first visit to Fort Christina Park, I found much to my disappointment that it was closed due to vandalism. (It has since been repaired and reopened to celebrate the 375th anniversary of the founding of the New Sweden colony.) But it's still a sad commentary relating to a number of historic sites along the Delaware. When you lose a link to your past, it's difficult to relate to the future.

But just as the rivers played such an important role in the creation of Wilmington, they are also a revitalizing ingredient. It's a scenario that has played out in many an urban center: industry creates growth, industry starts to fail, decay sets in, inhabitants leave to find work elsewhere, and abandoned industrial areas become re-purposed real estate. Wilmington is no different. The Wilmington Riverfront project has been in development since the 1990s and now features once-busy marine cranes as benign monstrous sculptures along a picturesque walkway beside the Christina River. An ambitious effort has established cultural and learning centers, fine restaurants, outlet shops, luxury apartments, and the Judy Johnson Field at Daniel S. Frawley Stadium . . . home of those Blue Rocks!

Wilmington

16

MERCER & MIFFLIN

When Ann Cooper married James Whitall, she could not have imagined that she would be known to history as a heroine in the aftermath of a major battle in the Revolutionary War. And what an unlikely heroine she was. The mother of nine children, she kept a meticulous journal that gives an accurate description of farm life in eighteenth-century colonial America. It also gives us insight into the intimate misgivings of a grim and pious Quaker woman. She lived her life according to Old Testament teachings, believing that death was always right around the corner and that her family should be constantly made aware of it. She complained bitterly about her husband and children who "houf me every day I live. O it is as bitter as wormwood and gol; I think sumtimes there never was a mother so unhappy as I am."

For all her complaining, she seemed to have a pretty good life. In 1748 she and her husband built a beautiful brick house in the Flemish bond style on a prosperous 400-acre plantation along the banks of the Delaware with orchards, livestock, a grist mill, smoke house, shad fishery, and a ferry across the river. It was known as Red Bank.

And it was in one of their orchards that the Pennsylvania militia proceeded to build a fort in April of 1777. It was named Fort Mercer in honor of General Hugh Mercer, who had been killed at the Battle of Princeton four months previous. Defenses were needed to protect access to the port of Philadelphia (which Ann Whitall called Babylon) and surrounding communities. Another fort, Mifflin, was also built across the Delaware as well as an installation at Billingsport in what is now Paulsboro, New

Jersey. (That fortification was never completed.) The forts did little to stop British General Howe and his troops, fresh from their victory at Brandywine, from occupying Philadelphia in September of 1777.

But the Continental forces did manage to block and harass British ships trying to sail up-river to supply their troops. They constructed *cheveaux-de-fries*—huge caissons built of logs and planks. These contained long log spears tipped with iron sheathing that projected from the caissons at forty-five-degree angles. They would be towed to strategic locations on the river, filled with rocks, and then sunk just below the water line. Unsuspecting ships would be impaled and then bombarded with canon fire from the forts.

These installations proved enough of a nuisance to General Howe that he ordered their destruction. In October, a two-pronged attack was planned: three battalions of Hessian* Grenadier guards and light infantry under Colonel Count Carl Emil Kurt von Dunop were to cross the Delaware to Cooper's Landing (now Camden) and attack Fort Mercer by land. (The forces numbered between 1,200 and 2,500). They would be assisted by the sixty-four guns of the British warship Augusta, as well as the additional warships *Roebuck, Liverpool, Pearl,* and *Merlin*. Fort Mercer was under the command of Colonel Christopher Greene, recently appointed by General Washington with orders to hold his position at all costs. This would give the exhausted Continental Army enough time to move into winter quarters at Valley Forge. Given a force of only 400, Greene was forced to improvise and had an abatis of sharpened logs and brush constructed to further hamper the attackers.

On October 21, the Hessian troops ferried across the Delaware and marched to Haddonfield to bivouac. When word spread that the troops were in New Jersey, a blacksmith's apprentice named Jonas Cattell, full of youthful energy and patriotic vigor, ran all the way from Haddonfield to Fort Mercer, a distance of over eleven miles, to warn Colonel Greene of the impending attack. Armed with this valuable information, Greene was able to deploy his small group of defenders to their best advantage.

The German mercenaries wouldn't reach their destination until the following day. Their route required them to travel south on the Kings Highway, but local patriots destroyed the bridge over Big Timber Creek, forcing the Germans to backtrack and find another route, wasting valuable time and energy. This set the tone for what was about to happen. When the Hessians finally arrived at the fort, they formed battle lines. But before they attacked, Colonel Von Dunop stepped forward to declare "The King of England orders his rebellious subjects to lay down their arms; and they are warned, that if they stand battle, no quarters whatever will be given." Colonel Greene accepted the challenge for himself and his men. "We ask no quarters, nor will we give any." And with that, the battle began.

The Germans were able to breach the outer earthworks after forty-five minutes of cannon bombardment, but once inside found themselves caught in a cross-fire and were quickly reduced. The number of German casualties are thought to be somewhere around 500. They left Colonel Dunop on the battlefield; he was taken prisoner and later died of his wounds. The colonists lost far less proportionately, and the attack was repulsed. As for the British support vessels, the *Augusta* and the *Merlin* ran aground the next day and were set ablaze by the Americans, who sent fire ships crashing into them. Both ships were destroyed.

During the battle, Ann Whitall refused to leave her home. Legend has it that she was spinning yarn, and when a cannonball ripped through a nearby wall, she calmly picked up her spinning wheel and continued her work in the cellar. After the fighting was over, many wounded were brought to the house; American doctors ripped doors off their hinges for use as makeshift operating tables. Ann pitched in to help, scolding the agonized soldiers for coming to America to conduct war and telling them that they "ought not complain who had brought it upon themselves." But she was also kind in her treatments, using her vast experience with herbal cures. Naturally, she blamed the whole conflict on her family, who brought judgment upon themselves for "sleeping at meeting" and for "Sunday skating and fishing."

The battle was a tremendous success and morale boost for the Americans. It also had much to do with influencing the French to provide aid to the struggling colonists.

WHILE ACCOLADES were heaped on the defenders of Red Bank, Fort Mifflin across the river received praise of a different sort. Situated on Mud Island, the fort is a tranquil oasis of history near the Philadelphia International Airport, near the confluence of the Schuykill River. In late fall 1777, however, it was anything but tranquil. Two thousand British troops and 250 warships began the largest bombardment of the Revolutionary War. For five days the assault continued, at one point raining down 1,000 cannonballs on the fort in an hour. The fort could respond with only ten cannon of its own. Finally, exhausted of ammunition, Major Simeon Thayer evacuated what was left of the 400 defenders in the middle of the night of November 15. They silently rowed to the mainland, leaving a skeleton crew behind to set Fort Mifflin on fire, but left their flag still flying. The determination of the Fort Mifflin defenders and the heroes of Fort Mercer allowed Washington's Continental Army to withdraw to Valley Forge, where they spent a harsh but productive winter, emerging in the spring as a cohesive fighting unit.

As early as 1771, the British made plans to build a fortification on Mud Island, considered to be of extreme strategic importance for the defense of Philadelphia. Construction faltered due to politics and lack of funding, and it took the efforts of Benjamin Franklin to restart the project. It was finally completed in 1776 and then reduced to rubble the following year. The ruins of the fort sat idle until 1794, when Pierre L'Enfant, the planner of Washington, DC, supervised its reconstruction. (During this time the facility was named for Thomas Mifflin, a Philadelphia merchant, officer in the Continental Army, and the first governor of Pennsylvania.) Casements were built, along with a barracks and a Commandant's House.

The fort was in a ready state when the War of 1812 began, but saw no action.

Occasional construction and upgrading continued, and by the time of the Civil War it was used not only for river defense but to house military and civilian prisoners. Four were executed at Mifflin, including Union army

soldier William H. Howe, accused of desertion and murder. Howe staged an attempted escape of two hundred prisoners, which was quickly quelled. Despite writing to President Lincoln asking for clemency, he was hanged in 1864 before a paying audience.

Upgrading and modernization continued on the fort right up to World War II, when anti-aircraft guns were installed to defend the nearby Philadelphia Naval Shipyard. By 1962, the old fort had outlived its usefulness and was deeded to the City of Philadelphia. However, it is still an active base for the US Army Corps of Engineers. Fort Mifflin is the oldest active military base in the US, and since its construction pre-dates the Declaration of Independence, is the only military base in use that is older than the country itself.

The fort is open to the public through much of the year, hosting educational and living history programs and events. There are, of course, reports of paranormal activity on the grounds. The History Channel and Travel Channel have named it one of America's "most haunted locations." Fort Mifflin hosts candlelight ghost tours and "sleeping with the ghosts" events. You can find out for yourself: http://fortmifflin.us.

While Fort Mifflin was eventually reconstructed, Colonel Greene ordered Fort Mercer destroyed on November 20, 1777, when it was clear he was about to be attacked by an overwhelming force of about 5,000 British regulars. All that remains today are shallow trenches. But the grounds contain tastefully employed monuments and plaques and a collection of artifacts. The Whitall house is still standing and in superb shape, having been well-tended by generations of the Whitall family. It is currently under the care of the Gloucester County Parks and Recreation Department and is on the National Register of Historic Places. The house is open for tours year-round, displaying well-preserved artifacts, period furniture, and archives.

The Headless Hessians

After the battle of Fort Mercer was over, the dead were buried in long trenches next to the river bank. After a few years of New Jersey winters, the bank began wearing away, exposing some of the remains. Neighboring youngsters and others with too much time on their hands discovered the bones and began running around at night, rapping on the Whitalls' windows and uttering ghostly cries. Stories began circulating that the old battlefield was haunted. Naturally, Ann Whitall was not amused and persuaded her sons to re-inter all the bones that had been disturbed.

According to legend, among the Hessians were two whose heads had been blown off. When they were re-buried, the heads were placed with the opposite bodies. This caused considerable consternation to the two departed German soldiers, who were now unable to continue their endless sleep wearing the wrong heads.

The two would arise on moonlit nights and wander through the countryside around the old fort. It was reported, according to tradition, that they wandered as far as Haddonfield, far from their final resting place. Each was trying to find the other; each was attempting to locate his own head.

They wandered all over the old battlefield for years without ever meeting one another. They frightened old and young alike. Sometimes one of them appeared, and a short while later a second apparition appeared, its long red coat swaying in the moonlight as the evening breezes gently moved it to and fro. After one had gone on, the other phantom would return and fade away amidst the trees on the banks of the Delaware.

So for years these two unfortunates floated through the meadows, woods, and streams, with an occasional glance through the windows of the Whitall Mansion, and from there on to Woodbury Creek and as far as the Lowe House, where their leader Count von Dunop had passed away.

Years passed into decades and decades into centuries as the two moved and floated over the countryside, until early in the twentieth century. One night, they met at the spot where the Lowe House had stood on the other side of Crown Point Road. They finally exchanged their heads and immediately fell into dust.

17

CAMDEN

When I was just out of high school, I drove a delivery van for a dental supply company in southern New Jersey. It was a source of constant embarrassment to me because on the back of the van was the company slogan: "Be true to your teeth, or they will be false to you." The author of the slogan was also the owner of the company and he thought it was extremely witty. But he was a nice man despite his fondness for corny humor.

My delivery route would sometimes take me on Route 45, which ran from the large growing fields in Salem and Cumberland Counties up to Camden. I would often wind up in back of a truck loaded with red, ripe tomatoes headed for processing at the Campbell Soup Company. The road would be littered with squashed tomato road kill. Despite the turnpike jokes, New Jersey is, after all, the Garden State.

Campbell's began in 1869 when Joseph A. Campbell and Abraham Anderson started selling canned food products. What made Campbell's unique and started it on its way to becoming one of the largest food companies in the world was its introduction of condensed soup, the process developed by John T. Dorrance, a nephew of the general manager. Campbell's also became recognizable for its unmistakable red and white packaging and clever advertising campaign introducing the Campbell kids, two rosy-cheeked, well-fed children gracing the packaging. Its vintage labels, dolls, and other promotional materials are now highly collectible Americana. Artist Andy Warhol got in on the act in the 1960s when he produced the iconic pop art silk screens featuring Campbell's soup cans. Campbell's corporate office is still in Camden and remains an economic mainstay in a city that has been in a sad and steady decline for many years.

In 2012 the FBI ranked Camden first in violent crime in cities with over 50,000 residents. Three of its recent mayors have been jailed for corruption and its school system and police department are operated by the State of New Jersey. Two out of every five residents are below the national poverty level. It is often referred to as one of the worst cities in America.

Hard to believe now, but Camden was once in direct competition with it's neighbor across the river, Philadelphia, as a major industrial manufacturing center of the northeast. In addition to Campbell's Soup, there was the Esterbrook Pen Company, American Nickel Works (the only nickel refinery in the country, supplying the US Mint), major rail lines, carriage manufacturers, meat processors, cigar makers, and endless others.

IT WAS IN BAD SHAPE in the 1960s when some of my friends and I had a band. We used to practice in Ken's sister's apartment on Cooper Street. Neighbors would stand in a small yard in the back of the building and bang on the windows with clothes props to make us shut up, but we couldn't hear them. Invariably, Camden's finest would be summoned to silence what we believed to be fine music. We would be issued a stern warning, and then resume once the police had exited. After a while, the neighbors stopped complaining or caring, much like the city itself.

Cooper Street is named for the family who operated a ferry at its base to carry passengers and commerce back and forth across the Delaware River to the newly established city of Philadelphia. The first ferry operator was William Royden, granted a license in 1688. He was to provide "good and sufficient boats which were to be in readiness at all times to accommodate people's actions." The rates were six pence per person, 12 pence for man and horse (or other beast), and 6 pence per head for swine, cattle, and sheep.

Daniel Cooper took over Royden's post in 1695 and the ferry service remained in the Cooper family for the next 150 years. It became known as Cooper's Ferry, operating from Cooper's Landing. There was also Cooper's

An old mile marker that now resides with others at Red Bank Battlefield Park

Point (another ferry landing), the Cooper River nearby that drains into the Delaware, and Cooper Hospital, where my father and I were born. (Some older South Jerseyans still pronounce it "Cupper.") Other ferry systems were established at Market Street, Federal Street, and Kaign's Point, and stayed in business until the Delaware River Bridge opened in 1926. The bridge was later renamed in honor of Benjamin Franklin.

Taverns, hotels, and pleasure gardens were built near the ferry landings; the Benjamin Cooper House, one of the oldest, is still standing and used by the Camden Ship Repair Company. During the British occupation of Philadelphia, the house served as headquarters for British Lieutenant Colonel Abercrombie. Years afterward, the house became a notorious saloon known as the Old Stone Jug. In 1773, another Cooper named Jacob began to lay out forty acres of family land into streets and lots and named it in honor of English lawyer and politician Charles Pratt, the first Earl of Camden, a sympathizer of the American revolution.

Three years after the Delaware River Bridge was built, the Radio Corporation of America purchased the Victor Talking Machine Company, manufacturer of the famous Victrola, from its owner, machinist Eldrige Johnson. Johnson had invented the technology that made recording to a disc a lucrative new industry. People crossing the new bridge from Philadelphia could look to their right and see a brick factory tower with a stained glass image of a dog listening to a Victrola. "His Master's Voice" and the dog Nipper became instantly recognizable icons of RCA Victor. The facility was on the waterfront, just off—you guessed it, Cooper Street. RCA Records soon became known world-wide and a major force in the burgeoning communications industry.

Before being purchased by RCA, Victor had its own recording facility turning out some of the finest recordings of its time under the Victrola label. The original "recording laboratories" were located on Front and Cooper Streets. Historic recordings were made there in 1918—Karl Muck with the Boston Symphony and the Philadelphia Orchestra under maestro Leopold Stokowski. Victor later purchased the nearby Trinity Baptist Church, which gave them much more room and better acoustics. It also came with an Estey pipe organ that Fats Waller used in his recordings of the 1920s and 1930s. Enrico Caruso's final recording and Vladimir Horowitz's first recording were done there. Joining them was a seemingly endless parade of artists that included such diverse talents as Jelly Roll Morton, Duke Ellington, the Carter Family, Louis Armstrong, Jimmy Rodgers (the Singing Brakeman), and Bix Beiderbecke.

In the 1940s, RCA began issuing a budget label named after its home city, RCA Camden, that featured re-issues of historic classical and popular recordings on 78- and 45-rpm discs. Budget and Camden were two words that would soon become synonymous. You could purchase a recording by the ever-popular Snooky Lanson at the bargain price of just seventy-nine cents!

An unidentified young lady about to christen the USS Sonoma in 1912 at New York Ship

RCA is under the umbrella of Sony Entertainment. In 1984, RCA moved away from Camden and most of the factory was demolished, except for the original RCA Victor buildings that have been declared national historic buildings. They have since been renovated as luxury apartments.

DURING WORLD WAR II my father was one of more than 30,000 people employed by New York Ship Building Corporation in Camden. It came by that name because in 1899, when the company was formed by industrialist Henry G. Morse, it was intended to be located on Staten Island. But a 160-acre farm on the Delaware just south of Camden had a much more attractive price tag. The name was already incorporated, so a state-of-the-art shipyard was built with backing from financial biggies Andrew Mellon and Henry Frick. New York Ship initially landed lucrative government contracts to build warships and by 1917 was the largest shipyard in the world. So large, in fact, that entire towns sprang up in Southern New Jersey just to house the workers, including Yardship, now known as Fairview. More than 600 ships were constructed there, including aircraft carriers, battleships, submarines, and landing craft. Battleships USS *Utah* and USS *Oklahoma* were both sunk at Pearl Harbor on December 7, 1941. The *Oklahoma* was righted and sold for scrap, but the *Utah* still rests in the mud near Ford Island, a memorial to the unknown dead entombed there.

New York Ship also built luxury liners, barges, and ferry boats; in 1959, the first nuclear-powered cargo ship, the NS *Savannah*, was launched. The aircraft carrier USS *Kitty Hawk*, finished in 1961, was one of the last major shipbuilding projects at the yard. Too large to be constructed on the ways, a special drydock was built just for the *Kitty Hawk*. She turned out to be the first and last ship New York Ship ever constructed in a drydock. Orders from the Navy eventually began to dry up and New York Ship closed up shop in 1967, leaving many employees jobless. My father had been an electric draftsman at New York Ship and was able to find work across the river with the Philadelphia Electric Company. I still have his case of mechanical drawing tools.

In an odd twist of fate, New York Ship built the first Navy destroyer sunk in World War I: the *Jacob Jones* (DD-61). It also built the first US Navy ship

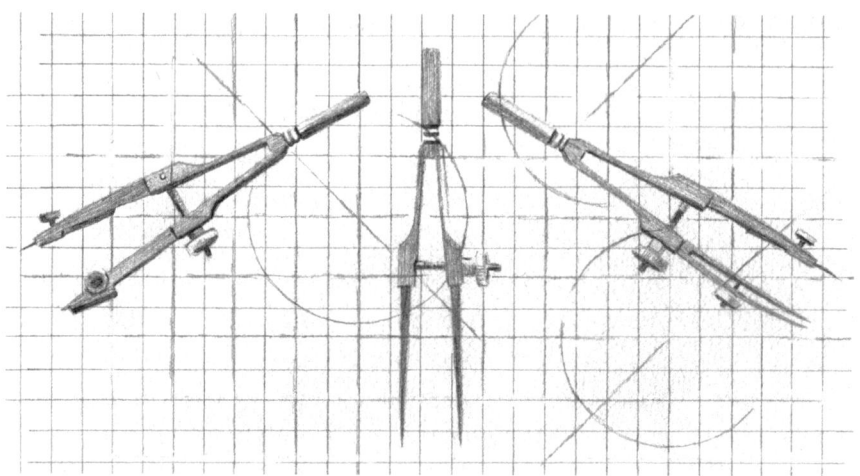

sunk in World War II: the *Reuben James.* Both were torpedoed by German U-boats. Another *Jacob Jones* (DD-130), launched less than a year after the first one was lost, was also sunk twenty-five years later.

The *Jacob Jones* destroyers' namesake was a Delaware Valley native born near Smyrna, Delaware, in 1768. An officer in the US Navy, he served under Commodore John Barry, for whom the Commodore Barry Bridge over the Delaware is named. Jones saw action in a number of conflicts, including the War of 1812, and received a gold medal from the United States Congress.

Reuben James was also born in Delaware, around 1776. A Boatswain's Mate, he served aboard the first USS *Constellation.* He also served as a volunteer on the American frigate *Philadelphia* with Lieutenant Stephen Decatur and was involved in a battle with Barbary Pirates at Tripoli in 1804. He was highly acclaimed for saving Decatur's life during hand-to-hand combat with the pirates. After the ship named for him was lost, it was memorialized in a highly patriotic song written by Woody Guthrie.

THERE WAS AN original Sears, Roebuck & Company store in Camden. I remember my parents taking me there to buy school clothes in the days before malls. My mother loved to browse and would drive me crazy because she walked so slowly. My Dad would lag behind looking at tools. Early on, Sears had only operated as a mail-order business. But as the public became more mobile and abandoned farms for jobs in the city, Sears followed the consumers.

In 1971, Sears, too, left Camden for the nearby Moorestown Mall. Built in 1927 as a columned temple to commerce, the Sears building was one of the first to be built with its own parking lot. It was also one of only twenty-seven Sears stores in existence. After the store was abandoned, it was declared a historic site. Preservationists fought to preserve the eighty-six-year-old icon but finally lost out to Campbell's, which plans to develop the property as an office park.

ALL THE MEMBERS of our band, except me, were natives of Camden, and Frank's father was a devotee of all things Sears. He played and sang country and western music whenever he could and had a Sears Silvertone guitar. He also had a Silvertone reel-to-reel tape recorder that he had covered with contact paper for some reason. We used to "borrow" the tape deck to record our music and sophomoric comedy sketches. We would play the pieces over and over again and laugh ourselves silly. Silvertone products were sold exclusively by Sears through their catalog and retail stores, and though the partnership ended over thirty years ago, Silvertone is still fondly remembered. Silvertone guitars were part of the careers of many musicians including Chet Atkins, Bob Dylan, Jimi Hendrix, Muddy Waters, and a host of others. They are true collector's items these days. When the Sears closed in Camden, a little piece of Frank's father must have shut down with it.

As for our band, all our hard work and practicing paid off. Our first gig was playing at a friend's birthday party, whose father happened to work for

Campbell's Soup. At the end of the night, we were stunned to discover our payment was a case of Campbell's rejected Pork & Beans. We headed back to the apartment on Cooper Street, tired and hungry, and chowed down on our beans served over toasted rye bread. Mm, mm, good!

Across the street from the courthouse sits the Walt Whitman House, the only home he would ever own. Whitman bought the house, which was built in 1848, for $1,750. He called it his "shanty," or sometimes his "coop," perhaps an omen of things to come for Camden. He spent his last years here welcoming a host of worldly visitors such as Oscar Wilde, Bram Stoker, and Thomas Eakins, who painted Whitman's portrait from a photo he had taken. His health slowly fading, Whitman continued his writings, including his final edition of *Leaves of Grass* in 1892, known as the "deathbed edition." His friends and relatives questioned his judgment in buying the shabby house on what was then Mickle Street, but he seemed to enjoy it: "Camden was originally an accident—but I shall never be sorry. I was left over in Camden. It has brought me blessed returns." Walt Whitman died on March 26, 1892, just days before his seventy-third birthday.

EFFORTS ARE UNDERWAY to revitalize the Camden riverfront through the promotion of the Cooper's Ferry Partnership, a name that still resounds. In addition to the RCA Victor apartments, Camden is home to the Adventure Aquarium; the Camden River Sharks minor league baseball stadium; the River Line, a rail service running from Camden to Trenton; and the Battleship New Jersey, anchored on the waterfront across the river from where she was built at the Philadelphia Naval Shipyard. There are also plans for the Philadelphia 76er's basketball team to construct a practice facility along the waterfront.

THE ILLUSTRATED DELAWARE RIVER

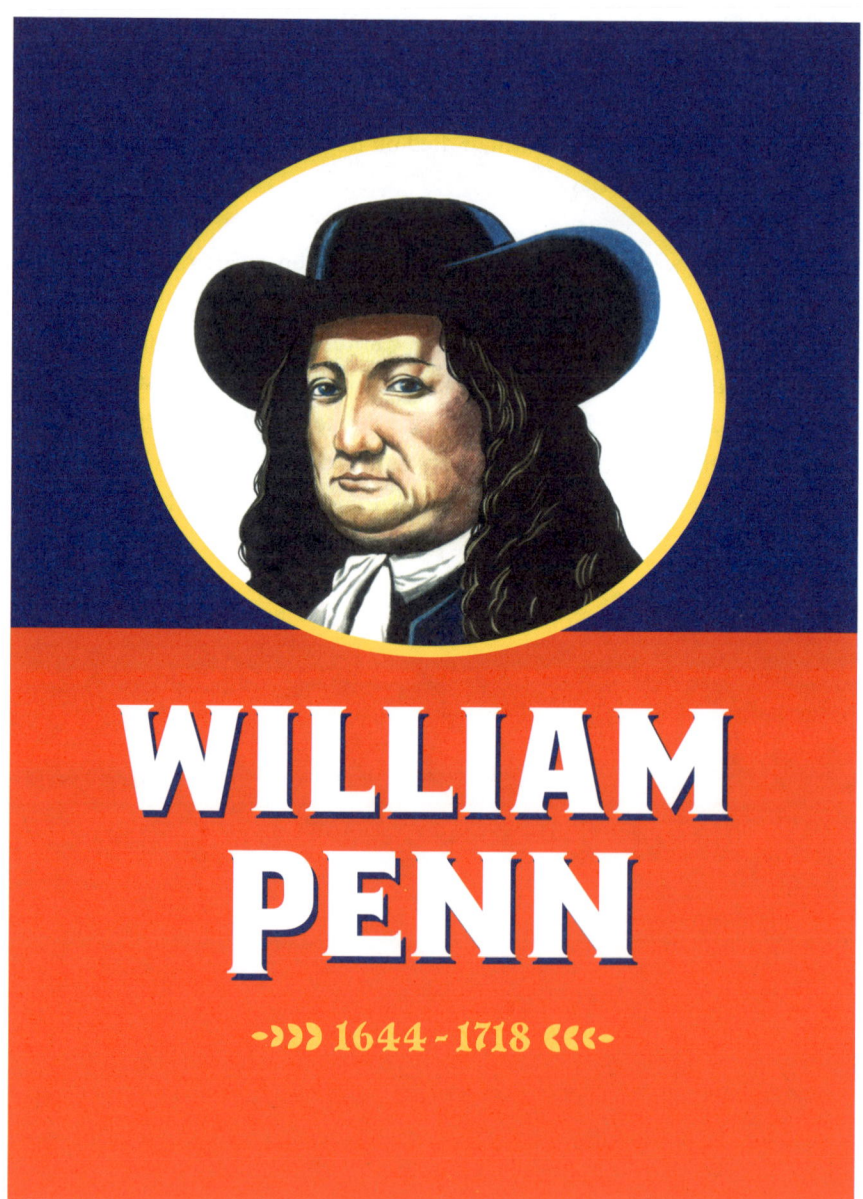

WILLIAM PENN

1644 - 1718

18

Penn

There is probably no one man, living or dead, who has left more of his fingerprints on the Delaware Valley—and beyond—than William Penn.

Consider this: Pennsville, Pennsgrove, Port Penn, Pennsport, Penn's Landing, Pennsbury, Penn Treaty Park, William Penn Highway, William Penn School District, William Penn High School, William Penn Middle School, William Penn Charter School, William Penn Elementary School, William Penn University, William Penn Foundation, William Penn Tavern, William Penn Life Insurance Company, William Penn Realty Group, William Penn Hotel, William Penn State Forest, William Penn Collection, William Penn Family Dental Pc, William Penn Memorial Fire Tower, and the William Penn Poodle Club—just a smattering of the entities named for him.

Pennsylvania, however, is named for Penn's father, Admiral Sir William Penn. The land that now defines the commonwealth was a gift from Charles II to young William in payment for debts that Admiral Penn had accrued for services rendered to his king.

Penn spent only four years in America, but in that time set the tone for what would eventually become a model for civilization the likes of which the world had never before seen. And it was done without the use of force or bloodshed.

My earliest impression of William Penn was probably like most: the pleasant face of a middle-aged gentleman dressed in formal colonial garb on the front of a Quaker Oats canister. The Quaker Oats company simply used the illustration to identify its company with the trustworthy Quaker. Another misconception is that a statue of Benjamin Franklin graces the top of Philadelphia's City Hall. That is actually William Penn. My own wife has made this error.

The Penn Family Crest, which can be translated as "The Line of Right as Well as Glory"

Penn was born in 1644 into a life of privilege. His father rose through the ranks as a naval officer to become Admiral of the Royal Navy under King Charles I. Then came the English Civil War, Oliver Cromwell's rise to power, and the removal of the monarchy, along with Charles's head. But Admiral Penn continued to thrive. For victories achieved, Cromwell bestowed upon him an even more glorious title: General of the Sea. As a bonus, he was given a confiscated estate in Ireland known as Macroom Castle, complete with a small army of servants. Even though Penn was a career military man, he secretly still maintained loyalty to the crown. When Cromwell died, Penn was sent on a secret mission to Holland and personally brought Prince Charles back to England to be crowned Charles II. For his service he was made Commissioner of the Navy, a cabinet position, and was thenceforth known as Admiral Sir William Penn.

Young William greatly admired his father, but was an introspective lad who took advantage of his father's position to bury himself in books, a luxury available only to the very wealthy. They moved from their home on Tower Hill in London to a country estate in Essex, where William's education continued and he developed a love of horticulture.

He also began to experience deep religious feelings, which became even stronger during an extended stay at the Irish estate. At around the age of fifteen he wrote, "the Lord visited me and gave me divine Impressions of Himself." His newfound belief was enhanced when a missionary named Thomas Loe visited the estate. Loe was trying to spread the teaching of an itinerant preacher named George Fox. Fox was the founder of a new Christian sect called the Religious Society of Friends, more commonly known as Quakers. It was during this formative period of his life that Penn developed a deep sense of equality, tolerance, and decency. So deep, in fact, that it would land him in prison on more than one occasion. It would also bring him close to knowing the executioner on a personal level.

Penn's education continued at Oxford, where he arrived as a gentleman scholar with a personal servant. He grew into a studious and rather humorless young man, temporarily burying his moral consciousness. Probably because of peer influence, he leaned more toward Puritan ethics. (H.L. Mencken described the experience of being a Puritan as "having the haunting fear that someone, somewhere, may be happy.") But unlike his aristocratic counterparts who felt entitled to harass and persecute minority groups, Penn developed sympathy, particularly for the Quakers. There was something in their apolitical leanings, unlike the Anglicans and Puritans, that appealed to his sense of fairness. They believed all people to be equal under God, including the king. The rights of the individual were foremost. Obviously, this did not sit well with the monarchy, which declared the Society of Friends an unauthorized form of worship, punishable by imprisonment or deportation.

During Penn's matriculation at Oxford, a radical new concept—rational thought—began to spread throughout the centers of learning. This was also frowned upon by the king. One of his instructors, John Owen, appointed university dean, was fired for injecting this new process into his teaching. A group of loyal students including Penn followed Owen to his home for seminars but were threatened with punishment for their involvement. Young William rebelled against newly enforced regulations meant to quell such thoughts and behavior and was expelled. Admiral Penn reacted so violently to young William's expulsion that he forced him from their home with a cane. Eventually Penn's mother eased the situation, allowing her son to return home. But for fear of ruining the Admiral's career and his mother's social standing, his parents sent young William to Paris to complete his education and improve his state of mind.

PENN WAS A BIT of a paradox. His sense of equality made him care deeply for the condition of the common man, but he also enjoyed the finer things afforded to a person of privilege. Perhaps he took them for granted. He returned from France after two years as a sophisticated and nattily dressed young gentleman. He never relinquished his fondness for fine clothes and wigs. But the wigs grew out of necessity: young William contracted smallpox at age three and lost all his hair, remaining bald for the rest of his life.

Young William returned to his studies, intent on becoming a lawyer, and also acted as an emissary between his father, who was preparing for battle with the Dutch, and Charles II. Admiral Penn was soon disabled by gout, and in 1666, William was sent to Ireland once again to manage the family affairs. This time, contrary to his later stand as a pacifist, he took part in suppressing a local uprising. He seemed to relish the experience and even had his portrait painted proudly wearing a suit of armor, the only life image of him that exists. (After becoming a Quaker, he refused any more portraits, as it would have been considered inappropriately vain.)

Penn eventually regained his senses and began to attend Quaker meetings. He was arrested at one meeting, and rather than easily escape charges, he proclaimed himself a member, finally joining the Society of Friends. After release from jail because of his social position, his father called him to London, greatly distressed by his son's actions. He feared retribution from the crown not only for William but for himself, and banished William from the house, denying his inheritance.

Newgate Prison, Old City Gate, London

Penn, now homeless, began to live with Quaker families and became a close friend of George Fox. They traveled together through England, Holland, and Germany, with Penn developing the basis of Quaker theory. In his first piece, entitled "Truth Exalted," he railed against the doctrine of the Holy Trinity and the hypocrisy of the Puritans. Then in 1668 Penn was imprisoned for writing "The Sandy Foundation Shaken," a similar missive that blasphemed the established churches. He was held in the Tower of London, within site of his boyhood home at Tower Hill. Given writing materials in hopes that he would compose an apology, he stubbornly refused and instead penned another scathing critique entitled "No Cross, No Crown." He was eventually released after eight months, thanks to the negotiations of a royal chaplain.

William Penn spent the next several years in and out of jail, mostly on charges of agitating against the intolerant attitudes of the church. Finally, his father realized that young William had a great deal of integrity and was taking a courageous path through life. And a very dangerous one. The Admiral bailed William from his incarceration at notorious Newgate Prison and put in motion a plan that would eventually result in the founding of a new order in a new land.

The old Admiral appealed to King Charles and his brother James, the Duke of York, to help with his radical son. The proposed plan would involve a mass migration of Quakers to North America. In 1677, a group of prominent Friends that included William Penn would purchase the province of West Jersey, the half of the current state that had been given to the Duke. Two hundred Quaker settlers would then journey there and establish the town of Burlington on the Delaware River. In 1682 they purchased East Jersey as well. In the meantime, in a moment of generosity, the king granted Penn a land charter as a reward for Admiral Penn's long and loyal career. He now held the title to 450,000 square miles of land in North America, making Penn the world's largest non-royal landowner. Penn wanted to call the land grant New Wales, but the King decided on the Latin "sylvania," meaning forest or woods, and "Penn" after the Admiral.

In 1682, Penn wrote "The Frame of Government," a constitution for the governing of the royal charter. Penn called this venture his "Holy Experiment." It would provide for religious tolerance and political freedom, progressive ideas for the time, and the very basis for what the United States would eventually use for its own constitution. The people who settled Pennsylvania would have more real freedom than had ever been known in Europe, more even than the grim, intolerant Puritans who were already established in North America.

Penn, skilled as a lawyer, theoretician, and scholar, now had to become a real estate promoter, which he tackled with the same fervor. Leaving his wife Gulielma (known as Guli) and children behind in England, Penn set sail on the ship *Welcome*. In October of 1682 he arrived amid great fanfare at what is now New Castle, Delaware, and took control of the new Pennsylvania Territory. Control is perhaps too strong a word, because even though this was Penn's brainchild, he purposely limited his power so that the new society could be run much like a Quaker meeting using "open discourse."

William Penn was a brilliant man in most respects but paid little attention to his own business affairs. He would soon find himself back in England defending not only the limits of the Pennsylvania Colony but his personal property as well.

THE ILLUSTRATED DELAWARE RIVER

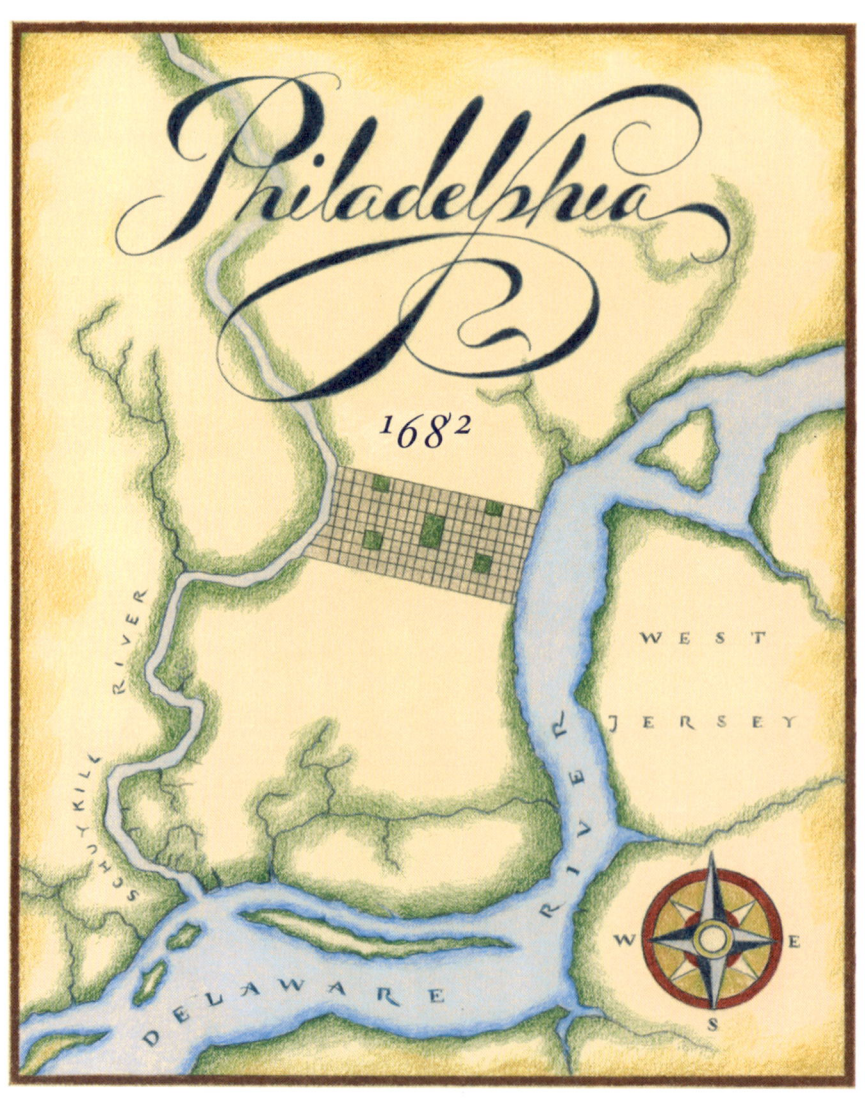

19
ΦΪΛΑΔΕΛΦΕΙΑ (Brotherly Love)

William Penn had grand ideas for his new colony of Pennsylvania, and to make them work, he needed grand designs. He recruited fellow Quaker Thomas Holme as his surveyor general and gave instructions on how to lay out the capital: plots were to have sufficient ground around the houses for gardens and orchards "that it may be a green country town, which will never be burnt and always wholesome." Penn had witnessed the destruction caused by the great London fire of 1666 and wanted to avoid the congestion that could cause such massive devastation. He chose a promising piece of land stretching between the Delaware and Schuykill Rivers. As befitting his classical training, he joined two Greek syllables: phila (love) and adelphos (brother) and called the new city Philadelphia.

Even though the royal charter granted this huge parcel of land to Penn and his colonists, he did not feel comfortable as the sole owner since the territory already had inhabitants—the Lenni Lenape. Penn's unerring sense of fairness led him to purchase the land from them. His relationship with the Indians was unique; many Europeans before him were prone to taking advantage of and abusing them—and in some extreme cases slaughtering natives as if they were pests. Penn insisted upon scrupulous dealings, winning their life-long respect. Legend remains that a combination land purchase and peace treaty took place in the Indian village of Shackamaxon by the river under a stately elm tree. There are no records of the transaction, but consistent family lore makes the event seem likely. Voltaire, the well-known philosopher and admirer of Penn, remarked that Shackamaxon was "the only treaty between the Indian nations and Christians which was never sworn to and never broken." That would come much later, long after Penn was gone and the usual relations between whites and Indians would resume.

Penn, memorialized by Alexander Calder's statue atop Philadelphia City Hall

Today, the event is memorialized in Penn Treaty Park at the river's edge, at the intersection of North Delaware Avenue and Beach Street. What was once an Indian village is now known as Fishtown, and Shackamaxon remains only as a street name. A sugar refinery opened at the foot of the street in 1881. The refinery is long gone, but the memory lingers in the form of the Sugar House Casino.

Penn actually got a rather late start at colonization in the New World. The Spanish were sending colonists from the time of Columbus, a well-established Jamestown colony in Virginia dated back to 1607, and Puritan enclaves from the 1620s in Massachusetts and New Haven had continued to expand. The prosperous Dutch city of New Amsterdam had been renamed New York eighteen years earlier, when the English took control. And European settlers had been in the Delaware River Valley for nearly two generations—before Philadelphia was even thought of. Swedes and Finns had wandered northward from the defunct New Sweden colony, buying land from the Indians and putting down roots. And Dutch settlers were still to be found, refugees from the also dismantled New Netherland colony. Quakers were on the move, too, some crossing the Atlantic from England and Holland, and some simply crossing the Delaware from earlier settlements in West Jersey to get a head start staking out property before Penn would arrive. Finding themselves shelterless, many lived in man-made caves dug horizontally into the river bank, or on top of it, creating cavities much like a cellar or basement. Temporary walls were then built around them of mud or earth and covered with limbs, bark, or other organic materials.

The Indians had originally recycled muskrat burrows for the same purpose for use during winter hunting trips. As primitive as these dwellings were, they got the Quaker settlers through the winter of 1681 before plots could be laid out and houses constructed. John Key, the first English child born in Philadelphia County, was brought into the world in one of these humble dwellings on July 20, 1682. He was also one of the first children born in the Commonwealth of Pennsylvania. To commemorate the occasion, William Penn gave young Key a plot of land. At the end of Key's life, Benjamin Franklin reported his passing in the Pennsylvania Gazette on July 16, 1767, noting that Key had been born in a cave on the river bank.

Some of the caves were actually rather spacious, accommodating people such as Francis Daniel Pastorius, a German scholar and lawyer who came to buy land from Penn on behalf of the German Society. He eventually founded the community of Germantown.

As the cave-dwellers gradually moved into houses above the river bank, some of the abandoned dwellings became "caves of ill-repute," used for drinking, gambling, and other illicit services. The businesses became so successful that the newly established court system decreed that they "be pulled down" and "demolished." Many of these new patrons were Quakers, but that doesn't mean they were saints. Penn, back in England by now, also demanded that the caves be evacuated in an official decree.

A small number of these old caves survive today in the form of basements for the buildings that were eventually constructed on top of them. Shorn up with bricks or other building materials, some now serve as wine cellars or exercise rooms.

Penn essentially became America's first city planner. Unlike Boston or New York, where meandering cow paths became major roadways, he introduced a grid of street patterns broken up with shaded squares for markets and congregating. His obsession with maintaining open areas also applied to the waterfront. Delaware Front Street, the first street built in Philadelphia, ran atop the bank closely paralleling the river. The name was eventually shortened to Front Street. Penn envisioned the street as a promenade where people could stroll while enjoying fresh river breezes. He also prohibited the construction of any buildings that would block the view from Front Street. This would prove impractical as industry began to develop along the docks and river's edge. Penn's solution was to create a series of granite steps placed strategically along the waterfront that acted as conduits to funnel fresh air to the upper reaches of the newly developing city. Due to numerous changes to the waterfront's profile over the last 300 years, however, only one set of steps remains.

Penn must have done an excellent job of recruiting settlers, for in the first year of the city's existence, at least thirty ships arrived from England, Holland, Germany, Sweden, Finland, Ireland, and Wales. This cultural diversity was not found anywhere else in America (not even in the early Dutch town of New Amsterdam, whose liberal attitudes carried over from its namesake in Holland). The early arrivals were people of means and brought with them a level of sophistication that attracted other wealthy colonists.

The sun shone brightly on the new town of Philadelphia in the Commonwealth of Pennsylvania, but the skies were darkening for William Penn. Even before he was awarded the Royal Charter for Pennsylvania, there was a dispute concerning adjacent lands claimed by Lord Baltimore. It seems he had also been given a land grant some years previously and due to inadequate surveying and inaccurate maps, was convinced Penn's land was overlapping his own.

Penn also received word that his wife Guli was not well. She had given birth while he was gone and the child had lived only a week. Then a rumor began circulating that Penn had been killed in the colonies. After only two years in America, it was decided that Penn should return to England to sort out his troubles.

Upon his arrival, he spent only a week with his wife, who had now recovered, and family before setting off for London. On a visit to the king and the Duke of York, he found that political conditions had deteriorated and doubted that the land dispute would be settled in his favor. But in 1685, Charles died and his brother was crowned James II. James appointed Penn to the royal court. Arbitrators were commissioned to settle the Pennsylvania border dispute and temporarily denied Lord Baltimore's claim. (The matter would not end for many years, however, eventually leading to the surveying of the Mason-Dixon line, long after Penn and Lord Baltimore had passed away.)

But Penn still had a large problem. His trusted business manager, Philip Ford, had been embezzling a substantial amount of money from Penn's estates. Although a brilliant business man, Penn was often blasé about the wording of important documents, trusting associates more than he should have. Before embarking for America, Ford thrust a number of papers in front of him to be signed. One was a deed actually transferring ownership of Pennsylvania to Ford himself, who then demanded rent for the purloined property. He and Ford worked out a deal that financially swept the matter under the carpet while Penn made plans to return to Pennsylvania.

Penn finally set foot again in Philadelphia; what was to be a brief visit to England had turned into 18 years. Guli died in 1694, and he brought with him a new wife, Hannah Margaret Callowhill. When Penn had left Philadelphia, it was basically a frontier town perched on the edge of a vast wilderness, and now it contained more than 10,000 inhabitants and 400 houses, most of which were built of brick. One of the earliest houses was constructed in 1683 on the south corner of Front and Mulberry (now Arch). Industry was still limited to household manufacturing such as candle making and weaving, but there was no shortage of imported goods. Almost anything available in England could also be found in Philadelphia. And his plan for a religiously tolerant, democratized society was working. Quaker grammar schools were open to all and turning out an educated workforce. Thanks to its literate population, Philadelphia was becoming a leader in the higher disciplines of science and medicine.

Penn had started building a mansion for his family during his first visit, and now he took up residence. Named Pennsbury Manor, it still

exists today as a memorial, rebuilt in the 1930s with funds provided by the Society of Friends. It sits at the edge of the river about twenty-six miles north of Philadelphia. Penn commuted to the city in a highly prized barge that was powered by sail and six oarsmen when the winds or tides were not favorable.

And once again Penn proves to be an enigmatic individual—he was a slave owner. Hard to fathom for a man with such a sense of decency and equality. Quakers in general had mixed feelings about slavery; they did not agree with the concept but felt it was a necessary evil. There was so much hard labor involved with homesteading that most admitted they could probably not have survived without it. It was an accepted part of life in those times. Eventually, the Quakers freed their slaves and became some of the leading advocates of abolition.

Another home industry began early in Philadelphia—the brewing of beer. It began the same year that William Penn arrived to take up residency, when William Frampton opened a brewery on Dock Street. At the time of colonization, Europeans were not particularly fond of drinking water. They didn't trust it, as many diseases could be contracted from water. It had acquired a social stigma that made it unacceptable even when safe to drink. Beer was another

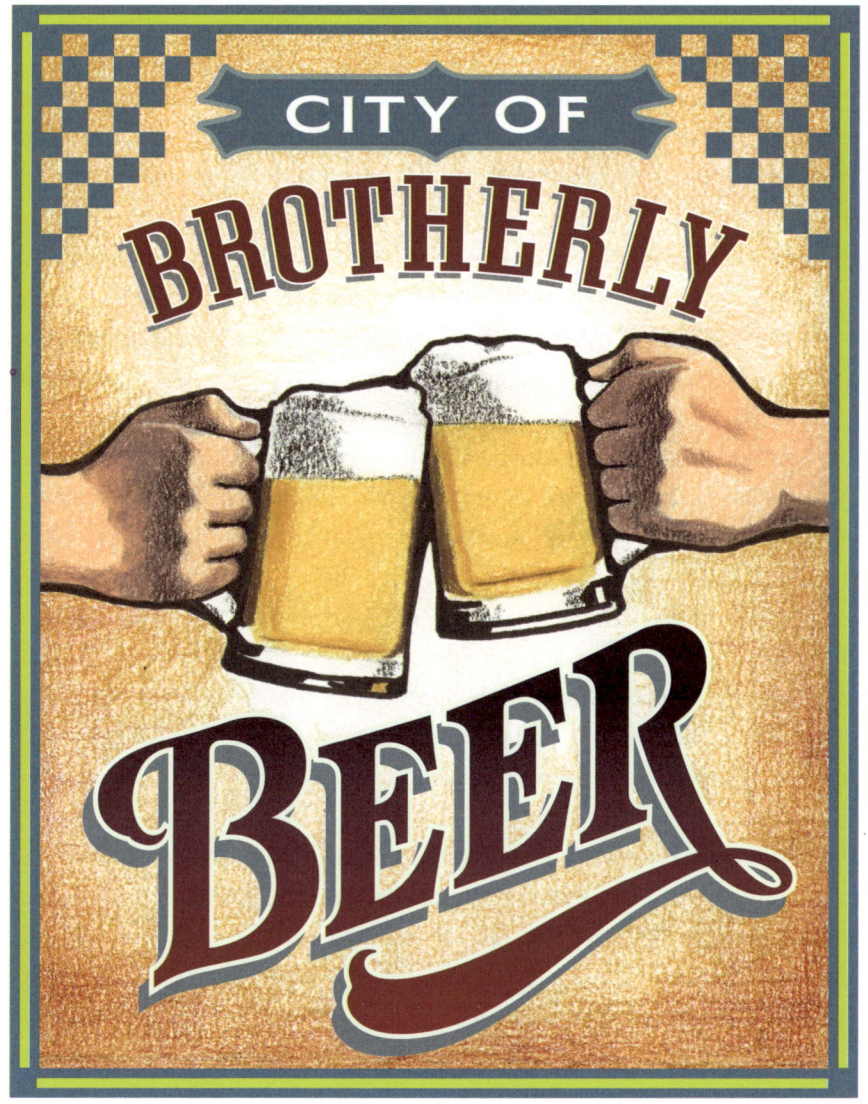

matter. This was the traditional colonial beverage until tea and coffee surpassed it. Many homes contained small breweries where it was made fresh to be consumed throughout the day. Even the founding fathers such as Benjamin Franklin brewed their own. A number of personal recipes survive to this day. (I am puzzled as to why it never occurred to these supposedly intelligent people that beer was safe to drink because the brewing process involved boiling water.)

With increasing population and demand, commercial breweries began to appear. By the time of the War of Independence, it has been said that Philadelphia had one tavern for every twenty-five men. By the nineteenth century, Philadelphia was known as the greatest brewing city in the Western Hemisphere, and by the twentieth century more than 100 breweries were operating within the city and it's immediate suburbs. There is even a section of the city still known by it's unofficial name of Brewerytown. Ironically, one of the city's neighborhoods that produced vast quantities of beer was the old Indian village Shackamaxon.

Unfortunately, the Eighteenth Amendment put many brewers out of business. Only the largest, such as Schmidt's, survived. But when Schmidt's eventually closed in 1987 it left Philadelphia without a single brewery for the first time in 300 years. However, local craft breweries began to emerge in the 1990s, some of them in the same neighborhoods as the old breweries. Happily, new brewers seem to be popping up nearly every day. There is even a gentleman with the nom de plume of Joe Sixpack who writes online reviews of local, national, and international brews (http://joesixpack.net). And you thought your job was tough.

PENN FOUND it necessary to return to England again in 1699 as threats by France were about to force the English crown to reclaim Pennsylvania to protect the colonies. And he found himself perpetually in financial straits. His oldest son William, Jr., had become a ne' er-do-well, ignoring his wife and children and running up huge gambling debts. Penn senior was just about broke, having invested so much of his own money in the colony and receiving very little in return. To make matters worse, his problems with Philip Ford resurfaced, when it was discovered that he had been diverting funds from Penn's estates and then asking for loans to cover the losses. Ford died in 1702, but the troubles worsened. Ford's widow, Bridget, threatened to sell Pennsylvania, for which she had legal title. Penn tried to block her claim, but she would not back down and demanded his arrest. Penn found himself in prison again at the age of 62. He was still highly regarded, however, and his imprisonment was considered an outrage. A group of prominent

Quakers arranged a deal with Mrs. Ford that essentially paid off back rents, and Penn was released.

But legal and financial problems continued to plague the aging dissenter, and in 1712 he suffered a stroke, followed by a second stroke several months later. He slowly lost his memory and became unable to take care of himself. Penn finally passed away in 1718, penniless, and was buried in an unmarked grave next to his first wife in Buckinghamshire, England.

Despite Penn's sorry ending, his "Holy Experiment" had been a great success and set the wheels in motion for a society—in fact, an entire country—based on his principals and ideology.

Philadelphia continued to expand and prosper, becoming by the mid-1700s one of the most important business centers of the British Empire. It also became home to some of the colony's most iconic personalities—among them Benjamin Franklin, scientist, philosopher, statesman, author, publisher, and ladies' man. Because of people like Franklin and Philadelphia's sophistication, it became known as the Athens of America.

Before long, a revolution took form on paper in a document composed near the banks of the Delaware, signed by members of every colony and carried out throughout North America until independence from Great Britain was finally realized. (And, oh yes, a small fracas took place as well.)

By 1800, Philadelphia had become the largest city in the United States. It gradually grew away from the river, to the west, north, and south, filling with immigrants who landed at the Washington Street Wharf, Philadelphia's equivalent of Ellis Island. A verse from an old traditional Irish song called "Lough Erne" goes:

> *When we got 'oer to the other side, we were both hail and healthy,*
> *Dropped our anchors in the bay, goin' down to Philadelphy.*
> *And for every lad linked with his lass, blue jacket and white trousers,*
> *And for every lass linked with her lad, blue petty coat and white blouses.*

Though still a fluid highway, the river itself became filthy and polluted, a disgraced body of water that had become the butt of many jokes. It was a place to stay away from. And to keep it further distanced from the rest of the city, a physical barrier was constructed. Interstate 95 now whisks travelers along the Delaware but offers little enticement to stop and visit. Perhaps the saddest part is that almost all of the past 300 years of waterfront history has vanished. The civic area called Penn's Landing has no bearing on the place he landed. That is covered by superhighway. (For a much more detailed experience, be sure to read *Philadelphia's Lost Waterfront* by Philly historian-in-residence Harry Kyriakodis.)

Old City Philadelphia is one of the most visited and tourist-friendly spots in the country, featuring Independence Hall, the Liberty Bell, Elfreth's Alley, and more. But the waterfront, not so much. If you should happen to already be in the city and are able to maneuver past I-95 to the waterfront, stop and visit; there is plenty to enjoy. The Independence Seaport Museum is home to an outstanding collection of maritime gear, artwork, and immigrant memorabilia. Permanently docked near the museum is the USS *Becuna*, a submarine commissioned in 1944 that saw plenty of action in World War II, Korea, and Vietnam. Tied up right next to it is the USS *Olympia*, known as Admiral Dewey's Flagship. The only remaining steel-hulled warship of its kind, it became a symbol of America's emergence as an Imperial power when it was a member of the fleet that destroyed the Spanish Navy at the

Battle of Manila in 1898. Interesting to see how war was waged then. Officers went to sea with their servants—the interior of the *Olympia* is reminiscent of the drawing room of a country estate, with ornate oak and walnut paneling and sturdy tables and chairs scattered throughout the decks. Large-caliber guns next to them poke out of a porthole. The men would stand ready for a battle . . . or a card game.

The Delaware River is cleaner now. For all the changes it's gone through, it's still a valuable resource, and for that William Penn would be proud.

The Illustrated Delaware River

20

Burlington

In the middle of the Delaware River, about twelve miles north of Philadelphia, sits an island, and in the middle of the island is a lake. The Lenni Lenape called this Matennecunk, which roughly translates to "island of pines." The first European presence in the Delaware River Valley appeared on this island in 1624. A small group of fur traders in the employ of the Dutch West India Company built a *factorij*, a small, primitive outpost, and called it Fort Wilhelmus after William of Orange. And they called the island Verhulsten after the director of the New Netherland colony. Later that same year, Captain Cornelius Mey arrived on his ship the Nieu Nederlandt from Amsterdam. With him were a group of Walloon settlers, French-speaking Dutch from the southern part of the Netherlands that would eventually become Belgium. (The lake on the island didn't appear until modern times; more on that later.)

They were part of several companies of colonists and businessmen with whom the Dutch would try to establish a legitimate claim to the region. Mey also brought immigrants to Fort Orange (modern-day Albany, New York) and set up another trading post called Fort Nassau farther south on the Delaware near present day Gloucester, New Jersey. And while he was at it (as we've seen previously) he named the southern tip of New Jersey for himself, and the northern tip of Delaware (Henlopen) for a place in his homeland of Holland.

The English had previously claimed the entire northeastern seaboard from Virginia into Canada, dating back to its discovery by John Cabot in 1497. In the mind of King Henry VII, the claim was made legal by documentation—Jus Gentium, Law of Nations, "that whatever waste of uncultivated country is discovered, it is the right of that prince who has been at the charge of discovery." But little was done to use the territory, so for many years the law was more like "you snoozeth, you loseth."

Matennecunk was probably so appealing to the Europeans because it was easily defensible—not so much from the Indians, who they wished to deal with anyway—but from other nationalities with less savory intentions. Despite the strategic advantage, the Walloon settlers found life a bit too harsh for their liking and left for another island named Manhattan. Swedes then arrived to take control of the island from their newly formed colony in Delaware, and they continued fur trading with the Indians. The Dutch returned, however, in 1655 when Peter Stuyvesant declared an end to the New Sweden colony during the "War of the Forts." It remained in their possession until the English took over all of the New Netherlands colony in 1664. It reverted back to the Dutch again in 1673 after a brief but ineffectual rebellion that resulted in the English finally re-taking possession for good the following year.

Peace broke out, but relations with the native population were strained when the first murder in New Jersey took place in 1671. One Peter Alricks became the first tenant on the island under English rule and employed two Dutchman named Peter Veltscheeder and Christian Samuels. The story goes that a Lenape brave named Tashiowycan blamed the two employees for the death of his sister. He recruited another Lenape man, Wyanamettamo, to help him gain revenge and the two Dutchmen were soon dispatched. In the aftermath, the tribal leaders learned of the incident and decided on swift Indian justice. The two murderers were invited to a dance celebration, got drunk, and were then clubbed to death. This was also the place where African-Americans first saw the Delaware River—as slaves of the early Dutch settlers.

After the final takeover of the Dutch colonies, things changed—not physically but on paper. Charles II gave an extensive land grant to his brother James, the Duke of York, that included all of the New Netherlands territory. New Amsterdam became New York, and the land to the south became New Jersey. Later that year the Duke gave New Jersey to John, Lord Berkeley; and Sir George Carteret (bailiff of the Island of Jersey, from whence we get New Jersey), dividing it between them. They set about framing a constitution declaring personal rights and religious liberty, one of the first in North America. New Jersey was now West Jersey and East Jersey, with a dividing line between the two that was not always clear.

Eventually Lord Berkeley sold his half of New Jersey to the English Quaker John Fenwick, who purchased it in trust for another Quaker, Edward Byllinge. But a dispute arose, mainly because Byllinge had no money to back the purchase. So the matter was turned over to uber Quaker William Penn to act as arbitrator. He divided West Jersey into 100 parts. Fenwick receiving one-tenth for his trouble, and the rest was reserved for sale to appease the creditors of Byllinge. Penn himself was appointed trustee along with two of the creditors, English Quakers Gawen Laurie and Nicholas Lucas, to dispose of the remaining ninety percent. Penn then solicited other Society of Friends members to buy it up and start a new life in a new land.

And so, between 1677 and 1678, five vessels sailed for West Jersey with 800 emigrants, mostly Quakers. On the first trip, the *Kent* sailed up the Delaware after making stops at New Castle and the old Swedish settlement at Raccoon Creek. From there the emigrants made their way on foot and by canoe up the Delaware to a place called Chygoes Island, directly across from Matennecunk. They had heard glowing reports about this place from George Fox, who had passed through on a missionary tour several years earlier.

They purchased the land from the Indians and laid out plans for a town they first called Beverly. No, wait, let's make that Bridlington; no, hold on—Burlington!

The next wave of settlers arrived in December of 1678 on board a ship named *Shield of Stockton*. Legend has it that when they arrived at the new town of Burlington, the weather suddenly turned brutally cold, causing the Delaware to freeze. The ship's line was tied to an enormous sycamore tree next to the bank, and the passengers walked to shore on the frozen river. The tree served as a memorial for many years until it died. A bronze plaque now serves as a permanent reminder.

OVER THE YEARS, the small settlement grew quietly but steadily, gaining more and more colonists who cleared land for planting, built mills, set up shops, and performed the usual communal necessities. Assemblies were met, legislation was enacted, magistrates elected, and in 1694 the first town meeting was held. Burlington prospered to such an extent that it became the capital of West Jersey even though the division was reunited in 1702. Politically, though, the state was still formally seen as a West Division and East Division with the New Jersey Assembly alternately meeting between Burlington and Perth Amboy.*

The last Royal governor of New Jersey was William Franklin, the recognized illegitimate son of Benjamin Franklin. He had an estate in Burlington called Green Bank but actually presided over state affairs at Perth Amboy. The senior Franklin also spent a short spell in Burlington in 1726 while waiting for a boat to take him to Philadelphia. It's said he bought some gingerbread and was given supper by a friendly woman at what is now known as the Revell House. (Built in 1685, it is the oldest house in Burlington County and possibly New Jersey).

Franklin senior and junior were at extreme odds on the matter of colonial independence—Benjamin was a rabid patriot and his son a staunch Tory Royalist. In the spring of 1776, William was placed under house arrest and on July 4 he was officially taken into custody and removed to a prison in Connecticut. He was eventually released during a prisoner exchange, moved to New York City (at the time under British occupation) and then to Britain. He met one last time with his father when the senior Franklin was returning to the US after his diplomatic tour in France, but their differences were never resolved.

Burlington has long been acquainted with more than its share of historic luminaries. When asked who the first president of the United States was, most people would answer Washington—but they would be wrong. There were a number of presidents before Washington was finally elected—presidents of the Continental Congress, one of whom was Elias Boudinot, who spent his final years in Burlington. He also served as a Supreme Court lawyer, director of the United States Mint, trustee of the future Princeton University, and was an advocate for abolition, American Indian rights, and religious tolerance.

At 457 High Street is the house where James Fenimore Cooper was born. Author of *The Last of the Mohicans*, *The Leatherstocking Stories*, *The Deerslayer*, and many other tales of the early frontier, he is considered the first true American novelist. The house is now the headquarters of the Burlington County Historical Society and exhibits copies of all of his writings including an original manuscript.

The Cooper and Lawrence houses, home of the Burlington County Historical Society

Remarkably, the house next door is the birthplace of James Lawrence, American naval hero of the War of 1812. Unfortunately he is remembered most in defeat when he gave the command, "Don't give up the ship!" He succumbed to wounds suffered during the battle but will be forever remembered for standing toe-to-toe with a much more heavily armed British warship. Earlier in his career he received praise for accompanying Steven Decatur to Tripoli and defeating the Barbary pirates who had been harassing American shipping.

Not far from these two houses is the former residence of Oliver Cromwell, an African American soldier who fought in the Revolutionary War. He accompanied Washington in crossing the Delaware in December 1776 and participated in the battles at Trenton, Princeton, Brandywine, Monmouth, and Yorktown. General Washington personally signed his discharge papers.

Just a couple of blocks from Cromwell's home on Wood Street is a house that was rented by General U. S. Grant in 1864 at the urging of his former artillery instructor at West Point, who insisted his family would be safe from harm for the duration of the war. (An unsubstantiated but colorful legend has it that years before, General Grant arm-wrestled then Presidential candidate Abe Lincoln at the Blue Anchor Inn around the corner.)

After the war was over in April of 1865, General and Mrs. Grant were invited by his former sparring partner's wife, Mary Todd Lincoln, to attend a play at Ford's Theatre in Washington. The general declined so that he and Mrs. Grant could travel to Burlington to see their children. Later that night in Philadelphia as they dined at Bloodgood's Hotel, Grant received the shocking news of Lincoln's assassination. Taking a ferry across the Delaware to Camden, they continued to Burlington. At six a.m. Grant rushed back to Philadelphia to board a special train commandeered to take him back to Washington. Little did Grant realize he had also been briefly considered as a target in the bizarre plot to kill off a number of high-ranking government officials.

At the end of Wood Street, on the banks of the Delaware, stood a house that was the summer home of Philadelphia Judge Edward Shippen. It's hard to believe that this bucolic location had a connection to a scandal during the Revolutionary War that could have rocked the rebellion to its foundations.

Judge Shippen had three daughters and the youngest, Peggy, was her father's darling, a stunning, blue-eyed blonde with a beguiling personality. The Shippens were loyalist members of Philadelphia society, and when the British occupied the city, Peggy found Major John André quite to her liking. Unfortunately, the next year the British had to evacuate the city, returning

General Benedict Arnold *Peggy Shippen Arnold*

control to the Americans. This time around, engaging in the company of patriots, Peggy met General Benedict Arnold, a heroic veteran of many battles. Smitten, he courted Miss Shippen and they eventually were married, he a thirty-eight-year-old widower with three boys and she a spoiled young socialite of nineteen.

Soon after the marriage, Arnold found himself sinking deeply into debt. Peggy suggested he could ease their financial burden by working for the British. She contacted her old and dear friend Major André (who was actually a spy) and hatched a plan in which Arnold would provide documents to the British describing fortifications at the American defense post of West Point. In return he would receive 10,000 pounds and a commission in the British military. Major André was captured, however, with the clandestine documents that included Arnold's signature. André was executed, and Arnold and his young wife escaped to New York City. They eventually moved to London and lived the rest of their lives there, held in contempt by both the British and Americans.

AROUND THE CORNER from Grant's house on Union Street is an impressive stone building that looks like it could have been designed by Edward Gorey.

But it houses one of the oldest continuous libraries in the country. Originally chartered by George II in 1758, the library traveled from home to home sponsored by some seventy original patrons (including William Franklin) until a permanent location was built in 1789. There it continued until its contents outgrew its limitations, and a newer, more spacious building was constructed in 1864. To step into this building and view the second-floor balcony, which is filled with exquisitely aging volumes still in their original nooks, is an extreme rush for a historyphile. The original charter is still there along with much of the original collection of 700 books. The oldest dates to 1551. This was also the first library to print a catalog, in it's inaugural year. As if this remarkable collection isn't enough, the Library Company is also in possession of two pristine first editions by John James Audobon: The Vivaparous Quadripeds of North America and Birds of North America, complete with hundreds of hand-colored plates. It gives me chills.

BURLINGTON FAIRLY glimmers with history, laying claim to New Jersey's oldest pharmacy, oldest volunteer fire company, and one of the colony's oldest printers. The print shop was located on High Street where Isaac Collins turned out New Jersey's first weekly newspaper, The New Jersey Gazette. Ben Franklin also put in an appearance, printing the first colonial currency in 1728 on a copperplate press. But before either of these accomplishments, this same spot was the office of Samuel Jennings, the first Provincial Governor of West Jersey from 1681 to 1684.

During the post-colonial era, Burlington was the third largest port in North America, and fittingly, a landing for the country's first steam-powered boat. John Fitch, a self-taught scientist/mechanic who had contemplated the idea of a steam-powered vehicle for some time, developed a boat propelled by twelve canoe-like paddles. After exhaustive trial and error and wrangling and cajoling with politicians, Fitch was finally able to demonstrate his invention. On August 22, 1787, Fitch got a head of steam up on his boat and under the dubious gaze of a number of delegates to the Constitutional Convention, set the boat in motion against the current of the Delaware River. It achieved the breathtaking speed of three miles per hour. The delegates immediately granted Fitch a patent and he began the first steamboat passenger service in the US, sailing between Philadelphia, Wilmington, Trenton, Bordentown, and

Mount on the Burlington Island carousel now residing in Seaside Heights, New Jersey

Burlington. But customers did not take to the new self-propelled technology, possibly because of the undependable nature of early steam power. Fitch was soon out of business. He died drunk and frustrated, taking his own life in Kentucky in 1798. This left Robert Fulton to happily but erroneously claim history's place as the inventor of the first successful steamboat.

Matennecunk, which had been renamed Burlington Island, became a trust of the City of Burlington and was rented out for farming. The revenue was used for education for the city's children. Early in the twentieth century it became Island Beach Park, a family picnic resort, and eventually blossomed into an elaborate amusement park complete with a large wooden roller coaster and a miniature railroad with replica Reading Railroad locomotives. It received thousands of visitors from river excursion cruises and ferries working both the Pennsylvania and New Jersey sides of the Delaware. It all came to a sorry end, however, in 1928 when a fire devastated the park. Then in 1934 another fire completed the destruction. Only the carousel survived, and it was restored by local resident Linus Gilbert. It found new life at an amusement park in Seaside Heights, New Jersey, and survived Superstorm Sandy in 2012. After well over 100 years, it is still being enjoyed today.

As for that lake in the middle of the island—it was created by a sand-mining company that unwittingly dug a quarry on the site of the early Dutch, Swedish, and English settlements. Any trace of their existence is gone forever. Fortunately, noted archeologist and naturalist Charles Conrad Abbott unearthed some artifacts prior to the mining. Born in 1843 and a graduate of the University of Pennsylvania, Dr. Abbott received world-wide acclaim for his discoveries of human habitation along the Delaware from glacial and pre-glacial periods. In addition to archeological studies, he penned many books about the wildlife, plants, and habitats that he studied right on his own farm between Bordentown and Trenton. The area is now known as Abbott Marshlands and encompasses a rich treasure of naturally preserved wetlands. Learn more at http://www.marsh-friends.org.

ANOTHER GREAT walking town, Burlington will take you way back—you'll almost believe Ben Franklin is walking beside you eating gingerbread.

21

The Bend in the River

"My heart and myself are three thousand miles apart; and I had rather see my horse, Button, eating the grass of Bordentown than see all the show and pomp of Europe."

Such were Thomas Paine's feelings when he wrote these words while living in France after the American Revolution. He had purchased a house in Bordentown at the corner of Farnsworth Avenue and Church Streets in 1783 and lived there off and on until his death in 1809. It was the only property he would ever own.

Born in England, Paine emigrated to Philadelphia at the urging of none other than Benjamin Franklin, who wrote for him a letter of recommendation. Franklin's suggestion turned out to be a wonderful idea, for shortly after his arrival in America, Paine authored one of the most incendiary works ever written: *Common Sense*. At just forty-seven pages and costing two shillings, it began to be sold on the streets of Philadelphia in January of 1776. Within three months 120,000 copies had been purchased and shared, sending an electric shock throughout the colonies. It bolstered the cause of the revolution, reinforcing the belief that freedom was the noblest of all things to fight for. John Adams declared, "Without the pen of the author of *Common Sense*, the sword of Washington would have been raised in vain." Paine continued to write more inspirational works, such as the *Crisis Papers*, from which Washington read aloud to his troops: "These are the times that try men's souls."

Paine's career continued not only as an author, but as a military aide, political activist, statesman (negotiating France's involvement with America), and helping to organize the Bank of North America. When the American Revolution was over, he moved to France and penned *Rights of Man*, another political tract encouraging the French in their own revolt. Paine was also an inventor, receiving a British patent for an iron bridge design, developed a smokeless candle, and worked with John Fitch in developing steam engines.

His intensely radical nature deepened over time. While in France, he attacked President George Washington as an incompetent commander and wrote to him, "the world will be puzzled to decide whether you are an apostate or an impostor; whether you have abandoned good principles or whether you ever had any." He returned to America to no great welcome and finally passed away in 1809. Only six mourners attended his funeral. His obituary read simply: "He lived long, did some good and much harm." His house in Bordentown is now a dentist's office.

Bordentown is not the largest town on the Delaware, nor the oldest, but it packs more history in it's one square mile than most. Founded in 1682 when Thomas Farnsworth, an English Quaker, moved his family up the river from Burlington, Farnsworth Landing quickly became a trading post. It was a strategic location at a broad bend in the river offering the shortest overland route between the Delaware and New York Bay. In 1717 Joseph Borden arrived and began buying up property, and by 1740 he had established ferry services and stage lines linking New York and Philadelphia. Farnsworth Landing gradually became known as Borden's Town.

An increasingly important transportation hub, it housed not only important visitors but distinguished residents as well. Francis Hopkinson, the first graduate of the University of Pennsylvania, lived here in a house that is listed on the National Register of Historic Places. It was used as headquarters by the British during the Revolution. Hopkinson was a delegate to the Continental Congress, a signer of the Declaration of Independence, and the son-in-law of the town's prominent namesake, Joseph Borden. Colonel Borden's house was burned by the British during the war, and as a British officer apologized for the act, it is said Mrs. Borden reacted: "This is the happiest day of my life. I know you have given up all hope of reconquering my country, or you would not thus wantonly devastate it." The house was soon rebuilt and is still standing today on Farnsworth Avenue.

The British saw the potential in occupying the town during the Revolution, which they did—on three different occasions. The first was in 1776 when a number of British posts were scattered across New Jersey. They withdrew after the Battle of Trenton. (These troops were Hessians commanded by Colonel Von Donop, whom we've met previously at the Battle of Red Bank). In May of 1778 they returned to destroy the Pennsylvania Navy, which was moored there and burned much of the town to secure a safe route to New York. The third occupation was in June of 1778 when the actual evacuation of Philadelphia took place.

Patience Lovell Wright was another Bordentown resident who had a part in the American Revolution. She worked as a spy for Benjamin Franklin and was America's first sculptor. After her husband died, Patience started molding in bread dough and other materials to amuse her children. She became so proficient that it became her occupation and she moved to New York to create tinted wax likenesses. In 1771 much of her work was destroyed in a fire. But her reputation had grown internationally and she moved to London to open a new studio. Here she created busts and statues of many notables of English society. It was also here that she learned of the impending storm in the colonies and agreed to work clandestinely with Franklin for the good of her native home. It was not difficult, as many of her artistic subjects were British government officials. She had merely to keep her ears open and report what she overheard. Her life-sized statue of William Pitt (Lord Chattam) still stands in Westminster Abbey, and her childhood home also still stands on Farnsworth Avenue.

Other Bordentown artists included portraitists Gilbert Stuart, Samuel Bell Waugh, and landscape painters Charles Lawrence and George Bonfield.

Another of Bordentown's notable women was Clara Barton. Born in North Oxford, Massachusetts, in 1821, Clarissa Harlowe Barton was painfully timid as a child but also extremely intelligent, becoming a teacher by the age of 15. Around 1850, Clara arrived in Bordentown after teaching in Canada and New England. She was dismayed to find many school-age children engaged in everything but schooling due to the social stigma of having to attend a "pauper school." She finagled funds from the town fathers and in

1852 took over a one-room brick schoolhouse. It was an instant success. In 1854, she moved to larger quarters to accommodate the increasing enrollment. The building was used until 1954, when it was demolished to make room for a more modern facility. A replica of her original school is now displayed in Bordentown's historic district. Clara later founded the American Red Cross after risking her life many times to bring supplies and relief to soldiers during the Civil War.

Joseph Bonaparte's Monogram

There was another of Bordentown's inhabitants who did not have a list of accomplishments like these other distinguished residents, but is perhaps better known—the King of Spain. I am not kidding. Joseph Bonaparte, older brother of Napoleon, was actually the King of Spain and Naples and Sicily. These were not titles he was born to, being the spoils of conquest, but they weren't meaningless, either. He truly was one of the crowned heads of Europe. Arriving in New York in 1815 under the assumed name Count Survillier, perhaps to distance himself from his unpopular brother, he made his way to Philadelphia, staying in center city and later in Fairmount Park. Bonaparte fled Spain after his brother's defeat at Waterloo, bringing with him only a suitcase full of jewels. However, he had the foresight to bury much more at a Swiss refuge.

A year later he moved to Bordentown's Point Breeze, on a high bluff overlooking the Delaware and Crosswicks Creek. On his property, originally consisting of a house and 200 acres, Bonaparte began building a new estate that would take three years to finish and comprise over a thousand acres of sculpted landscape with winding carriage lanes and an artificial lake spanned by an arched stone bridge. Under the house, connecting to the river bank, were a series of brick-lined tunnels perhaps built with the intention of an escape route should any of his European enemies come looking for him.

The next time you travel north on Route 295, as you approach Bordentown, look for a road sign announcing "Scenic Overlook." On your right, above a small marina on Crosswicks Creek, you will see a hill with Victorian-era houses on its summit. It is on that hill, a little to the north, that Bonaparte's estate once stood. He received many guests there, including former guerilla leader General Mina, who invited him to become King of Mexico. He declined.

His finances running low, Bonaparte enlisted his secretary Louis Maillard to return to Europe and retrieve the remainder of his fortune in Switzerland. He did so, after a harrowing journey that included being shipwrecked in Ireland. Maillard was also assigned to return with Joseph Bonaparte's wife, Queen Julie from Belgium, but she was under doctor's orders not to travel. Maillard did bring the ex-king's two daughters, Zenaid and Charlotte, back to Bordentown to live with their father. With his fortune now intact, he completed his estate and was said to be hospitable to neighbors who would drop by to spend a quiet afternoon. He also received distinguished visitors, such as John Quincy Adams, Henry Clay, and Daniel Webster.

In 1820, the newly completed mansion caught fire while Bonaparte was visiting Philadelphia. He returned just in time to watch the roof collapse. It seems many of his neighbors were there, trying to save as much as they could. Bonaparte had to stop some of them, as they were in danger of risking their own lives. He soon after wrote a letter to William Snowden, Justice of the Peace of Bordentown, in gratitude for all that his neighbors had done for him remarking: "I cannot omit on this occasion to repeat what I have said so often, that the Americans are the most happy people that I have known; still more happy, if they understand well their happiness."

Bonaparte rebuilt the estate, took at least one mistress, Annette Savage, fathered another daughter, and returned to Europe in 1839 to live out the rest of his days with his wife.

Apparently, he did not take all his belongings with him as various pieces show up from time to time at local antique auctions. A piece or two of Joseph's furniture has even been featured on the PBS Television Series *Antiques Roadshow*. Some of his items and furnishings are on display at the James Fenimore Cooper House in Burlington. His second mansion was torn down, and the only reminder of the Bonaparte estate is the building known as the gardener's cottage, which also housed his secretary, Louis Maillard. That building sits apart from the rest of the compound on the grounds of a Catholic missionary order. At some point in time, someone decided to tidy up the original plaster siding with a faux stone exterior. (Ugh.)

THE SAME YEAR that Joseph Bonaparte was arriving in America, naval architect and inventor John Stevens was convincing the New Jersey Legislature to authorize him "to erect a rail road from the River Delaware near Trenton to the River Raritan at or near New Brunswick." This was effectively the approval of the first railroad act of the United States. But it would not be until 1825 that he actually built and tested a steam locomotive at his estate in Hoboken, the first constructed in America. And finally in 1831, track would start to be laid at Bordentown for the Camden and Amboy Railroad using rails milled in England and delivered in sixteen-foot sections. Also delivered was a primitive steam locomotive that Stevens had purchased. Called the John Bull, it arrived disassembled with no instructions or diagrams. Stevens hired Isaac Dripps, a Belfast native, to put it together. Eleven days later, Dripps and his crew had the engine running on a short length of track. Weighing in at ten tons, the John Bull was named for the portly fictitious British mascot, much like the American personification of Uncle Sam. It made its trial run that same year carrying New Jersey legislators and two of the Bonaparte family as wary but excited passengers. After a long and

illustrious career and a number of modifications, the locomotive was finally retired in 1893. Now on display at the Smithsonian, it is the oldest operable self-propelled vehicle in the world. Look for a video of its 150th anniversary run on YouTube (it's not hard to find).

Bordentown continued its importance as a trade center with the building of the Delaware and Raritan Canal, which connected the Delaware and Raritan Rivers. Construction began in 1830. With Bordentown as the southern terminus, the canal ran forty-three miles to New Brunswick with fourteen locks in between. It was successful from the start, transporting coal from Pennsylvania to developing industries around New York Bay and the Lower Delaware Valley. It reached its peak in 1866 transporting nearly three million tons of anthracite coal.

But nothing lasts forever. As railroads proliferated, the canals were abandoned. Bordentown began to feel abandoned, too. As railroads were re-routed, it lost its edge as a major commercial center, resulting in economic decline. But what has been bad for business has been good for history. Bordentown survives as a sleepy river town and a largely intact example of what eighteenth and nineteenth century life was like.

Continental Lane, the route the Continental Army took after crossing the Delaware to New Jersey

22

The Crossing

We have come to a place in the river where a momentous military event took place. It was not a large battle and didn't last long, but had it's outcome been even slightly altered, our country's history might have been far different. We would probably have gained our independence from Great Britain—eventually. Or we might all be driving on the wrong side of the road.

The event came to be known simply as Washington's Crossing. The truth is that the campaign took a great deal of luck, determination, and a massive storm from Mother Nature to help. On December 27, 1776, an army of exhausted, half-frozen, half-starved men were rejoicing and recovering on the Pennsylvania banks of the Delaware. They had just spent more than sixty hours in snow, sleet, freezing rain, and fierce winds to wrest the city of Trenton from British control. The occupying troops were Hessians and Jägers on the payroll of Great Britain. Despite what every school child has been taught, they were not hung over from Christmas partying; they were a well-trained, highly disciplined fighting force on high alert for any kind of surprise attack. Many of them were exhausted from illness and constant duty with little rest. They were ordered to sleep fully uniformed with ammunition belts on and weapons at the ready. Even the artillery horses had been kept fully harnessed and on edge for over a week because of rebel forces sneaking across the river from various locations in Pennsylvania. The rebels would set fire to buildings and snipe at them, and when British dragoons or Hessian foraging parties ventured from the protection of Trenton, they would be attacked.

So when a vicious nor'easter set in on Christmas night, their vigilance relaxed. But around eight o'clock the next morning when Hessian Lieutenant Andreas von Wiederholdt stepped out of a makeshift guardhouse for a breath of fresh air, he thought he spotted dark movement in the dim morning light through the heavily falling snow. Figures started to appear, first just a few, then increasing in numbers until there were too many to count. Shots rang out and he shouted inside, "Der Feind!" The Enemy!

American soldiers numbering 2,400 under the command of General George Washington surrounded the village of Trenton, and after less than two hours of fierce fighting, forced the surrender of the German occupants. It was a decisive American victory that completely changed the climate of the Revolutionary War.

During the previous year, the Continental Army had suffered defeat after defeat, losing control of New England and New York, retreating south through New Jersey. Many volunteers were lost, too, through casualties, illness, and desertion. Morale was at an all-time low, and the consensus was that the revolution was on the verge of collapse. The bedraggled army limped through central Jersey and crossed the Delaware River into Pennsylvania to lick their wounds and regroup. They simply were not experienced enough to fight toe-to-toe with professional British and German soldiers.

The British followed them, leaving occupying forces from Newark and Hackensack down through Mt. Holly, Bordentown, and Trenton. Their next objective would be to take control of Philadelphia, the capital of the North American colonies and the second largest city in the English-speaking world. During his retreat, Washington had wisely ordered all river craft to be removed from the Jersey side of the Delaware and taken to Pennsylvania. But the British were in no hurry. Winter was setting in and they would wait until Spring.

Washington was well aware of the situation and instead of waiting, he needed to do something decisive—any action was better than another defeat. He had a plan in mind but gathered his commanders and advisors to get their input. This was what eventually made Washington so successful—although he didn't have the extensive military training and background of his adversaries, he had an open mind and was willing to engage in discourse. The decision to cross the Delaware and attack Trenton was horribly risky; it had to be planned and executed perfectly.

The Continental Army would be given a three-day supply of ammunition and cooked rations. They would start to cross the river at McConkey's Ferry under cover of darkness, boat all the men and equipment to New Jersey,

The Crossing

The Inn at McConkey's Ferry

then assemble and march ten miles south to Trenton and initiate a two-pronged attack that would began at four a.m. on December 26. Another crossing would be enacted just below Trenton to prevent the enemy's retreat. In addition, crossings would also be made at Bristol, Pennsylvania, over to Burlington.

There were problems almost immediately; getting the army moving was like trying to get a teenager out of bed. Then the storm struck. The wind had been gradually building from the Northeast all day and around midnight it hit hard. Men and horses and boats were enveloped in blinding rain, then snow, then sleet. A number of men died from exposure before ever getting started. The river currents were becoming stronger and ice sheets were forming that battered the shoreline into a jumbled mass. Every moving being was soaked and aching from the cold. Getting the army across the river was a monumental task and took far longer than anticipated. Anyone else would have called it a day, but Washington was determined to get the job done. And they had just begun. There were now ten miles to slog through unfamiliar territory in a blinding nor'easter. They soon discovered they also had to overcome yet another obstacle—Jacob's Creek—a large tributary of the Delaware at the bottom of a ravine with steep banks 100 feet deep. The heavy cannons had to be taken apart and hauled down and up by hand, then reassembled and hitched to the horses again. They might have given up completely if they had known what else was going on—the force that was to cross just below Trenton found it impossible to do so. Huge sheets of ice backed up by the tidal flow and falls made an impenetrable blockade on the Jersey side.

Still further downstream, Colonel Cadwalader's men called off their first attempt at Neshaminy Ferry because of the same problems, then tried to cross at Bordentown, but were again thwarted by the ice and swift currents.

The campaign seemed doomed. But Washington urged his troops on until another incident that nearly caused him to lose it altogether. About two or three miles from Trenton, a group of soldiers were spotted: Virginians from Adam Stephens' Fourth Regiment. They were on an unauthorized mission of revenge: several days earlier one of their men had been shot and killed in a boat by Hessians, and Stephens had taken the matter into his own hands on Christmas night, the very night the Continental Army was trying to initiate the most secret mission of the war. The Virginians staged their own raid on Trenton, killing four Hessians and wounding eleven. The entire town was alerted, and the Germans gave chase but Stephens' men got away. When Washington heard this story, he was furious, more angry than anyone had ever seen him. "You, Sir, may have ruined all my plans by having put them on their guard!"

By now the army was far behind schedule and Washington realized the element of surprise was probably lost, but at this point there was no turning back. Surprise was not really a factor, anyway. British agents in the rebel camps informed the Hessians that the Americans would be coming. But the Germans felt they had little cause for concern. The Hessian troops were seasoned veterans who soundly defeated the rebels at every turn and had little regard for their undisciplined fighting skills. In a supreme gesture of arrogance, Colonel Johann Rall, in command of the German occupation, said, "Let them come. We will go at them with the bayonet." His was not the only such display. Colonel Von Donop, with his force of Jägers, quickly chased off a small group of colonial militia as they tried to occupy Mt. Holly. His men remarked that the Americans "run so fast, they had not the opportunity of killing any of them." Von Donop was so unconcerned with the rebel threat that he decided to stay in Mt. Holly instead of positioning his troops close by Trenton, in case they were needed.*

However, Stephens's reckless act probably contributed to the successful capture of the town. Colonel Rall no doubt assumed the raid was the attack his spies had predicted and resumed his duty of keeping the town secure. He probably also believed that an entire army would not be foolhardy enough to attack in such miserable conditions. When he awoke the second time in a day to the sound of gunfire, he began to suspect something larger was afoot. And indeed it was. The Continental Army stormed through the small town,

A Jäger

creating havoc with the eighteen artillery pieces they had just dragged through a raging storm. In a relatively short time they killed twenty-two Hessians including Colonel Rall, wounded eighty-three, and captured 918. They also acquired muskets, bayonets, swords, and six German cannons. Washington reported that he lost only a few officers and privates. Unofficially, though, many more died of exhaustion, exposure, and illness.

The British were utterly shocked by Washington's first victory. They couldn't believe they had underestimated the Americans' resolve. But there was more to come. Many of the Continental Army regulars' terms of service were soon to expire, but Washington convinced them that if they stayed on for another month, they would do their country a great service. To sweeten the deal, he offered each man $10 in hard cash. The victory created a new-found confidence, and within days new recruits started pouring into the camps along the Delaware. The timing was fortuitous, because on January 2, a large, angry force of British and German troops marched on Trenton from Princeton, about ten miles away. But Washington was ready for them. He positioned his troops along a three-mile front just south of Trenton and repulsed attack after attack at the bridge over Assunpink Creek. This was the second decisive victory for the rebels in less than a week, although it has barely been recorded. The Battle of Princeton followed on January 3, 1777, yet another

American triumph over superior fighting forces. By this time winter was closing in rapidly and the American Army was exhausted and low on supplies. Washington gradually took his troops north to Jockey Hollow near Morristown to hunker down for the winter. The war would continue for another six years.

When the Revolution was finally over and Lord Cornwallis surrendered his troops to the American forces at Yorktown, he remarked to Washington that history would record this as his greatest victory. But what he grudgingly admired the most was Washington's capture of Trenton.

THE LITTLE VILLAGE where all this commotion took place began as many of the towns along this part of the river did: with a vanguard of Quaker colonists drawn to relocate at the urging of William Penn. In this case, a gentleman named Mahlon Stacy from Sheffield, England, led a group eager for political and religious freedom. In 1679 they began settling around Stacy's humble gristmill along the Assunpink Creek, which flows into the Delaware. It did not take long before a wealthy businessman from Philadelphia named William Trent started buying land along the river, Stacy's included. By 1719 Trent had acquired enough land and reputation that the village began to be called Trent-towne, later conveniently shortened to its present title. The village prospered and became another strategic location for a ferry terminal from which travelers could obtain overland transport to points north, chiefly New York.

After the Revolution, the town became the national capital for a few brief months in 1784 while entertaining members of the Continental Congress. Trenton was considered for the permanent capital, as were Princeton, Kingston, New York, Philadelphia, and Annapolis, Maryland. The idea was to steer clear of big cities, rife with merchants, investors, and politicians who might try to nationalize the fledgling government. The choice finally came down to two locations: one on the Potomac River near Georgetown, and the other on the Delaware at Trenton. We all know the outcome, probably influenced by Washington himself because Mt. Vernon was just a few miles from the Potomac site.

Trenton was made the state capital in 1790 due to its central location, although the New Jersey Legislature had met there often before.

Trenton marks the spot where the Delaware no longer is navigable. The earliest explorers called this place "the falles." There are no cascading torrents, only minor rapids strewn with rocks. But they are just enough of an impasse to halt shipping any farther north. The rocks are all that remain of ancient mountains, spread between the Appalachians and the coastal plain. This is also as far north as the tides reach—about 100 miles.

SPANNING THE DELAWARE River over the "falls" at Trenton is a steel truss bridge. First opened in 1806, it was the first to cross the Delaware. Needless to say, it has been rebuilt many times since then, but the original supports still stand next to the latest version. Emblazoned on the side of the bridge in giant neon Futura letters is the slogan "Trenton Makes, the World Takes." That was an apt statement when some of the largest manufacturing operations on the eastern seaboard were located here.

The Roebling Company, manufacturers of wire products, from bridge cables to elevator hoists, began in Trenton in 1848 as the brainchild of John Augustus Roebling (coincidentally born the same year as the first bridge over the Delaware). An engineering genius who emigrated from Prussia, Roebling developed a method for manufacturing wire rope, which became an indispensable building material. He rose to prominence from one of his first projects—a double-decked bridge over the Niagara River that carried a rail line on one level and passenger vehicles on the other. Roebling also designed a number of canal aqueducts, which were essentially bridges for boats that carried canal barges over a number of rivers on the coal routes in the Northeast. He is probably best remembered as the designer of the Brooklyn Bridge, although a construction mishap took his life, leaving his son Washington to oversee its completion. Later, in the 1930s, the Roebling Company would

provide the cables used to suspend the Golden Gate Bridge, spinning the thousands of miles of wire on-sight—an innovative first.

Despite the patriarch's untimely death, the company continued, outgrowing its Trenton facilities, and moved about ten miles south, still on the river. There Roebling built its own steel mill, along with an entire town to house its workforce.

More than 600 dwellings were constructed, from row homes for laborers to semi-detached houses for skilled workers and larger detached homes for management. The homes were leased from the Roebling Company, which took care of maintenance, including mowing the lawns. The first company town of its kind, Roebling contained an inn, general store, private stores, schools, repair shops, stable, boat house, recreation center, and even a ball park.

John Augustus Roebling

Many of the families, mostly immigrants, lived here their entire lives, some of them buying the rentals when they were offered for sale.

To learn more, visit the Roebling Museum (www.roeblingmuseum.org), located in the former gateway to the old mill, which houses a startling display of artifacts and memorabilia.

Pottery was another huge industry that grew along the river, its exact beginnings shrouded through time. It's possible that the early European settlers admired the quality of the original inhabitants' handiwork and found that the native clay was of exceptional quality. Trenton and East Liverpool, Ohio, were the two major pottery centers in the US in the nineteenth century, Trenton taking the title of the "Staffordshire of America." Lennox became the largest and best known of the commercial pottery houses of Trenton, known to this day for exquisite design and quality. The company produced some of the finest dinnerware available and was commissioned by President and Mrs. Wilson in 1918 to produce 1,700 pieces for the White House. Lennox also created services for Roosevelt, Reagan, Clinton, and George W. Bush. Unfortunately for Trenton, Lennox ran out of room and moved to a new facility in Pomona, New Jersey, in 1954.

Thomas Maddock's Sons was equally successful, but not as glamorous. Although it also produced exceptional china tableware for the White House, its specialty was more practical—sanitary ware, in other words, toilets, sinks, drinking fountains, and wash basins—and the company became the world's largest producer of these products. Originally begun as Millington, Astbury & Poulson in 1859, it was later joined by a young Thomas Maddock, who made his way to Trenton by way of New York from his birthplace in England. He entered into a partnership with M.A.&P., and eventually took over the business, bringing in his offspring.

I was fortunate to meet one of his descendants, also named Thomas Maddock, an extremely spry, energetic gentleman in his mid-seventies with a thick shock of snowy hair. Maddock is a guide at Washington's Crossing Park on the Pennsylvania side of the Delaware. He has more knowledge of Washington's crossing than most because he and his family lived in the park in a house that dated to the late eighteenth century. The park was created in 1917; later, when Maddock was still a child, the park commission decided that their house was not authentic enough, since it was a wooden structure rather than stone. So they moved it about three-quarters of a mile away. It had originally stood just a stone's throw from McConkey's Ferry Inn, the tavern where Washington and his aides met and organized the crossing on that miserable Christmas night in 1776. Maddock has early memories of the river freezing over, and if Washington had been lucky enough to have the same conditions, the Continental Army would have had a much easier time of it. It's doubtful anyone will ever see the river freeze over again.

THE WORLD TOOK other products from Trenton: its clay was used for bricks; anvils were made for forging iron, including one of the largest ever made, and the largest bathtub ever made—for the 350-pound President William Howard Taft. Trenton also supplied the world with farm tools, watches, cigars, mattresses, and linoleum. But like other river towns, much of Trenton's industry hit the skids after World War II. Wilmington, Delaware; Camden, New Jersey; and Bristol, Pennsylvania, were sent in a gradual downward spiral from which they never recovered. But downtown Trenton still thrives and is one of the busiest state capitals in the country. However, it has almost totally lost touch with its origins as a river town. You can still see the Delaware and the rapids streaming under the bridges, but only from the highway that skirts the river. A high fence now keeps people away. No walking along the bank, no fishing, no boating, no riverfront activity at all—and that's a shame.

23

The Canals

When Washington crossed the Delaware, he used Durham boats that were sixty feet long, eight feet wide, and only forty-two inches deep, capable of carrying fifteen-ton loads of iron ore. They were sturdy, flat-bottomed affairs designed to maneuver over rocks and rapids going downstream, and easily poled going back up. But even these large boats were not big enough to haul the immense amount of raw materials demanded by the increasing number of towns and industries springing up along the river. Larger and larger rafts, made of timber felled up in the mountains, would be lashed together and then disassembled and used for masts and spars once they reached the shipyards downstream. Cumbersome and crudely constructed coal carriers would be broken apart for lumber once their loads were delivered. But this watery freeway was anything but smooth sailing. Spring run-off, heavy rains, and drought-induced low water made for hazardous shipping, not to mention running a gauntlet of ice flows during the winters. It was a long journey, particularly if products were bound for New York—down the river, around Cape May, and out into the open ocean, which presented its own hazards. Sometimes if conditions were bad enough, rafting and boating could only be accomplished a few months of the year. The answer to a more consistent mode of transportation was a spider web of canals begun in the late-eighteenth century.

The first ones connected the Great Lakes to Canadian cities and then the Great Lakes to the East Coast of the US by way of the Erie Canal. Most followed an existing river to tap into a consistent water supply. The canal system along the Delaware was no different. The Delaware and Raritan Canal was begun the same day in 1830 that the Camden & Amboy Railroad went into business. A year later they merged. And in 1871 the entity was leased by the Pennsylvania Railroad Company. The D & R canal was begun at

Bordentown, ran through Trenton, and then abruptly turned northeast to connect with the Raritan River at New Brunswick. From there, transportation could continue by boat and barge to New York City. About 80 percent of the cargo transported was coal to supply the industrial revolution, now in full mode.

A feeder canal for the D & R began about twenty-two miles upstream at Bull's Island and followed the Delaware down to Trenton, where it supplied water to the main route. Hard to imagine today, this whole canal system was dug mostly by Irish immigrants using hand tools. When it finally opened in 1834, the main line ran for forty-three miles through fourteen locks seventy-five feet wide and seven feet deep. There were also pivot bridges, culverts, and one aqueduct. The locks were operated manually by lock keepers who lived with their families in houses next to the canal. A few of these dwellings still exist today, quaint and picturesque, most of them of stone construction. Mules were originally used to haul the barges along the canal on a tow path until steam-powered boats took over; steam was also used to operate the locks later on.

The Canals

The canals proved an immediate success, and why not? They reduced time and distance and provided controlled conditions, unlike the adventures of river shipping. By the 1850s, the time of greatest prosperity, more than 1,400 barges were working the canal carrying 1–2 million tons of freight per year. But while the canals were performing as well as expected, the railroads were doing it even better. The canal systems continued to operate well into the early twentieth century, but with steadily declining loads, and the D & R finally closed in 1932.

Meanwhile, on the other side of the river, the Delaware Canal ran from Easton south to Bristol. Again, the main cargo was coal, for which the country had developed an unquenchable need. Begun in 1827 and built by the State of Pennsylvania, it leaked so badly because of poor design that it was soon shut down. Through the intervention of Josiah White, cofounder of the Lehigh Coal and Navigation Company, it was repaired and reopened the same year as the D & R canal.

Both canals had access to each other at various crossing points along the river, as well as offshoots that would allow traffic to flow all the way to New York Harbor. In fact, much of the Northeast had a network of canals connecting cities as far-flung as Evansville, Illinois, and Albany, New York.

A few canals are still in use today, but the D & R and Delaware Canals are not. They have become recreational parks where Adidas and Nikes pound the towpaths in place of mule hooves. The rest of the Delaware Canal, nearly sixty miles long, is a National Heritage Hiking Trail. The trail runs just west of the lower portion of Washington's Crossing State Park and continues north close to the river.

Close by, you'll find Bowman's Hill Tower and Wildflower Preserve. This 125-foot stone tower was built in the early years of the Great Depression to employ laid-off workers, and it indeed kept them occupied for a couple of years using stone quarried from Pennsylvania and New Jersey. A visitor taking the elevator and a set of stairs to the top is rewarded with a stunning, fourteen-mile radial view of the river valley. The tower was originally conceived as a historic shrine to commemorate the pivotal crossing of the Delaware in 1776. It seems that members of the Continental Army camped around the base of Bowman's Hill in the days preceding the campaign and used the summit to keep an eye on enemy movements.

View of the Delaware from atop Bowman's Hill Tower

The tower and adjacent wildflower preserve occupy a farm once owned by Jonathan Pidcock, the first European settler in the area. The hill's name may come from Thomas Bowman, a well-known English merchant who traded up and down the river in the seventeenth century, or (and you'll like this one better) it may have been named for John Bowman, ship's surgeon to Captain Kidd. It has been said that he retired here after returning from the sea and that the doctor and a bit of Kidd's treasure may be buried somewhere on the hill.

Back in New Jersey, the Delaware & Raritan canal towpath has also become a haven for bicyclists, strollers, and runners. Nearly all of it remains intact and is a designated National Recreation Trail. Only a portion in Trenton that has been covered over (although the water still flows underneath) and a section in Bordentown are inaccessible.

The Evolution of New Hope and Lambertville

We have reached a point on the river where we start to leave the deep history of the Dutch, Swedes, and English Quakers behind and continue on to more contemporary times. Not that what we've seen so far has been ancient history; in the grand scheme, America still has the new car smell. Europe has socks that are older than us.

As we continue north up the river from Trenton, we come to New Hope on the Pennsylvania side and Lambertville across the river on the Jersey side. These two low-stress, little river towns attract visitors in droves looking for rural charm that hardly exists anymore.

Let's start with New Hope. Situated on land originally used by the Lenni Lenape for hunting, fishing, and planting, it was later sold to a Robert Heath by our old friend William Penn. Heath established a mill, and a small community grew around it. Before long a ferry business was established and changed hands several times before John Coryell bought it, giving the little village a name: Coryell's Ferry. This provided a river crossing for people who, unlike those traveling by boat to Bordentown or Trenton, took the York Road overland from Philadelphia to New York City. It also happened to be about the midway point between the two cities.

During the Revolution, the ferry was used often by both British and American forces. It is almost certain that General Washington worked out a good deal of his plans for the invasion of Trenton at Coryell's Inn on the Pennsylvania side before finalizing the river crossing at McConkey's Ferry. Here we also find General Benedict Arnold commanding a post before his terrible lapse in judgment.

Like so many villages and burgs that took advantage of the river's power supply, Coryell's Ferry became a mill town. When Prime Hope Mills burned down in 1790, the owner, Benjamin Parry, rebuilt it and called the new facility New Hope Mills. The title seemed to bring a certain dynamic with it and gradually, Coryell's Ferry took on its present name. The town also took on a new industrial presence when the Delaware Canal passed through, providing transportation for any number of New Hope's manufactured goods. An outlet lock was even built to connect with the D & R Canal across the river. The Union Mills Paper Manufacturing Company was one of the few employers that kept going after the canals shut down. In fact, it was just about the sole large-scale business remaining, supporting entire families.* It finally closed in 1970. The mills have since been converted into exclusive condominiums.

New Hope began to attract people with a deep appreciation for the river's natural beauty. Painters such as Edward Redfield and William L. Lathrop began to create an artists colony that became known as the New Hope School, or, the Pennsylvania Impressionists. They strove to capture images of the Bucks County countryside through use of color and lighting. The artists painted plein air to vividly capture the moment. Redfield could often be found on a cold winter day, his canvas tied to a tree, painting for hours at a time. He would eventually become one of the most highly decorated artists in America. Word soon spread of this new artist-friendly community and painters from all over began to settle there. New Hope had something else to offer, too: close proximity to galleries in Philadelphia and New York. Eventually, some members of the colony moved farther north along the river to Phillips Mill, where an art community still exists. Many of the remaining artists, seeking privacy from the influx of tourists, fled to the countryside, and there is no real "art colony" there any more. The rural and scenic area around the river continued to attract artists of all types, however. In 1939 a group of art enthusiasts including Moss Hart purchased one of Parry's old gristmills and turned it into the Bucks County Playhouse, a summer stock theater that brought widely known thespians to it's stage. It became a highly valued off-off Broadway venue for newly minted plays and musicals. Broadway legends like Grace Kelly, Walter Mathau, Liza Minnelli, Helen Hayes, Jessica Tandy, and Hume Cronyn sharpened their skills here.

Just down the street is entertainment of a different sort, in a venue that is only slightly younger: John & Peter's. A legendary mecca for musicians

who perform original material, this intimate club opened in the early 1970s, and has been featuring live music seven days a week, 365 days a year ever since. This book would run far too long to list all the artists who have performed there, but here's a short list: Clarence "Gatemouth" Brown, Penn & Teller, John Sebastian, Loudon Wainwright III, Nora Jones, Ween, Tiny Tim, Stanley Jordan, Townes Van Zandt, Chris Smither, Maria Muldaur. The place was even featured in Ken Burns's documentary *Jazz*. And, of course, yours truly performed here, too, with the band Hucks Buxter and the Crash Bunnies. (The band's real name has been changed to protect the innocent.) Needless to say, good times were had by all. New Hope is today very much a tourist destination with restaurants, shops, and galleries. On the weekends, it may take a good forty-five minutes to travel a mile on the main drag through town.

Across the river, Lambertville is only slightly less congested. Both towns began with ferries owned and operated by the Coryell family, including John, whom we met earlier, and his father, Emanuel, who was the only white man in the region when he arrived on the Jersey side of the river in 1732. Until after the Revolution, both towns were called Coryell's Ferry. The Coryells' fortunes were very much tied to the Revolution. In addition to Washington's planning the Trenton raid at the West Bank Coryell's, Cornelius Coryell, son of Emanuel, was praised for his service as a guide on the Jersey side. Washington's army came by this way again over a year later after the brutal Valley Forge winter and crossed the river, camping in an orchard that has since become part of the Lambertville business district.

In 1812 a US senator under Jefferson's administration applied for a post office to be created at Coryell's Ferry. His petition granted, he named the village after himself, and made his nephew, Capt. John Lambert, the postmaster. This infuriated the Coryells, who refused to accept the new designation, calling it "Lambertsvillainy." In time, they got over it and the town is now proudly known as Lambertville. Also in 1812, bridge construction was begun to link the two Coryell Ferry villages. It was completed two years later, becoming the second bridge to span the Delaware. Captain Lambert then oversaw the construction of a new tavern. This "respectable hostelry," as he called it, survives to this day on Bridge Street and is known as the Lambertville House.

The old train station, now a restaurant aptly named Lambertville Station

Lambertville's industrial history closely parallels that of New Hope. The D & R feeder canal ran through town and was used extensively to ship products manufactured there, from underwear to rubber bands. But whereas an arts colony rejuvenated New Hope after the canals' decline, Lambertville was neglected. It wasn't until the early 1970s that overflow from New Hope, coupled with a more affluent society's desire for quaint country living, brought new life to the town. You'll find much of the same atmosphere now in Lambertville, but without the crush of New Hope. Replacing old storefronts are now galleries, eateries, shops, and B & Bs. The Lambertville House serves as one of the swankiest hotels along the river. Then there is Lambertville Station, a historic rail stop that has been converted into a large restaurant. It was there that my wife and I and about fifty other wedding guests boarded a restored Black River & Western Railroad passenger car headed toward Ringoes, New Jersey. It was one of the finest wedding ceremonies I've attended. Anyone can book a pleasant ride through the countryside: www.newjerseytrain.org.

One of the country's most highly regarded auction houses resides here, too. Rago Arts deals in contemporary fine art, estate sales, and jewelry. Owners David Rago and Suzanne Perrault are featured regularly as decorative ceramics and porcelain appraisers on the PBS series *Antiques Roadshow*.

24

Fish & Floods

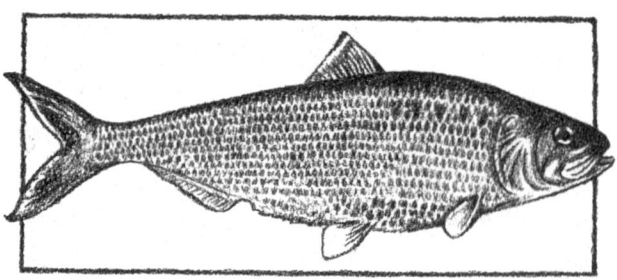

American Shad

In addition to manufacturing, fishing kept river people in groceries. Every year shad made their run up the Delaware to spawn. Many of the workers at Union Mills Paper would leave their jobs for ten weeks starting April 1 to take advantage of the run. They would use a haul seine, a long net harnessed to a horse on shore with the other end attached to a boat that would drift downstream. When the net was played out, they would row back to shore, creating a U shape that would trap the struggling shad. On good hauls, they could catch as many as a thousand fish. The fish would be packed in crates of a hundred, with a few extra small males thrown in, and shipped on the four p.m. train to New York's Fulton Fish Market. There were runs on the Hudson and Connecticut Rivers, too, and by the end of the fishing holiday, the market would be glutted.

This early spring extravaganza continued for hundreds, if not thousands, of years with fairly consistent results. During the brief period of spawning, rivers along the east coast of North America would literally turn silver from the millions of shad returning to their birthplaces. The Lenape used weir traps to ensnare and then spear the fish. They were then eaten fresh or preserved for later. One method of cooking was to attach the fish to wood planks and set them around an open fire to roast. West Coast tribes also used this technique, but with salmon instead of shad. (A modern approach is to soak a cedar plank in water for a couple of hours, then place fish fillets on it and cook over a gas or charcoal grill. Yummy!) It didn't take long for the earliest European settlers to catch on to this yearly food feast. Peter Lindestrom, an engineer with the Swedish colony at Fort Christina, wrote glowingly about shad. Seventeenth-century Dutch writings would describe dinners of smoked shad, cheese, ham, and fowl with cabbage and good Dutch beer. It has also been said that Washington's starving troops benefitted greatly from the spring run of 1778.

One of the earliest records of shad catches was 8,385 fish within a two-week period. But sometime after World War II began a steady decline. Carefully kept records indicate that in 1953 the shad catch was exactly zero. The river had become so polluted that the shad couldn't make it past Philadelphia—they were literally being asphyxiated from lack of oxygen. Efforts to clean up the river had begun in the mid-1950s, but it took many more years and the Federal Water Pollution Control Act to get the water back to healthy conditions for the fish. It took a lot of money too—a half billion dollars to increase the oxygen level by barely two milligrams per liter, the bare minimum needed for fish to breathe.

American shad (the species in the Delaware) are the largest member of the herring family and average twenty to thirty inches long. They are common all along the east coast of the US. Unlike their West Coast cousins, Pacific salmon, which die after spawning, shad can come back to procreate more than once. At one time called the "poor man's salmon," it was considered food only for the destitute. It would be a disgrace for anyone to serve shad to a guest. But plenty were eaten in private.

The shad have returned, not in the numbers they once were, but enough to celebrate. The Shad Festival takes place every Spring, the third weekend in April, when Union Street in Lambertville is closed off and crafters and vendors suddenly appear like daffodils.

Shad has a delicate flesh that can be prepared many ways, but some complain that they have an inordinate amount of bones. Even better is shad roe—the egg sacs, one of my favorite delicacies. Here's a recipe for two servings (or one if you're a pig like me):

1 large pair shad roe
6 tablespoons butter
flour for dredging
¼ cup chopped fresh parsley
salt and freshly ground pepper
1 tablespoon fresh lemon juice

Rinse the roe in cold water, pat dry, and carefully separate the two lobes. Melt the butter in a saute pan over low heat. Roll each roe gently in flour and place in the pan. Turn the roe to coat on all sides with the butter. Cover the pan and cook over low heat for 10 minutes. Turn the roe, sprinkle with the parsley, cover, and poach 10 minutes more.

Sprinkle the roe with salt and pepper and the lemon juice. Serve garnished with more lemon and some chopped chives. *Bon appetite.*

NOBODY REALLY thinks of shad roe as caviar (even though it is fish eggs), yet caviar was another early product of the Delaware River waters. From 1870 to 1900, 75 percent of all Atlantic sturgeon caught in the US were found in the Delaware, making it the "caviar capital of North America." Picture, if you will, an aquatic creature that looks as if it would be at home in the Jurassic period. Armor-plated, this stunningly ancient-looking fish was once prized worldwide for the supreme delicacy of it's eggs. These primitive "living fossils" are one of the oldest fish species on earth, with relatives dating back 350 million years. They could grow as long as twelve to fifteen feet, weigh over 800 pounds, and live for up to 100 years. A bottom feeder, the sturgeon has rows of bony plates running the length of its body and what are known as "barbels" on it's snout that help guide food to its toothless mouth. Like shad, the Atlantic sturgeon lives most of its life in the Atlantic and returns to eastern rivers to spawn. As indestructible as it appears, it is now an endangered species. Over-fishing and pollution have driven it to near extinction. By 1901, New Jersey catches of sturgeon were just 6 percent of what they had been a decade earlier. And because they take up to fifteen years to reach sexual maturity, there was no way for the species to stay ahead of the harvest levels.

It is estimated that there are now less than 300 spawning adults in the Delaware, down from over 180,000 spawning adult females from 100 years ago. Though they are no longer fished, the sturgeon may be facing their biggest challenge to date—the Delaware River Deepening project, which is dredging the main shipping channel for more marine commerce. The Army Corps of Engineers claims there is no danger to the sturgeon, but the National Marine Fisheries Service and the Delaware Riverkeeper disagree. We can only hope that "life will find a way."

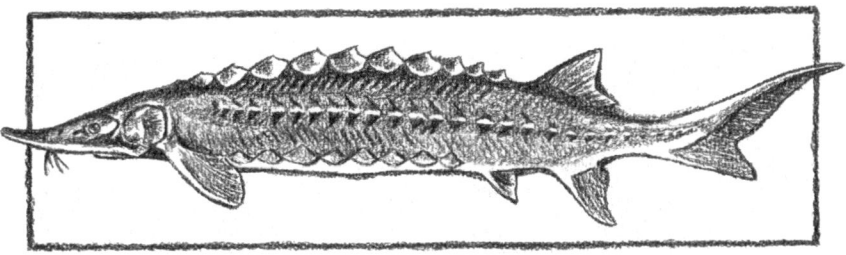

Atlantic Sturgeon

Floods, too, can affect the fish population, and the Delaware has had more than its share. One of the worst and most vividly remembered occurred in 1955. In 1957, my parents sent me to a summer camp near Shawnee on the Delaware. I can still remember all the talk about the great flood that had taken place two years earlier. There was still debris here and there throughout the camp. Travelers on some of the roads along the river can still see high water marks painted on rocks. In less than a week during August, Hurricanes Connie and Diane dumped more than twenty inches of rain over the Delaware Valley. The resulting flood swept away bridges, homes, resorts, and businesses and took the lives of nearly 100 people. Corpses were still being found thirty years later. The Army Corps of Engineers estimates that if the same flood were repeated today, it would cause damages in excess of $2.8 billion. Following the disaster, serious consideration was given to the construction of a dam north of the Delaware Water Gap. At the time, the Delaware was the longest river east of the Mississippi that was not dammed. The plan would have provided a hydroelectric power operation, reduced downstream flooding, and created a thirty-seven--mile-long reservoir. Opposition from local residents and businesses stalled the planning, and eventually it was scrapped altogether. More about this failed plan later.

Flooding continued, resulting in more damage and deaths, such as Tropical Storm Allison in June 2001 that caused $35 million in damages and seven fatalities. Then in a stretch of two years, from September 2004 through June of 2006, the river flooding caused close to $745 million in damage in New York, New Jersey, and Pennsylvania.

Yet folks continue to live on or near the river. Take the dreamy little river towns like Stockton, Frenchtown, and Milford in New Jersey, or Lumberville, Point Pleasant, and Erwinna in Pennsylvania. Smaller and even more laid back than New Hope and Lambertville, one trip through them on a fall afternoon and your head will be filled with the thought "I need to live here." Newcomers have arrived to replace the old timers who have passed on. Like Robert Rando, who with business partner Caroline Scutt owns the Book Garden in Frenchtown, up the street from the river. In addition to current best sellers, the store features a collection of vintage publications and prints and contemporary artwork, creative toys, and children's books.

Rando had a previous life as a biochemist with over 100 journal publications and fifteen patents to his name. After a lifetime of moving his family all over the country for his career and then a debilitating automobile accident, he decided it was time to settle down, and when the opportunity presented itself, bought the bookstore. In addition, Robert has become a fiction writer using the nom de plume Saverio Monachino (his grandfather's name). The store is more than just a commercial enterprise, it has become a community hot spot with Rando also hosting Spark, a writer's workshop series held during the winter months. You can find out more about this intriguing little gem at: www.bookgarden.biz.

For more literary adventures, visitors need look no further than Two Buttons, a shop that features exotic imports from South Asia. It is owned by Elizabeth Gilbert, author of *Eat, Pray, Love*, and her husband Jose Nunes.

FRENCHTOWN IS one of these sweet river towns with a long history and has become a thriving tourist destination. I remember an early 1970s excursion with some of my musician friends. We cruised up Route 32 in Pennsylvania, the scenic country road that hugs the river from Morrisville up to Riegelsville. We eventually crossed the Uhlerstown Bridge and stopped at the first drinking establishment we saw—the Frenchtown Inn. It was a small country bar in an old hotel that had seen better days. We had a few beers and a couple of bags of peanuts and were on our way again.

The inn has come a long way since then. A premier restaurant with three dining rooms and a bar, it consistently ranks among the best in the state. More than ten other dining establishments occupy this tiny burg of 1,500 inhabitants. There are no French restaurants; Frenchtown is not really French, anyway. It

Uhlerstown-Frenchtown bridge. Notice how the supports are angled on the upstream side to deflect debris, like the prow of a ship.

takes it's name from Paul Henri-Mallet Prevost, a Swiss national born in 1756 to a family with French Huguenot ancestry. He arrived in America after a long, harrowing escape from the French Revolution in a story that would rival anything written by Robert Louis Stevenson.

Prevost left Paris one step ahead of the guillotine, escaped to Geneva, then traveled to Germany, Holland, and England, finally landing in New York City in 1794. He arrived in New Jersey nearly a year later. Frenchtown was then known as Alexandria, after James Alexander, who immigrated from Scotland in 1715. Prevost purchased nearly 1,000 acres in and around the town, brought his family from Switzerland, and lived what is described as a quiet life in a fine house on the Delaware River. Somehow, over time the town took on the pseudonym for the Swiss aristocrat who everyone mistakenly believed was French. The town seems to enjoy a name change every now and then. The first inhabitants, the Lenni Lenape, called it Nishisakawick, or "two outlets of a stream near a house." Archeological evidence seems to confirm the existence of a house-like structure dating to 2,800 years ago. The first white people were farmers who built a ferry to unite with Bucks County in Pennsylvania. Originally known as the London Ferry, it later was called Sherard's Ferry, Calvin's Ferry, and then became Alexandria when it was laid out as a town complete with grist and saw mills and a river freight business. The mills were later converted

An old, funky, but charming storefront window typical of Frenchtown

to factories, the river shipping was taken over by the canal, and then the Belvidere Delaware Railroad arrived, part of the Pennsylvania Railroad System running from Trenton north via Phillipsburg and eventually Belvidere, New Jersey.

All the industry is gone now, but because of it's natural scenic beauty and charm, Frenchtown is *très bien*.

The Volendam Windmill in its current state

25

The Windmills of Your Mind

Just a few miles north of Frenchtown, still right on the river, is Milford, New Jersey. Milford hasn't quite found its tourist groove, but is on it's way.

The main road branches as you enter the town. If you turn left, you will come to yet another of the fifty-plus bridges that cross the Delaware. To the right, Route 519 (north) leads all the way to Phillipsburg, at the confluence of the Lehigh River. Along the way, you'll find one of the quirks that make back roads so enjoyable.

In the course of research for this book, I've acquired quite a few guide books and travelogues, some helpful, some not so much. In one of them I found an attraction that seemed to speak to me—a windmill museum in, of course, Holland (New Jersey). Provided with directions that seemed only slightly vague and after a quick study of Google maps, I felt fairly confident. Not that many roads—rural area—there was probably some kind of signage for it—how hard could it be to find? I'm going to condense this for you. After several hours of tracking through the hilly countryside of Hunterdon County, back-tracking, fighting gnawing hunger pangs and the wicked urge to relieve myself with no Super Wawa or fast food chain in sight, I finally found a road sign that looked promising. It took only a few more false turns and some well-worn oaths, and there I was, staring at an authentic six-story Dutch windmill that was... closed for business. And looked like it had been closed for a long time.

Two of the mill's four arms were missing, severed by a storm some years back. There was also an old, weathered sign advertising "Charlie Brown's Christmas Tree Farm." Obviously, quite an enterprise at one time.

The windmill was the brainchild of Poul Jorgenson, a skilled engineer and toolmaker who spoke seven languages. Born in Denmark, he never forgot the kindness of a miller who allowed neighborhood children to sweep the mill's floors for leftover flour during the harsh times of World War I. This experience prompted Jorgenson to build a real working mill to teach people about the milling industry. He traveled throughout many countries studying, sketching, measuring, and photographing all types of milling operations so that he could incorporate the best features into his dream. After his retirement, Jorgenson began work on the mill in 1965, and along with his wife, May, built the entire structure by hand, using only the outside help of steel workers and masons. Incredibly, he and his wife were both in their sixties, carrying fieldstone and wrestling lumber up six flights to lay flooring. Not to mention being able to somehow install the one-ton millstone. They wound up with a working mill that could grind grain into flour, powered by the wind gathered by four sail arms sixty-eight feet long. The top or cap could be rotated to meet the direction of the wind.

They called their creation the Volendam Windmill Museum in honor of a town in Holland, and probably also because they were in Holland Township. Poul Jorgenson died a short time later, but May carried on until she passed away in 1993. Other family members stepped up to continue the operation, but the attraction closed after the wind arms were damaged in 2007. There's a sadness to the place, a broken and empty windmill sitting on a wind-swept hill.

IF YOU DOUBLE back down Route 519 through Milford (and maybe stop at New Jersey's first brew pub, the Ship Inn) and cross the bridge into Upper Black Eddy, Pennsylvania, you're on your way to another attraction. Turn north onto Route 32 and in a short distance you'll see a sign for Ringing Rocks County Park.

You're in for a strange sight: Seven or eight acres of open field strewn with boulders, as if some giant poured them out of an immense bucket. But that's not the weirdest part. There's a reason it's called Ringing Rocks. If you bang on them with something hard, like another rock, they make a hollow metallic sound, like a hammer on an anvil. There always seems to be plenty of visitors testing them out, many using their own hammers. The boulders are composed of diabase—volcanic basalt containing large amounts of iron and aluminum. In the nineteenth century Dr. J. J. Ott collected rocks of sufficiently varied pitches to play tunes accompanied by the Pleasant Valley Band. A rock concert?

There is endless speculation about how this field of boulders came to be. The first thought is that it was created by a receding glacier, but glaciers were not known to have traveled this far south. And glacial deposits would be in a valley or hollow, but this boulder field is on top of a hill. There are fringe explanations of meteorites, comets, strange magnetic fields, and, of course,

The Ringing Rocks

paranormal activity, but most likely the rocks went through thousands of years of freeze-thaw cycles that broke them up into so many boulders.

Near the rock field is a lovely little waterfall that may not have much water, depending on the time of year you visit, but is well worth the short hike.

THE DELAWARE gets noticeably narrower the farther north you travel; from Pennsylvania to New Jersey, bridges jump across like children's sticks laid across a stream. One of the more picturesque spans connects Riegelsville, Pennsylvania with Pohatcong Township, New Jersey, which brings us back in contact with our old friends, the Roeblings. It replaced a covered bridge constructed in 1837, which replaced Wendel and Anthony Shenk's ferry. The covered bridge was swept away during what became known as the pumpkin flood of October 1903. Constructed with Roebling's famous "wire rope," the current bridge opened in 1904. It withstood the infamous flood of 1955, one of the few that survived, and is one of the last continuous-cable, multi-span suspension bridges remaining in the country. Originally a toll bridge, it was purchased by the Joint Commission for Eliminating Tolls and you can now cross it for free. For a time, both towns were named Riegelsville after Benjamin Riegel, a third-generation Pennsylvania German who moved back and forth between the two states, becoming successful in both. Born in Pennsylvania, he purchased a farm in New Jersey, then in 1823 bought a grist, saw, and oil

The Riegelsville Bridge, circa 1904

mill complex in Musconetcong. Moving back to Pennsylvania in 1832, he built a house and then an inn that still thrives today with quaint rooms for rent and a fine restaurant.

Riegel kept his business interests in both states, selling his New Jersey sawmill to his son John, who enlarged the facilities and converted it to paper mills. It was one of the largest employers in the area, in existence for nearly 100 years. It ceased operating in 2003 and is now an abandoned hazardous-waste site with an uncertain future.

The Riegels were not the only successful businessmen in the region. When the canals and then the railroads were built along the river, Riegelsville found itself in the midst of the northeast iron and coal corridor. A number of intrepid industrialists took advantage of the massive shipping opportunities and prospered, building majestic gilded-age mansions along what is now Easton Road, on a hill overlooking the river.

The industrial aspects of Riegelsville have long since dried up, but all is not quiet in the seemingly sleepy little river town. The place seems to be teeming with paranormal activity. Legend claims that from prehistoric times, the local natives considered this a sacred spot and came here to have their spirits cleansed. When Europeans arrived, they desecrated this holy area, upsetting the spirits to no end. And now there are over twenty supposedly haunted locations, which can be visited during walking tours every October.

For those who prefer more anchored footing, there are plenty of hiking trails, mostly along the D & L Canal, and the Appalachian Mountain Club plans to develop the Pennsylvania Highlands Trail, a network of conserved greenway that will include more than 130 miles of trails.

Just a few miles from Riegelsville, Pennsylvania, is the old town of Durham, where the Durham boats that General Washington commanded for the river crossing were built. It is also the site of one of the earliest iron furnaces in the US. The boat-building operation met a need to transport the iron and other freight down river. The first boats were thought to have been built around 1730. At the height of their use, about 1,000 were working the river. Some of the cargo was critical weaponry—iron products like shot and cannonballs to be used by colonial troops. There is an odd New Jersey connection here: at approximately the same time (mid-eighteenth century), the village of Batsto in the middle of the Pine Barrens also produced iron products mined from bog ore found in the swamps. It, too, supplied the Continental Army with munitions and supplies during the Revolution. Since neither source of iron ore was of exceptional quality, it's been hinted that Batsto ore was mixed with Durham iron to make a better product. And on the grounds of Batsto are the remains of an old ore barge that some speculate could have been an exact likeness of a Durham boat. But it's not that unusual. Durham's boats also found their way north for use on the Mohawk River as well as the Hudson and Niagara and into Lake Erie, though they were often altered to accommodate different conditions. Some were even fitted with sails. To be sure, Washington was grateful for the Durham boats in more ways than one.

THE ILLUSTRATED DELAWARE RIVER

Drawn with (what else?) Crayola Crayons

26

THE FORKS

When you were a child, you undoubtedly let your creative urges flow by drawing gorgeous pictures—landscapes, still lifes, space aliens, parents, animals—or you filled in ready-made images or connected mysterious dots in coloring books. And the artistic medium you used was a small wax cylinder to which dye had been added—a crayon. Who can forget the lovely, warm aroma as you created your latest masterpiece, which might make it to the coveted refrigerator door gallery. The most popular manufacturer was clearly announced on it's label—Crayola—which was peeled away as the crayon was worn down.

Since 1903, Crayola® Crayons have been manufactured in Easton, Pennsylvania, where the Lehigh River empties into the Delaware. Edwin Binney and C. Harold Smith started their business by manufacturing lamp black from charcoal, then moved into barn paint and carbon black for car tires. After producing slate school pencils, they introduced dustless school chalk. It was only a matter of time before they came up with inexpensive wax crayons. The first offering was a box of eight that contained red, orange, yellow, green, blue, violet, brown, and black. You can still use those primary colors or go wild with inch worm®, mango tango®, wild blue yonder®, or jazzberry jam®.*

Today Crayola makes much more than crayons: markers, dry-erase products, modeling clay, and digital creative tools are just a sampling of the current Crayola adventure. You can visit their downtown facility right on Centre Square, aptly named the Crayola Experience. Most of an entire day can be spent learning how crayons are formed, designing your own crayon label, making wax sculptures, playing in a giant water table, creating puzzles, and checking out the world's largest crayon—fifteen feet long and weighing in at 1,500 pounds.

Easton has had more than crayons to make the town colorful. At least thirteen taverns, including the Bachman Publick House, were in abundance during colonial times despite a sparse population. Even though the pubs were used to conduct the King's Royal Court sessions and other civic business, rowdiness and general shenanigans were quite normal.

The town was formally founded by William Penn's son Thomas in 1752, but its roots go back years earlier when the land became part of the infamous Walking Purchase discussed in chapter one. The Lenape translation came out as "Ye Hurry Walk." After William Penn died in 1718, his sons inherited his sizable estate of Pennsylvania—and along with it a great deal of debt. While John and Richard Penn remained in England, Thomas and land agent James Logan began selling off parcels to an ever-increasing influx of colonists. They were not as scrupulous as the senior Penn had been in compensating the native inhabitants. The illegal and shameful Walking Purchase provoked resentment that lasted many years and persuaded scores of the Lenape to join the French in their war against the British nearly twenty years later. (As recently as 2006, the Delaware Nation still sought to reclaim the land and was denied by the US Supreme Court.)

Thomas Penn optimistically decided to name this portion of the tract after the Easton-Neston estate in Northhamptonshire owned by his father-in-law Lord Pomfret. The Lenni Lenape called it Lechauwekink, the "place where there are forks in the stream." The early settlers called it the West Branch and North Branch of the Delaware. It was only later that the West Branch became known as the Lehigh River. During this time David Martin, the sheriff of Hunterdon County in New Jersey, secured from George II the rights to operate a ferry over the Delaware at these forks. Martin lived the life of a gentleman much farther downstream in Trenton. He became one of the first four members of Benjamin Franklin's American Philosophical Society. He later became the master of Franklin's Academy for Boys in Philadelphia while continuing as ferry owner. As his business grew, a small settlement grew along with it. Eventually William Parsons, a Philadelphia businessman and Franklin's compatriot, designed a town grid based on Penn's original plans for The City of Brotherly Love. It included a Great Square, which today is known as Centre Square. It became, as intended, a gathering place for settlers and travelers on the Pennsylvania frontier.

It is still the nerve center of Easton, hosting a vibrant farmer's market every Saturday from May through November. It's also open Wednesday evenings and becomes an indoor market during the winter. Ringing the immense monument to local heroes who served in the Civil War are produce and products from the surrounding areas, featuring organic and heirloom fruits and veggies, dairy products, artisan cheeses, baked goods, mushrooms, pasture-raised meats and poultry, and preserves, pickles, locally produced wines and beers, seasonings, honey, plants, and flowers. Also on-hand are artists, crafters, food vendors, and entertainers. Something for just about everyone.

DURING THE FRENCH and Indian War, which eventually became the Seven Years War, engulfing much of the world in conflict, Easton became a staging area for troops heading to battle. This was still considered the frontier, with western Pennsylvania and the Ohio Valley viewed as the far west. Indian attacks occurred within twenty-five miles of Easton, which became flooded with refugee settlers. In 1756 a truce was enacted and a long series of conferences took place between Pennsylvania Governor Robert Morris, his successor William Denny, and Indian tribal representatives, including Chief Teedyuscung. Many of these meetings took place in Easton's Great Square under makeshift

shelters, the air ringing with different spoken languages: English and German from the colonists colliding with Iroquois, Lenape, Shawnee, and other native tongues, the interpreters frantically trying to sort it all out.

One of the main points of dissension was the Walking Purchase. Finally, in October of 1758 negotiations reached their highest point. In attendance were more than 500 Indians from over a dozen tribes, including six Iroquois nations, the Lenni Lenape, and Shawnee. Pennsylvania Governor Denny, New Jersey Governor Bernard, and George Croghan, who represented the British Indian Agent, spoke for the colonists' cause. In what was to become known as the Treaty of Easton, Pennsylvania renounced claims to settle any farther west than the Appalachian Mountains and in return, the tribes would bury the hatchet. The Lenape also agreed to cede remaining claims to land in New Jersey for the sum of 1,000 pesos de ocho (pieces of eight). And though the war would not end until 1763, the French could no longer count on the Indians as allies. As for the Walking Purchase, it seems Teedyuscung's fondness for rum clouded his ability to negotiate reasonable demands, the result being that neither the colonists nor the Indians were able to take him seriously. The Walking Purchase was deferred to the British Indian Agent Sir William Johnson, who successfully buried it in His Majesty's legal system.

The war had taken a massive toll on Britain's treasury, and it tried to recoup the losses with revenue from the American colonies, leading to yet another war.

OVER AND OVER again in the history of the settlement of America, the treaty with the Indians was ignored. Instead of a military staging arena, Easton now became a jumping-off point for pioneers heading west into the Ohio territory. The British still hung on to their forts, forbidding the settlement of the territory, which along with increased taxes became a major factor leading to the Declaration of Independence. On July 8, 1776, Easton was one of three places where it was formally read in public; the others were Philadelphia and Trenton. Easton resident Robert Levers gave the public reading on the steps of the courthouse in the Great Square. (Another Easton citizen, George Taylor, businessman and politician, was one of the signers.) The courthouse bell was rung, thereafter known as the Northampton County Liberty Bell, and is still on display at the Northampton County Government Center. Another artifact of that historic occasion is the Easton Flag: a blue field occupied by thirteen red and white stripes in the upper left corner and next to it a large circle of thirteen eight-pointed stars. This is thought to be the earliest use of the "stars and stripes."

With the Indian wars and the Revolution behind it, Easton used the two forks for transporting the abundant natural resources of the region—grain and lumber; Durham boats were ideal for transporting the grain. The lumber was transported by rafts, then broken apart down river to be used in shipyards. (It's been claimed that one of the spars for the USS *Constitution* "Old Ironsides" arrived this way.) The grain was also shipped after being processed into a more convenient cargo—whiskey. Easton became the home of nine distilleries, the excess providing refreshment for boatmen, teamsters, and rafters. Unlike many other river towns whose origins were grounded in religious sobriety, Easton's atmosphere was lax. It was considered "a very wicked place—Sodom" to pious visitors and newcomers.

The abundance of coal passing through Easton made it one of the major industrial manufacturing centers of the country in the early nineteenth century. Mined in the upper Lehigh Valley, anthracite coal, harder and cleaner-burning than bituminous, was used to fuel the emerging Industrial Revolution taking place along the eastern seaboard. Canals began to be constructed: First the Lehigh Navigational Canal linking Easton with the coal mines up the Lehigh River, then the Delaware Canal, sixty miles down to Bristol just north of Philadelphia. Then the Morris Canal connecting the Delaware River at Phillipsburg (directly across the river from Easton) to Newark, N.J., and finally New York Harbor. This precipitated a new way of life. Entire families' existence revolved around the canals. A canal boat would either be leased from the coal company or owned outright. Papa would steer, Momma would do the washing and cooking in an 8×10 cabin, and the kids would walk the mules on the towpath and care for them. The offspring of a female horse and a male donkey,

*The house of Jacob Nicholas, a
Durham boat skipper, circa 1750*

mules were steady, reliable animals that ate less than a horse and generally had better health.

Lock tending would also be family affairs. Long days started at four a.m. and lasted until ten p.m. The lock tenders would not only operate the gates that allowed the boats to pass from one level to another, but they would also provide stables for the mules at night, direct canal traffic, and socialize as the boats passed through the locks, gossiping and often trading coal for baked goods. He might also be called upon to settle disputes between boatmen who didn't follow canal etiquette. Part of the proper protocol was for boatmen to signal their approach by sounding a horn within a quarter mile of the lock. The most popular instrument for this was a conch shell, probably acquired in Philadelphia from ships that had brought them from some tropical port.

In a display of opulence, Louis Comfort Tifffany and companions luxuriously outfitted a canal boat in 1866. For two weeks they traveled from Bristol to Mauch Chunk on the Delaware and Lehigh Canals, naming their boat the *Molly-Polly Chunker*, after their two mules and destination. Tiffany and company took many photos and kept a log called "The Good Ship Molly-Polly Chunker, Showing Forth the Perilous and Thrilling Adventures of Her Company on a Voyage Through Strange Countries Never Before Visited by Any Similar Expedition."

In the post-Civil War era, at least five iron foundries were established in or around Easton. Industry attracted jobs, which attracted immigrants, mostly from Germany. They brought their traditional customs with them, including the Christmas Tree, which many believe made its American debut in Easton. Its introduction is honored in Scott Park. Church services were held in German until the mid-1800s and a German-language newspaper, *The Pennsylvania Argus*, was published until 1917. And what respectable city would be without an institute of higher learning? The residents of Easton decided that education should play a key role in the development of their town and in 1826 a charter was issued to create a college. The aging military hero the Marquis de Lafayette had recently greeted members of Easton on his farewell tour of the US, and the new school was named in his honor. The campus of Lafayette College is set in one of the more majestic locations along the Delaware, on a hill overlooking the city and countryside.

The beginning of the Gilded Age saw Easton produce its own crop of tycoons. This is evidenced by the number of mansions still found in the downtown area, especially Millionaire's Row along North Third Street, many of them remarkably well-preserved. Unlike some other river towns, Easton maintains a progressive attitude while embracing it's historic, gritty soul.

The Illustrated Delaware River

The Water Gap looking east from Pennsylvania.

27

The Gap

Here's where the river takes an interesting twist—literally. Wending its way south from way up in the New York Catskills, it encounters a northern portion of the Appalachian Mountains, older than the Rockies and at one time just as massive. Water always finds a way, and over time the river ate its way through a 2,100-foot-high mountain ridge to form the Delaware Water Gap. A scenic treasure, this mountain pass has delighted visitors for thousands of years. The first to enjoy it were Paleo-Indians known as the Shawnee-Minisink. In fact, they were some of the first human inhabitants in the northeastern US, arriving on the heels of the receding ice age.

They had this beautiful corner of North America all to themselves until Dutch explorers began snooping around in the early seventeenth century. Making their way from New Netherlands settlements on the Hudson River, they were searching for any minerals that might have some value to the Dutch West India Company. On the New Jersey side of the Delaware, just north of the Gap, they found green malachite in the rock, indicating the presence of copper sulfide or copper ore. They then constructed a 104-mile road, (probably following an ancient Indian trail) to haul the ore back up to present day Kingston, New York (then known as Esopus), on the Hudson River, where it was shipped to the Netherlands. (Strangely, the Dutchmen's earliest explorations led them to believe that the Delaware River, the southernmost border of New Netherlands, was in a nearly tropical climate. Later they discovered that the Delaware headwaters were nearly the same latitude as the Hudson.)

But this is mere conjecture. There is no proof of early Dutch mining; however, copper was mined here between 1753 and 1918. It proved to be of such low grade that no one was able to make a success of it. But someone created the road and to this day it is known as the Old Mine Road. It is also generally believed to be the oldest commercial road in the US.

The road, which parallels the river, is the historical backbone of what has become the Delaware Water Gap National Recreation Area. Despite the failed attempt at copper mining, Dutch and French Huguenot settlers gradually flowed into the region to try farming. And after the demise of the New Netherlands colony came English, Irish, and Scots immigrants down the old road from what was now known as New York. When pioneers from Philadelphia arrived in the 1730s, they were quite surprised to find European inhabitants thriving in what they believed was wilderness. When they saw that the settlers carted their goods overland to market in New York rather than by boat down the Delaware, it was revealed that the settlers didn't know where the river ran to.

BY THE 1750S there were still only some 600 settlers in the area, which created severe problems when the French & Indian War began. There were not nearly enough able men to raise a militia for protection, and as a result many fled east to Morristown and Elizabethtown. New Jersey then appropriated

Van Campen's Inn

£10,000 to build forts along the Delaware and roads to supply them. Those who remained flocked to Van Campen's Inn for protection. It was designated as a Yaugh House—a dwelling licensed under colonial law to provide food and shelter for travelers. At one point in 1763 it was reported that 150 settlers found refuge there from Indian attacks. The house was built sometime before 1750 by Dutch colonist Harmon Rosenkrans, who later sold it to his brother-in-law Isaac Van Campen. The inn had other lodgers as well. John Adams arrived on horseback on his way from Massachusetts to attend the Continental Congress in Philadelphia. General Horatio Gates and seven regiments of his men from the Continental Army camped on the grounds in 1776 while waiting out a snowstorm. They were on their way to assist Washington far down the river in the assault on Trenton. And much later in 1955, the house served as a shelter for nearby flood victims. That flood nearly put Van Campen's Inn in a precarious situation. But more about that in the next chapter.

FARTHER DOWN the Old Mine Road is Millbrook Village. It sprang up in the early nineteenth century when local farmer Abram Gari constructed a grist mill. The village, though never really bustling, held its own through several generations until its decline after the Civil War. Today, Millbrook has been revived as a superb example of an antique farming community. The place is staffed with costumed park rangers and volunteer crafters who display typical skills from the period.

This is where I met Wayne and Steve. They were the only two people actually performing said skills when I arrived for a visit one Saturday morning. Steve was making wooden buckets by hand with antique and hand-made tools—on a cooper's bench he made himself. This may seem a bit exaggerated, but his expertise was such that watching him work was mesmerizing. The seams on the bucket were indistinguishable. He then fashioned metal hoops, installed rivets and hammered them around the bucket, then trimmed excess wood away from the extended staves that would make the handles. It was all done with such fluid precision that it was like watching a sculptor at work. And this was just a wooden bucket!

Meanwhile, Wayne (a not-too-shabby woodworker himself and photographer) did some masterful whittling and provided color commentary.

The Cooper

We chatted for a while, found we had a bit in common, and I made plans to return for Millbrook Days, a yearly celebration they were obviously looking forward to. But minds like steel sieves were at work, coming up with the brilliant strategy (with no apparent purpose) to shut down the federal government, which includes the National Park Service, which operates Millbrook Village. Sadly, Millbrook Days did not take place.

After the wars were over and the Indians had been forced to retreat from their homelands and things began to settle down, Americans began to realize that they lived in an incredibly beautiful country. In the earliest era of European exploration, the land was considered abundant, but also a wilderness, something that needed taming if they were to survive. Trees and rocks needed to be cleared for farming, logs and lumber trimmed for shelter and storage and a thousand other things that we take for tranted in the twenty-first century. There was precious little time for enjoying your surroundings, no matter how picturesque they might be. But by the late eighteenth and early nineteenth centuries, technology started to provide more leisure time. People who worked in cities that were becoming increasingly overcrowded looked for opportunities to literally "take to the hills." The natural wonders of the Delaware Water Gap and its surroundings were a relatively short journey away from the grit, grime, and summer heat of the industrial climates of New York City and Philadelphia.

One of the first entrepreneurs to see the potential of exploiting the Gap's natural wonders was a gentlemen named Antoine Dutot. A plantation owner in Santo Domingo (now the Dominican Republic), Dutot was forced to flee the country during the slave rebellion of 1791. After landing in Philadelphia, he traveled upstream to the Delaware Water Gap. Falling in love with the surroundings, he purchased a large parcel of land and formulated a plan for an inland city that he would humbly name for himself—Dutotsburg. He built a sawmill and then a road leading to his future mountain metropolis. More than a dozen wooden buildings were constructed and a portion of property set aside for its eventual use for religious or educational purposes. A school was built that was used until 1969. Today the building is the Antoine Dutot School & Museum. One of its old rooms is furnished like a classroom from the 1920s complete with inkwells (for dipping pigtails into).

As early as 1820, out-of-town sightseers would stay in private homes. Dutot saw an opportunity, and in 1829 he began building a boarding house that could house twenty-five guests. He named it the Kittatinny House after the Gap's nearby mountain ranges. By 1860, it had been enlarged to accommodate 250–275 people and had become the most prestigious hotel in the second most popular resort town in America. The Gap was topped only by Saratoga Springs in New York State.

Dutot would not achieve the same success, however. The hotel soon had competition, fueled by the growing tourist trade. More hotels opened, each trying to out-do the other in luxury and convenience. These were full-fledged resorts featuring nature walks, sporting events, fishing, and boating that included moonlight cruises on the river. The Delaware House, Belleview House, Buckwood Inn, Castle Inn, and Glenwood all vied for tourist dollars. Early transport was limited, but eventually a stagecoach line was opened, carrying mail and passengers three times a week. By 1856 the Southern Division of the Delaware, Lackawanna, and Western Railroad was officially opened. This early trip could whisk passengers from New York City to Delaware Water Gap in six hours. Many visitors would stay for weeks on end, often for the entire summer. Papa would work in the city during the week and spend weekends at the resort with the rest of the family. The resorts had their share of celebrity guests as well. President Theodore Roosevelt visited in 1910 and was joined by other politicians, financial gurus, and members of high society. A young Fred Astaire vacationed here frequently with his sister in his younger days.

If trains made transportation easier and faster, the automobile changed the way people vacationed. Instead of staying in one place for weeks or months, they could motor to more and increasingly distant places. The Gap resorts lost their appeal, vacationers built their own summer houses, and Dutot's properties became derelict. He ran out of funds and in 1832 was forced to sell the Kittatinny House. Over the years it changed owners numerous times and had been rebuilt and enlarged still further when a fire destroyed it in 1931. By that time, the hotel could accommodate up to 500 guests. Offering a ball-

The Kittatinny House

room, bar, and evening entertainment, it also had a stream running through a basement kitchen. All that remains today are the ruins of a rock garden that surrounded a water fountain at the front of the hotel. The town's other resorts disappeared, too. In 1915, the Water Gap House caught fire and was destroyed in a matter of hours. The resorts faded into oblivion, leaving little evidence of existence aside from a few old postcards.

The name Dutotsburg would not survive, either. Today the town is called Delaware Water Gap—not as imaginative as Dutotsburg, but obviously more commercially marketable. This once bustling tourist village that welcomed hundreds of travelers through its train station now sees travelers of a different sort: backpackers hiking the Appalachian Trail that passes through the middle of town. Hikers pause on the 2,100-mile trail to browse shops, enjoy cafes, or spend the night in a real bed. The trail crosses the Delaware via Route 80, where hikers can climb to a spectacular view on top of Mt. Minsi.

Only one resort survived. The Buckwood Inn was part of a large recreation park created in the 1880s by New York businessman C. C. Worthington. It also featured a private hunting lodge, a state-of-the-art golf course, and a theater. It was built on the site of Fort Depuy, named for Nicholas Depuy, who made his way from the former New Amsterdam in 1727. Far ahead of its time, the dining experience at the resort featured locally grown products and even maintained a creamery featuring fresh milk, cream, and butter. But what really set the Buckwood apart was its Tillinghast-designed golf course. In 1912, Worthington invited a group of professional golfers to be guests at the inn, and the PGA and PGA Championships were born. Golf continued to be the main attraction at the Buckwood, and when Fred Waring bought the resort in 1943, the sport brought in even more celebrities: Bob Hope, Art Carney Lucille Ball, Ed Sullivan, President Dwight Eisenhower, and more. No one was more enthusiastic about the game than Jackie Gleason, who played his first round here.

When Fred Waring bought the resort, he renamed it the Shawnee Inn, after the Indian tribe he mistakenly thought originally lived on the land. Waring was one of the premier entertainers of his day, leading a choral group called the Pennsylvanians. (Incidentally, their music was produced on one of Camden's early Victor recordings.) To help promote the inn, Waring

FRED WARING

organized a choral workshop and broadcast radio programs from the Shawnee Inn throughout the 1950s. He also hosted a TV show and sold millions of recordings that featured his famous chorales positively swimming in an ocean of reverb. Known as "the man who taught America how to sing," he was also responsible for the Waring Blendor, although he did not invent it. Waring bankrolled the development of the appliance, which was invented by Frederick Jacob Osius. The blender is still popular today, selling for as much as $287 for a commercial model.

28

The Dammed

The recreational area around the Delaware Water Gap is about as lovely and serene as you can imagine in the overcrowded northeastern United States. But it was not always a place of leisure. For hundreds of years, people farmed here on strips of land that ran from the high ground down to the river and supported acres of fruit trees, nut trees, sugar maples, fields of melons, blackberries, and grazing for dairy cattle.

But in 1955 the Delaware flooded badly, setting in motion a plan that would change the Gap's communities forever. To reduce the threat of flooding, the Army Corps of Engineers commissioned a study to determine whether a dam would be feasible. The study cost $2 million and ran to eleven volumes. The proposed dam would be built at Tocks Island, six miles north of the Gap, creating a 12,300-acre lake thirty seven miles long with depths up to 140 feet. It would extend to the confluence of the Neversink River at Port Jervis, New York. The proposed plan would include fifty-eight water projects, take fifty years to complete, and cost in the neighborhood of $437 million. The dam would be used to create hydro-electric power and provide fresh water for New York City and Philadelphia. It would also be used for recreation, creating "the greatest inland resort in the Northeastern area," bringing in ten million visitors a year and adding $30 million to the local economy. It was also estimated that displacement of local residents would be minimal.

Despite the misgivings of many locals, the plan was approved in the early 1960s, and the National Park Service and the US Army Corps of Engineers started buying properties at basically pennies on the dollar, backed by the Federal Government's Right of Eminent Domain. Residents on both sides of the river were forced to leave although construction was still years away. Families who had farmed the land for generations were coldly and methodically turned from their lands and possessions. At least two landowners committed suicide.

Opposition began to mount, however, and feisty Shawnee area resident Nancy Shukaitis took it upon herself to lead the fray. Attending hearings in 1964, she argued that the dam would damage the environment. She said the Army Corps of Engineers "may have the will,
the know-how, but it had no moral vision." In addition to the loss of private property, massive amounts of wildlife would be condemned. Shukaitis formed the Delaware Valley Conservation Association, which quickly grew to include more than 1,000 members. Other concerned voices joined hers, including US Supreme Court Justice William O. Douglas.

In the middle of it all, the Vietnam War was draining the military economy. The budget for the dam was being shaved even before final plans were drawn up. All the property that had been acquired was now abandoned, inviting mischief. The Army Corps of Engineers placed ads in area newspapers to lease the now-derelict properties that they had so hastily acquired. They even advertised in New York's *Village Voice*. The counter-culture movement's "flower children" began arriving, intent on creating communes and self-sufficient co-ops. Many of the properties did not even have electricity or running water. In addition to the rentals, tents, lean-to's, and other shelters were put up. Eventually, the Corps decided that it didn't want to be a landlord and demanded the evacuation of the latest inhabitants. Most of them refused to go. Less savory individuals were drawn to the free property, and drugs and violence soon followed. Buildings burned down on a regular basis, caused by the squatters themselves or disgruntled locals trying to chase them out. Approximately three dozen buildings were destroyed between 1970 and 1972.

Finally in 1974, federal marshals armed with weapons and eviction notices forced many of the squatters off the land. Immediately following came bulldozers, demolishing the former hippie hovels (along with treasured property of former residents). The counter-culture occupation was over, and soon support for the dam would be gone as well.

Thanks to Nancy Shukaitis and others like her, the Corps of Engineers was forced to re-examine the project and came to the conclusion that the ground at Tocks Island was not stable enough to support the proposed 160-foot- high rock and earth dam. (Ironically, as early as 1942, tests conducted by the Corps came to the same conclusion. Drilling holes couldn't find bedrock as deep as 140 feet.)Immense opposition, increasing cost projections, and dwindling funds combined to put an end to the plan. In 2002 the dam project was officially abandoned, turned over to the care of the National Park Service and preserved as the Delaware Water Gap National Recreation Area.

The wounds left by this regrettable and unnecessary boondoggle are deep. Many of the people and their relatives who were left dispossessed have a deep resentment of the US government. And with good reason. Farms and homes that were inhabited for years are now the property of the National Park Service. It must be heartbreaking for former residents to see their homes slowly being reclaimed by the forces of nature.

The old fire siren in Walpack Center

Not just farmland but entire towns, such as Walpack Center, were abandoned. This was a lively and vibrant little town with roots reaching back to the eighteenth century. It was such a typical example of Americana that the 1934 film *These Thirty Years* was shot here. The brainchild of the McCann-Erickson advertising agency, the film depicts the rise of the automobile industry, or more accurately, the rise of Henry Ford. A propaganda piece disguised as a parable, it describes the rise of a young man who starts with nothing and becomes the head of a multi-million dollar industry, Ford Motor

A doorway in Millbrook Village

Company. All of the buildings on Main Street, where some of the movie was filmed, are now owned by the National Park Service, except for the school, which is used as a town hall. And the 150-year-old Rosenkrans House serves as a museum maintained by the Walpack Historical Society.

Another such town is historic Millbrook Village, which was a farming community long in decline but not in the dam's way. With the help of the Millbrook Village Society, the NPS moved some buildings that were threatened to new locations there to replace older structures that had long since faded away. Millbrook Village now contains roughly the same number of buildings that existed there in 1900. In 1981, the Park Service began restoring the nearby Van Campen Inn because of its historical significance. The Inn is now operated by the Walpack Historical Society. These are just a few that were saved, but many other historic sites would have become watery graves.

A little less historic, but still fascinating, was the presence of a dude ranch called The Lazy K Bar Ranch. Touted as the largest dude ranch on the East Coast, it hosted a broad range of celebrities and show business people. Founded in the 1930s, it featured trail riding, fishing, and swimming, and also provided entertainment in the form of rodeos, basketball on horseback, and singing around the old campfire. Singing cowboy Tex Ritter and the Lane Sisters, members of Fred Waring's radio show, were given screen auditions here.

The township of Walpack, which contains Walpack Center, has few residents—about twenty in a twenty-four-square-mile area. Although most of them would just as soon forget the dam, there are those who are just glad it was never built and happy to be able to share their remote and beautiful surroundings with everyone.

The town of Dingman's Ferry, on the other side of the Delaware, was also slated for flooding, but the Corps of Engineers relocated the entire community to a higher elevation. The town takes it's name from Andrew Dingman, another Dutch settler who arrived on the river from Kinderhook, New York, around 1735 and set up a ferry crossing. People wishing to cross had to summon him by ringing a bell. The ferry was operated by the Dingman family for over 100 years until a covered bridge was constructed in 1836. It was destroyed during a flood in 1847 when debris from the Milford Bridge farther upstream smashed into it. Along with the bridge, about 200 pigeons belonging to toll taker Andrew Dingman III were carried away and never seen again. The ferry was then called back into service. A second bridge was built around 1850, but within five years a massive wind storm lifted the entire structure from its moorings and dropped it into the river. Again the ferry was back in business. A third bridge was built in 1856, but it was poorly constructed and fell into the river around 1861. Andrew Dingman III once again oversaw ferry operations. The fourth bridge, still in use today, was fashioned from the remnants of an old iron bridge that spanned the Susquehanna River. It is the only privately owned bridge across the Delaware. Motorists wishing to cross to New Jersey are met by a toll-taker on foot, as the booth is situated to handle only traffic entering Pennsylvania. Dingman's is one of a number of narrow, two-lane bridges traversing the Delaware. This doesn't seem to bother daily commuters, but ever since I lost a side view mirror on the Washington's Crossing Bridge,

I tend to drive slowly and cautiously, which is no doubt annoying to experienced bridge commandos.

South of Dingmans Ferry, also in Pennsylvania, the town of Bushkill endured a similar relocation. Though Dingmans Falls is a popular natural attraction, Bushkill Falls are so spectacular that they're referred to as the Niagara of the East. The property that contains Bushkill Falls has been owned by the same family since 1904 and attracts approximately a quarter-million visitors per year.

Despite all the misery and negative energy the Tocks Island Dam Project provoked, there is a silver lining: an enormous parcel of land has been saved from development, free to all and forever protected.

A portion of Bushkill Falls

29
Tri-States

Of all the town names in the US, Milford is certainly a popular one. Only Montana, Nevada, New Mexico, North Carolina, North and South Dakota, Oklahoma, Oregon, Rhode Island, Tennessee, and Washington do not have a Milford. A few, like Louisiana and West Virginia, have a West Milford; South Carolina has the bucolic Milford Plantation; Mississippi has a New Milford.

There are four Milfords in the Delaware River watershed: in Delaware, New Jersey, New York, and Pennsylvania, but only the towns in New Jersey and Pennsylvania are on the river. Milford, Pennsylvania, has the distinction of being the home of the Deputy Delaware River Master. The purpose of this imposing-sounding position is to regulate the flow of the Delaware from the US Geological Service stream-gauging station across the river at Montague, New Jersey. The flow is regulated on two reservoirs north of the confluence of the East and West Branches, so the proud claim that the Delaware is the longest un-dammed river east of the Mississippi is perfectly legitimate.

The reservoirs exist so that New York City can have a share of the river—about half of its water supply. But, you say, New York City is outside of the Delaware River Basin, how can this be? It's like this: When New York began to outgrow it's local water supplies, it turned to the headwaters of the Delaware in the Catskill Mountains, which could be gravity-fed to the city. This gave rise to disputes with New Jersey and Pennsylvania, who also claimed water rights. After years of judicial wrangling, the US Supreme Court decreed in 1931 that the State of New York would be entitled to dip into the juvenile meanderings of the Delaware at the rate of 400 million gallons per day. So a reservoir was constructed. In 1952 this amount doubled and another reservoir was built. But the agreement stipulated that New York would have to share with everyone else downstream. So, in order to ensure enough water for users throughout the basin, water must be released from the reservoirs to meet a flow of 1,750 cubic feet per second registered at Montague.

But back to Milford. Its origins are partly based on the yellow fever epidemic that attacked Philadelphia in 1793. Those who could, like President George Washington, fled the city and returned when the crisis passed. Others, like John Biddis, moved his entire family far up the Delaware to a place known as Wells Ferry. After purchasing a large parcel of land, he built a cottage and divided his property into lots and laid out streets based on the existing grid of Philadelphia. He named the village Milford after his ancestral home of Milford Haven in Wales. (Another claim disputes this, saying that it was merely named after a mill and its adjacent river crossing.) Biddis was an ambitious and inventive man who had a number of patents to his credit, such as a new type of white lead paint, tanning gum, and a process for using wood pulp to make paper. Though Biddis moved back to Philadelphia, he remained connected to Milford and was later appointed an associate judge, one of the first in the area.

Other research places the first settler in the region a good bit earlier. In 1733, Thomas Quick arrived and pitched a tent. His ancestral ties are also somewhat vague—some sources state his homeland as County Ulster, some say it was Holland, and some claim both. Quick built a log cabin and began clearing the land for farming, which didn't seem to bother his neighbors, the Lenni Lenape. The following year, young Tom Quick was born, and here's where the story picks up momentum. As the youngster grew, he spent more time with the Indians than his family, learning their language and how to hunt, fish, and trap, and the ways of the forest. He nearly became an Indian himself.

Young Tom grew up living a life most boys would have found idyllic. But as the French and Indian War loomed, the Delaware Valley began to grow unsettled. Increasing numbers of settlers were encroaching on Indian lands. It didn't take much prodding on the part of the French to induce the Indians to drive the whites from their lands. As the story goes, young Tom was out with his father and brother-in-law on an errand across the river, when the senior Quick was felled by a round from a marauding Indian's rifle. Young Tom and the brother-in-law tried to drag the wounded elder Quick to safety, but he was dying and commanded them to run for their lives. The two men

The shadowy figure of Tom Quick

frantically made their way back across the frozen river. Tom paused after reaching the bank to see if they were being pursued, and saw, to his horror, his dead father being scalped.

Something snapped, and from this point on, Tom Quick swore vengeance on all Indians. Though he could have joined the British Army as a regular or scout, he preferred to exact his revenge as a lone assassin. Over the years, fact blended with fiction and he became the legendary Tom Quick, Indian Slayer, the Red Revenger, the Avenger of the Delaware. Many stories were told, such as the time he hunted with an Indian who agreed to keep the hides of their game while Tom would keep the meat. After a successful hunt in which seven deer were taken, Tom lingered behind the Indian carrying the hides and shot him in the back. He later told of his deed, saying he had shot a buck with seven skins. He supposedly murdered an Indian family canoeing on the Delaware. When asked why he killed even the children, he replied, "Nits make lice."

After the war was over and the hatchet was considered buried, Quick continued his independent rampage. Since there were still deep scars left mentally and physically on the settlers, they had no overwhelming desire to bring him to justice. To many he was a hero, but in today's world his actions would be associated with that of a psychopath.

On his death-bed he claimed to have killed ninety-nine Indians. According to legend, he begged to have an old Indian who lived nearby brought to him for killing, so he could claim 100 victims.

An even more far-fetched story persists that when he finally passed away, he was infected with smallpox. Supposedly, after his burial Indians dug up his corpse, cut it into pieces, and distributed them as souvenirs. The recipients then contracted the disease, thus Quick took more victims even after his death.

In 1889, Milford erected the Settlers Monument and transferred Tom Quick's remains there from his resting place in the nearby town of Matamoras. Legend or not, people eventually came to question whether someone of Quick's reputation should be immortalized. Then in 1997, someone took a sledgehammer to the monument, causing extensive damage. It was repaired, but not replaced. Much controversy has ensued, but for the meantime a plaque has been installed on top of the grave in the middle of Sarah Street which reads:

> THIS IS A GRAVESITE AND SHOULD BE RESPECTED AS SUCH. THIS MONUMENT AND ITS INSCRIPTIONS REFLECT A DIALOG AND MINDSET OF THE ERA IN WHICH IT WAS FIRST ERECTED CIRCA 1889, WHICH WAS 94 YEARS AFTER THE DEATH OF TOM QUICK.
>
> MANY STORIES HAVE BEEN WRITTEN ABOUT TOM QUICK BUT THERE IS NOT ENOUGH DOCUMENTED EVIDENCE TO SEPARATE TRUTH FROM FICTION. HOWEVER, RESEARCH INTO HIS LIFE CONTINUES TO BE ENCOURAGED BY THE PIKE COUNTY HISTORICAL SOCIETY.
>
> THIS GRAVESITE IS UNDER THE CARE OF THE MILFORD BOROUGH COUNCIL WITH THE APPROBATION OF MEMBERS OF THE CREE NATION, LONG RECOGNIZED AS PEACEMAKERS.

Milford has also produced citizens with far less surly reputations, such as Gifford Pinchot, the two-time governor of Pennsylvania. He was also the first chief of the United States Forest Service, and for this he is probably best remembered. From its earliest days, most of America's natural resources were considered fathomless, and it seemed nearly criminal not to exploit them. Pinchot taught the country otherwise. His father, James, had made a fortune through lumbering and land speculation, but was remorseful at the devastation it had caused. The senior Pinchot made a commitment to conservation and encouraged his son to become involved as a forester. Gifford studied at the French National School of Forestry and returned home to found the Yale School of Forestry with his father in 1900. Grey Towers, the family estate in Milford, was turned into a facility for developing forestry management.

Pinchot became well-known for his scientific conservation methods under President Theodore Roosevelt. But he encountered heavy opposition from timber companies, and at the other end of the spectrum, was at odds with preservationist John Muir. Pinchot believed in the commercial value of the forests, but in a highly controlled capacity.

Pinchot was elected to his first term as Governor of Pennsylvania in 1923; the following year he considered running against Calvin Coolidge for president, but decided against it. He was elected for a second term in 1931 after a brief hiatus. In his later years he advised President Franklin D. Roosevelt, wrote about his life in forestry service, and dabbled in inventions such as a fishing kit for lifeboats in World War II.

Grey Towers was turned over to the US Forest Service in 1963, becoming the only National Historic Landmark operated by that branch

Grey Towers

of the federal government. The estate is run by the Grey Towers Heritage Association, www.greytowers.org.

ANOTHER DISTINGUISHED Milford resident was Charles Sanders Peirce. Peirce (pronounced "purse") had a lengthy and rather rocky career in the sciences. Well-known and respected as an innovator in mathematics, statistics, chemistry, logistics, and research methods, he is widely regarded as America's most original philosopher and the father of Pragmatism. This was a theory (which I will try to interpret in my feeble terms) that encourages one to use thought not to explain things literally, but interpretively. His ideas were light years ahead of his time, many of them never discussed until after World War II.

Peirce came from good stock in Cambridge, Massachusetts. His father, Benjamin, was a mathematics professor at Harvard and a founder of both the US Coast and Geodetic Survey (USC&GS) and the Smithsonian Institution. Charles was employed by the USC&GS for thirty-two years, from 1859 to 1891. He carried out investigations, sometimes creating his own instruments for measuring scientific data. Peirce also held a second job teaching logic in the math department at Johns Hopkins University. But this job mysteriously disappeared after it came to light that Peirce's second wife was a gypsy—and that they had lived in sin before marriage.

Eventually, the USC&GS job dried up, too, and Peirce barely eked out a living doing consulting work. But he was a prolific writer. He was credited with over 12,000 printed pages and 80,000 handwritten manuscripts, all unpublished, on subjects that ranged from math and physical sciences to social sciences. He eventually bought 2,000 acres of farmland near Milford with money inherited from his parents. He remodeled the old farmhouse and called his estate Arisbe, after ancient Greek references. Peirce passed away in 1914, twenty years before his wife Juliette. She sold his papers to Harvard University, where they became neglected and largely misplaced. By the 1950s, however, efforts were underway to bring his work to light, and he is finally being appreciated.

Arisbe is now simply known as the Peirce House, in the care of the National Park Service, which uses it as the Delaware Water Gap Recreation Area's Division of Research and Resource Planning.

Tri-States

Although Milford is on the Delaware, the river's presence isn't felt as much as in, say, New Hope, Frenchtown, and Easton. To put the topography in perspective, take a hike up to Milford Knob. My friend Rick read that it was a forty-five minute hike with a spectacular view at trail's end, so off we went. The weather was threatening, but we plunged ahead, climbing at a steady pace. And we climbed some more, and then some more until finally reaching a summit where the trail followed the crest of the mountain. Getting to this point took more than the alleged forty-five minutes, but we were not deterred. But after another forty-five minutes of hiking and no destination in sight, we began to question the promised views. And it was starting to rain, steady enough to concern two aging adventurers tramping through wet leaves on top of wet rocks. We decided to head back and try another day. On the return, however, we somehow missed the trail that led down and kept walking on the crest. Nothing looked familiar, and yet everything looked familiar. We eventually came to a trail that seemed to head down, and with the rain continuing and darkness not far off, we took it.

We came down off of the mountain all right, but had no idea where we were. There was a golf course we hadn't seen on our way in, and you can't miss a golf course. Then we came upon a hiker's rest stop, complete with a map! We now realized we were miles away from where we had parked and would have to get to the public road indicated on the map and then walk five miles back up the mountain, or hitchhike. Hitchhiking sounded like the more practical choice, so I stuck out my thumb while Rick walked ahead. What were we thinking? People don't pick up hitchhikers anymore, it's just not done. There was a good bit of traffic including school busses, but we were largely ignored. Just when things looked bleakest, an old Volkswagon Jetta pulled to side of the road and we jogged to it as fast as our tired legs would let us. My sense of relief turned to apprehension when I saw the driver—a girl in her late teens or early twenties. I have a college-age daughter, and if she had ever offered a ride to a couple of hitchhikers, she would have been grounded for life, with no visiting privileges. We poked our heads in the car and explained our dilemma. She gave us a sympathetic look and said no problem, she would take us to our car, she had nothing better to do. She told us she had been driving in the opposite direction when she saw these two pathetic-looking guys hitchhiking in the rain (meaning us). She called her boyfriend and told him she was going to turn around and give us a ride. She was an angel, but she drove like a demon, as do most people who travel these mountain roads. Within moments she delivered us to the parking lot and our car. We climbed out, gave her a gratuitous amount of money and thanked her profusely. I also gave her my business card and invited her to visit my website and blog.

About a week later I received an email from our good samaritan, whose name was Ally. She wrote that the experience had touched her heart and that people just don't trust one another anymore and that she was happy to have helped us out. There was also a post script to the message: "You left your umbrellas in my car and I would love to return them to you because I'm sure you use them often."

Follow the river north from Milford, cross it, and you will now be in Port Jervis, New York. Taking Main Street south, you will come to the Laurel Grove Cemetery. (Interestingly, there are several headstones on one plot engraved with the name Quick, and one in particular labeled Tom.) A road runs through the cemetery and at its farthest end, you will be under the Route 84 overpass. Here on the bank of the Neversink River, amidst cigarette butts and empty beer cans, you will encounter two stone markers. One is the tri-states monument indicating where the boundaries of New Jersey, Pennsylvania, and New York intersect. If you stand on that stone, you will be in all three states at once. It was once inlaid with a brass National Geodetic Survey disk, which had disappeared. It replaces a monument dating to 1774 that effectively ended a border war, or "line war," between New York and New Jersey. One of many disputes between neighboring states in the early days of colonization, this one consisted of skirmishes and raids lasting over fifty years. Close by is a Witness Monument that indicates the merging of Pennsylvania and New York—in the river. You have now entered the realm of the Upper Delaware.

The Tri-States Monument, Port Jervis, New York

THE ILLUSTRATED DELAWARE RIVER

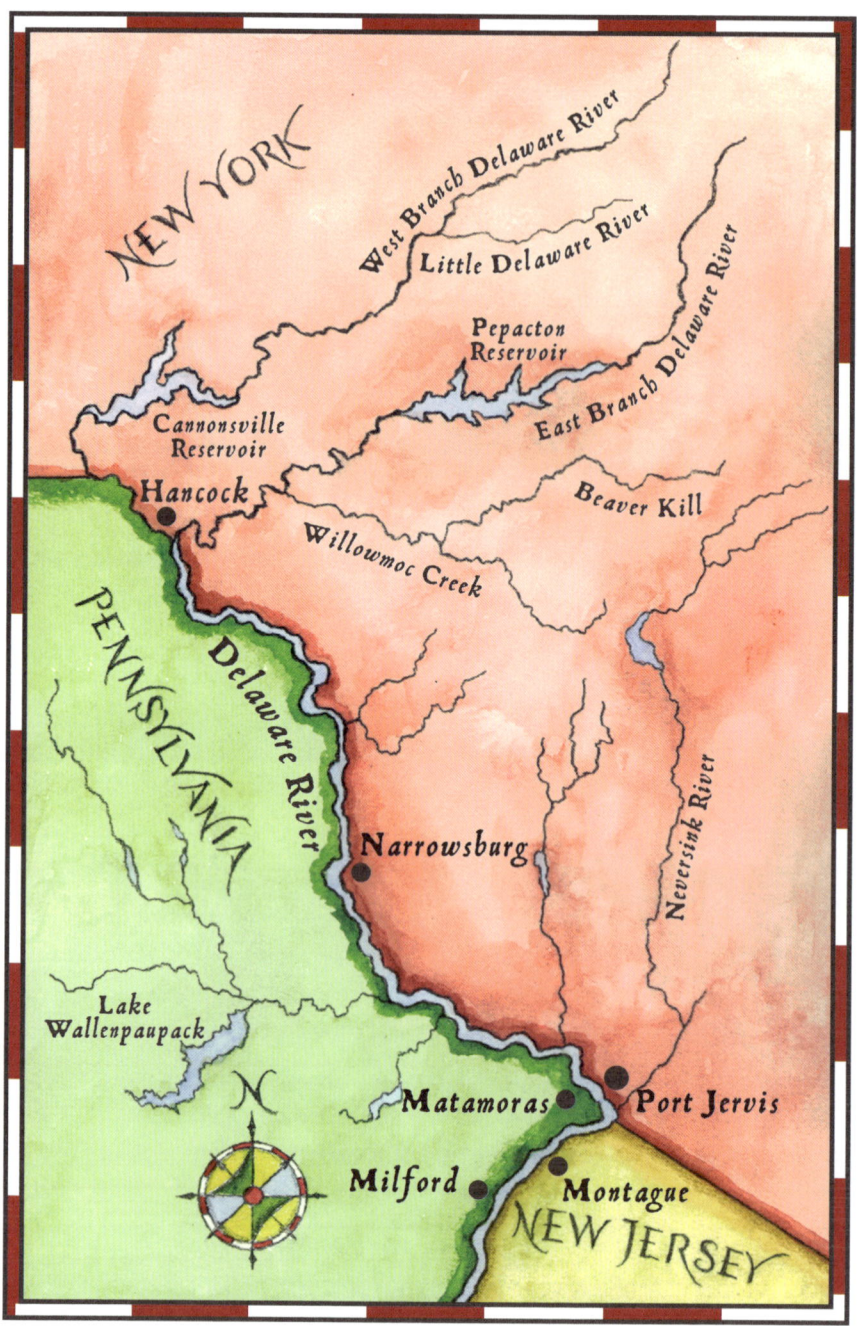

The Upper Delaware

30

The Source

Port Jervis is proud of the plug by *Budget Travel* magazine naming it one of the Coolest Small Towns in New York. This was in 2008. I am in no way a judge of cool, so I don't know if that assessment is correct. But I do know that Port Jervis is both shabby and picturesque and shimmers with history. It is situated where the Delaware makes a dramatic right turn, as if trying to avoid a collision with its largest tributary, the Neversink River. But it is unavoidable; the Neversink attaches itself to the Delaware like an old acquaintance trying to borrow money.

Once an energized industrial center and transportation hub, the city lost its manufacturing muscle through a combination of the Great Depression and changing technology. But a surging interest in outdoor recreation has brought new life to the scenic upper river valley, along with hikers, boaters, kayakers, and fishermen who have enjoyed its natural beauty for generations. The town sits under the trail-weary gaze of hikers on the Appalachian Trail passing by the High Point monument atop nearby Kittatinny Ridge, indicating the highest point in New Jersey. (A majestic height for those living in the east, more like a speed bump for Westerners).

Although there were scattered European settlers in the area, probably arriving here along the Old Mine Road, Port Jervis became a village in 1690 when it was called Mahackamack, or Magagkamack, or Mahackmeck—a Minsi name that roughly translates to pumpkin field. One of those early settlers was a Dutchman named Frederick Haynes who built a trading post of stone and logs that was later converted for defense during the French and Indian War. The structure remained, and when Haynes moved to New Jersey, he left it to the Deckers, his wife's family.

In 1779, Fort Decker, as it became known, was raided and burned prior to the Battle of Minisink, the most northerly of Revolutionary War conflicts. But a new house was built on its ashes in time to welcome the Delaware &

Hudson Canal that arrived in 1828. The canal barges brought coal from northeastern Pennsylvania to New York and New England. It also brought the chief engineer of the canal for whom the village would take a new name—John Bloomfield Jervis. The handsome stone structure is still known as Fort Decker and is now home to the Minisink Valley Historical Society (www.minisink.org).

After the canal came the New York & Erie Railroad, carrying its first passengers—President Millard Fillmore and Senator Daniel Webster in 1851. Growth and prosperity continued; by 1922 twenty passenger trains per day passed through town carrying travelers between Jersey City and Susquehanna, Pennsylvania. A connection center, the town also became an industrial city, home to burgeoning glass foundries and manufacturers producing everything from silk to cigars, gloves, saws, shoes, and stoves. Two daily newspapers, the *Port Jervis Daily* and the *Evening Gazette*— kept the population up-to-date on the state of the world.

The New York & Erie Railroad became simply the Erie Railroad, employing some 2,500 workers at its peak during the early twentieth century. Much of the railroad activity centered around a turntable and roundhouse used for repairs and re-routing trains. The roundhouse and much of the rail yards are gone, but the turntable is still operational, the largest in the US. It occupies a now-empty lot, watched over by a few vintage passenger cars and obsolete diesel locomotives—and, judging from the empty cans and scatterings of dry food, an abundance of stray cats. It is now just a curiosity visited by tourists and the occasional railroad buff, and of course the cats.

Leaving Port Jervis and heading north on Route 97, the scenery shifts from aging industrial to mountain-river-sky panoramas. The road is also known as the Upper

Delaware Scenic Byway. As it closely follows the river, you will begin to feel as if you are in a car commercial. That's because many advertisers, including BMW, Saab, and Cadillac have filmed their high-performance products hugging the twists and turns of this stretch of highway known as Hawk's Nest. It is small wonder; the road literally seems to hang dramatically on the mountain edge, shored up by sculpted stone walls. Guardrails are nonexistent here, but there are motorist pull-offs to enjoy the view without your hands on the wheel.

Just as you're tooling along in your luxurious ride, the cameras still trained on your best side, the wind whipping your hair in dramatic waves, you discover that something a bit more somber has disrupted the Hollywood fantasy along the stretch of river north of Hawk's Nest. At Minisink Ford, in July of 1779, in the midst of the Revolutionary War, 51 men lost their lives in a campaign far from the suburban battlefields of New York and Philadelphia. The Battle of Minisink began as a raid on Magagkamack led by Joseph Brant, a captain in the British Army and a chief of the Mohawk Nation. This was the action that left the village and Fort Decker in smoldering ruins. Brant, educated at Moor's Indian Charity School in Connecticut (which eventually became Dartmouth College), began his career as a soldier at the age of thirteen, fighting for the British in the French and Indian War. Well-educated and highly intelligent, he caught the attention of British officers and worked his way through the ranks but never really warmed to members of English aristocracy. He was even taken to London and received by George III, from whom he solicited support for Mohawk participation in the upcoming conflict.

After the raid at what was to become Port Jervis, a patriot militia force was raised under the command of Lt. Colonel Benjamin Tusten, a physician from the village of Goshen. They encountered Brant at Minisink Ford, and on a hill overlooking the Delaware were soundly defeated in an afternoon of brutal fighting. Those that did not run away were killed, including Dr. Tusten. The colonial force was comprised of not much more than farmers, clerks, and merchants; no match for the seasoned Indian veterans and Tories led by Brant. They are respectfully remembered at Minisink Battlefield Park, which maintains not only hallowed ground, but some excellent hiking trails. I'm not sure how they manage it, but many of the trails are paved with moss. It's like hiking on carpet.

Joseph Brant

Dr. Tusten also has a mountain named in his honor below Narrowsburg, New York. A moderately strenuous climb to the top pays off in a stunning view of the river down below.

Heading north (still on Route 97) and into the nineteenth century, you will encounter one of the most unique man-made structures on the river—the Delaware Aqueduct. Designed by a man known for engineering marvels, this is one of John Roebling's finest works. The aqueduct is actually a bridge for boats. The oldest wire cable suspension bridge in the country, it was originally built for the Delaware and Hudson Canal, which transported anthracite coal from the mines in northeastern Pennsylvania to Kingston, New York, on the Hudson. Rather than crossing the river where collisions might occur with timber rafts or ice floes, the canal boats could travel over the river with no interruptions. This one at Lackawaxen is the only remaining example of four originals.

Used for over fifty years, the aqueduct was converted to a toll bridge when the canal closed in 1898. It came under the possession of the National Park Service in 1980 and is now a toll-free bridge but has only one lane. You have to wait your turn. Despite numerous modifications and reconstructions, much of the existing ironwork is original. The suspension cables themselves were rendered on-site under the direction of John Roebling himself in 1847. Laboratory tests conducted in 1983 concluded that the cable was still viable after 140 years.

Within sight of the old aqueduct, on the Pennsylvania side overlooking the river, is a stately house with a covered porch running its entire length. This is the Zane Grey Museum run by the National Park Service. I would like to tell you what was in the Zane Grey Museum, but it was closed due to the government shut-down. However, I will tell you this: Zane Grey was an author and adventurer who nearly single-handedly created the idealized version of the Old West.

Born in Zanesville, Ohio, and trained at the University of Pennsylvania as a dentist, Grey spent time fishing the Upper Delaware. Here he met his first wife Lina Roth, whom he affectionately called Dolly. They moved to Lackawaxen in 1905, where Grey began pursuing his real love—writing. After spending time in Arizona hunting mountain lions and "roughing it," he returned to Lackawaxen and started writing stories about his experiences. In 1910 Grey published his first western, *Heritage of the Desert*, which became a best seller. *Riders of the Purple Sage* was published two years later and became an instant success. It propelled him to a career in which he would pen over ninety books and become one of America's first millionaire authors. An avid sportsman and adventurer, Grey even played professional baseball for a brief time in his youth. He participated in fishing trips all over the world and it has been claimed that he fished an average of 300 days a year throughout his adult life. Leaving Lackawaxen in 1918, he moved to California, where many of his books and stories landed on the silver screen. And on the small screen, as well, in Dick Powell's Zane Grey Theatre, a TV series based on his work that ran from 1956 to 1961. After living a legendary life, he finally caught the big one in 1939 in California. He was brought back to Lackawaxen and buried in the Union Cemetery.

Crossing back over the river to New York and continuing north on the Scenic Byway, there are opportunities to pull off the road and stop at one of the mobile eagle blinds. If you are lucky, you might spot one or two soaring on the thermals that prevail over the river and mountains at this part of the drive. State signage will inform you of proper eagle-watching etiquette: do not sit in your vehicle with the engine idling; move quickly from your vehicle to the blind; don't make loud noises—you get the idea. These are majestic birds, and not everyone gets an opportunity to watch them in their native habitat. The birds are so prevalent here that the nearby town of Narrowsburg boasts the title of Eagle Capital of New York State.

I COULD NOT tell stories about a river of this length without revealing its source. The Delaware River has two sources—the West Branch and the East Branch. In a quandary as to which is considered the true source, I did as any person in the communications age would do—I let Google decide. It says the West Branch is the primary source, on Mount Jefferson in

Jefferson, Schoharie County, New York, approximately 100 miles due north of Port Jervis.

The two branches converge at Hancock, where the confluence is known as the Wedding of the Waters. This area is traditionally known for timber. Many lumber rafts began their journey here on the way down-river to Trenton and Philadelphia. Raw lumber was supplied to Louisville Slugger for baseball bats; a few of them found their way into the hands of Babe Ruth. This region is also known for stone. The Empire State Building and the base of the Statue of Liberty contain bluestone quarried at Hancock. Fish are another abundant natural resource. Brook and brown trout, perch, bass, bullhead, and eels attract anglers from all over. And there are few better places to enjoy stunning fall foliage.

RICK AND I set out for Mount Jefferson from Port Jervis equipped with Google directions and a portable GPS. For a while they were both in sync, the scenery lovely despite cloudy, misty weather. We even crossed a bridge over the East Branch of the Delaware on our way to get to the West Branch.*

Somehow, we missed a crucial turn. We couldn't blame the GPS, as we didn't have an exact address. We were now wandering aimlessly in the bucolic Catskills, in need of a rest room and gas station. Before long, just the thing we needed appeared—a small, rustic building that served as a convenience store with gas pumps in front. I went inside to pay for the fuel and ask the cashier for directions. She was a small, rotund, middle-aged woman who's eyes lit up when I said we were lost and needed assistance. She clapped her hands and squealed, "Oh goody! I love giving directions!" But her expression changed from one of glee to emptiness, like a child who's been told there's no Easter Bunny, when I asked if she could tell us how to get to Mt. Jefferson. Crestfallen, she admitted she had never heard of it. But she rallied quickly and pointed to a Ford dealership down the road, suggesting they might know where it was.

Arriving at the Ford dealership, we entered a 1950s era showroom reminiscent of a hunting lodge. Instead of the latest models of Taurus, Focus, or F150s, trophy deer heads gazed down from the walls. We waited patiently for what appeared to be the only salesman while he spoke to an elderly couple who were seated on an old leather sofa near his desk.

When our turn came, we explained our reason for calling on him. This was a man dressed not to greet strangers with the intention of having them drive off in a new Flex, but a man who knew just about anyone who walked through the door, and who was confident that his clientele would come see him for a new ride when they were ready. He was stockily built, dressed for comfort in a polo shirt, shorts, and running shoes. He unfolded our map of the Catskills, laid it out, and proceeded to write down the directions to get us back on track. He even offered to photocopy the map and draw the route on it to make it even clearer,

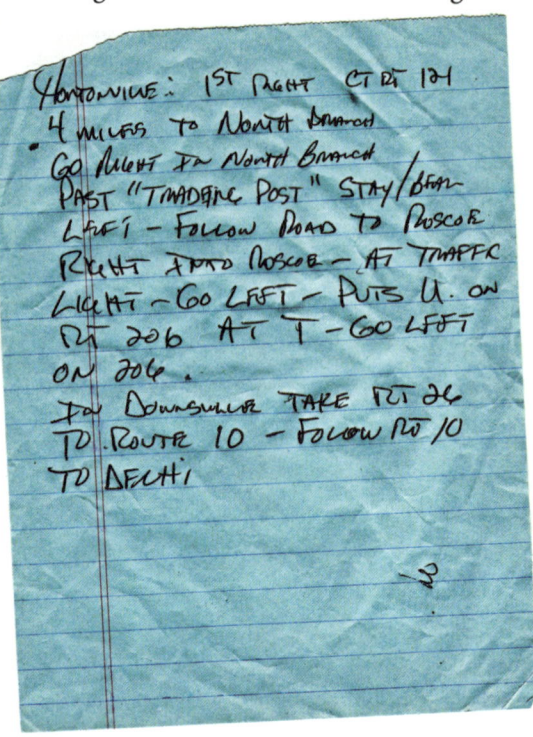

but we convinced him that wasn't necessary. His directions instructed us to go to Hortonville, then Roscoe, then Downsville, and then to Delhi, which would take us to our final destination.

He was such a helpful and pleasant guy that I felt I should offer him something for his generosity. All I had was my business card, so I handed it to him with an explanation about the book I was writing and an invitation to visit my blog. He broke out in a big grin, shook my hand, and informed me that we shared the same first name.

Following Hal the car salesman's impeccable directions, we soon entered the small, upstate New York college town of Delhi. Having been given the advantage of both verbal and written directions, we now knew that the name of the town was pronounced Del-high for future reference. We ate lunch at a small bookstore/cafe where I asked if anyone could direct me to the source of the West Branch of the Delaware. I really didn't expect to find a paved path leading to a marker saying, "here it is," so I figured some local guidance would be helpful. I did speak to one gentleman in the cafe who seemed to have first-hand knowledge and was glad to share it. But he was not as specific as I had hoped. We still had a good twenty miles to go. At this point the river is easy to follow, New York Route 10 hugging the high ground and the river meandering snake-like through the flood plain below, only about a dozen or so feet wide.

We were back to our Google directions, cruising through autumn-tinted rolling farmland muted by the light rain falling consistently now. We passed an old stone barn along the road that had a certain aged air about it and a blue historic marker that blurred as we sped past it. Checking it out later, I found that this was part of an enormous dairy business known as Sheffield Farms. In this barn in Bloomville, the first commercial pasteurization of milk in the US took place in 1892. We pushed on.

Next came Hobart, a remote village where we found a series of bookstores known as Hobart Book Village. It consists of five separate bookstores and a paper specialty/bookbinding shop. In a world where traditional books are gradually going the way of lava lamps, this is remarkable—a Jurassic Park of tomes.

We finally found ourselves nearly at our destination. The river had been easy to follow so far, but we lost it in a small-town street grid. We now had to follow the Google map blindly. We turned onto a small gravel road climbing a hill to what appeared to be someone's driveway, though it did have a road sign. We passed a well-kept residence and continued to what seemed to be an old unused access road. It was full of ruts and rocks and obviously hadn't been used for quite some time. A bit more climbing, and a larger residence appeared at the crest of the hill. This was the end of the line. Disappointed but not defeated, I managed to get the car headed back down the hill. It was raining harder now and I was glad to be off that grade. We backtracked and decided that maybe we had missed some minor detail. Not far from where we had turned back, the road veered sharply left, and out of the corner of my eye I spotted a small glimmer of ground water. I sprang out of the car and there it was—a tiny stream about eight inches wide, running down from the hill we had just left. The Source.

After following the Delaware for some 330 miles, my journey had come to an end. But it's not really the end, you know, the river keeps going.

Notes

Chapter 1

Lloyd E. Griscom, *The Historic County of Burlington* (The Burlington County Cultural and Heritage Commission, 1973); Jacob Ernest Cooke, *Encyclopedia of the North American Colonies, Dutch and Swedish Settlements* (New York: Charles Scribner's Sons, 1993), 142; Adrien Jorrisen Thienpont, *Journal of Middle Atlantic Archaeology*, vols. 14–15, 1998, 101.

"Philadelphia Firsts 1681–1899," ushistory. org, http://www.ushistory.org/philadelphia/philadelphiafirsts.html.

"Delaware Riverkeeper Network," http://delawareriverkeeper.org/delaware-river/index.asp.

"Thomas West, 3rd Baron De La Warr," Wikipedia, last modified January 2014, http://en.wikipedia.org/wiki/Thomas_West,_3rd_Baron_De_La_Warr; United States History, "Exploration and Settlement of Delaware," http://www.u-s-history.com/pages/h587.html; Jeffery M. Dorwart, *Cape May, New Jersey: The Making of an American Resort Community* (New Brunswick, NJ: Rutgers University Press, 1993).

"We Are Still Here!" leaflet produced by the Nanticoke Lenni-Lenape Indian Tribe; "About the Lenapes," last modified December 7, 2009, http://www.lenapelifeways.org/lenape1.htm; "The Life of St. Tammany," Monday, November 5, 2007, http://meeg-toomuchinformation.blogspot.com/2007/11/life-of-st-tammany.html; "The Walking Purchase," from a leaflet by William A. Hunter, Pennsylvania Historical & Museum Commission, 1972, http://www.portal.state.pa.us/portal/server.pt/community/things/4280/walking_purchase/478692.

Chapter 2

Jeffery M. Dorwart, *Cape May County, New Jersey. The Making of an American Resort Community* (New Brunswick, NJ: Rutgers University Press, 1992) 3; Albert Cook Myers, *Original Narratives of Early American History*. (New York: Barnes & Noble, 1912), 7–26.

Benjamin Ferris, *History of the Original Settlements on the Delaware*, 22–23; C. A. Weslager, *Dutch Explorers, Traders and Settlers in the Delaware Valley* (Philadelphia: University of Pennsylvania Press, 1961), Chapter IV, "The Swanendael Tragedy."

C. A. Weslager, *Dutch Explorers, Traders and Settlers in the Delaware Valley* (Philadelphia: University of Pennsylvania Press 1961), 102.

Lewes Chamber of Commerce, https://www.leweschamber.com/our-town/history-lewes-de; Lewes Historical Society, http://www.historiclewes.org/war%201812%20history.

Pam George, "The One That Got Away," *Delaware Beach Life*, Oct. 2010.

Pam George, "Raising the profile of the HMS DeBraak shipwreck," May 25, 2012, Delaware Public Media, http://m.delawarefirst.

org/27060-hms-debraak-shipwreck?wpmp_switcher=mobile.

James Scalli, "River pilots navigate risky duty, tiring hours," Dec. 6, 2004, http://www.freelists.org/post/seadog/River-pilots-navigate-risky-duty-tiring-hours; "Portrait of a river pilot," UD Messenger, vol. 8, no. 1, 1999; Eileen Stilwell, "Maritime's 'River Gods'"; Aug. 11, 2005, CourierPostOnline.com article, http://www.southjerseynews.com/river/pilotsa.html.

CHAPTER 3

Weslager, C. A. *Dutch Explorers, Traders and Settlers in the Delaware Valley 1609–1664* (Philadelphia: University of Pennsylvania Press 1961), 30.

Jeffery M. Dorwart, *Cape May County, New Jersey. The Making of an American Resort Community* (New Brunswick, NJ: Rutgers University Press. 1992), 2.

"Attractions in Cape May County - Historic Trail," June 20, 2012, Cape May County Department of Tourism, http://www.shorenewstoday.com/wildwood/history/in-another-time-indian-connections-ancient-and-modern-to-the/article_c6a82f69-3283-59d7-b70f-3f6587c16694.html.

Jeffery M. Dorwart, *Cape May County, New Jersey. The Making of an American Resort Community* (New Brunswick, NJ: Rutgers University Press. 1992, 3–5.

Paul Sturtevant Howe, "Mayflower Pilgrim Descendants in Cape May County New Jersey, 1620–1920," digital archive from the Library of Congress, https://archive.org/details/mayflowerpilgrimo2howe.

Jeffery M. Dorwart, *Cape May County, New Jersey. The Making of an American Resort Community* (New Brunswick, NJ: Rutgers University Press. 1992, 56-57.

Jeffery M. Dorwart, *Cape May County, New Jersey. The Making of an American Resort Community* (New Brunswick, NJ: Rutgers University Press. 1992), 63.

Jeffery M. Dorwart, *Cape May County, New Jersey. The Making of an American Resort Community*. (New Brunswick, NJ: Rutgers University Press. 1992), 120.

From a promotional booklet published in 1903 by the Cape May Real Estate Company, 101 Arcade Building, Philadelphia, reprinted in *South Jersey Magazine*, Summer 1996.

Emil R.Salvini, *The Summer City by the Sea. Cape May, New Jersey: An Illustrated History* (Wheal-Grace Publications 1995), 93-95.

Emil R.Salvini, *The Summer City by the Sea. Cape May, New Jersey: An Illustrated History* (Wheal-Grace Publications 1995), 224-226; Ben Miller. *The First Resort. Fun, Sun, Fire and War in Cape May, America's Original Seaside Town* (Cape May, NJ: Exit Zero Publishing, Inc. 2009), 224–226.

"Battery 223," FortMiles.org, Official Website of the 261st Coast Artillery 2014, http://www.fortmiles.org/intel/firepower/batteries/batt223.html; Emil R.Salvini, *The Summer City by the Sea. Cape May, New Jersey: An Illustrated History.* (Wheal-Grace Publications 1995), 95–96.

"Concrete Hulk of Atlantus Arrives to be Used as Dock for Jersey-Delaware Ferry," from the *Cape May Star and Wave*, June 12, 1926, reprinted in *South Jersey Magazine*, Spring 2001.

CHAPTER 4

Shirley R. Bailey, *South Jersey's Oyster Industry* (Millville, NJ: South Jersey Publishing Co), Introduction.

Notes

"O.T.C. History," Specialty Brands of America, March 2, 2010, http://americanhistory.si.edu/collections/search/object/nmah_1329398.

Shirley R. Bailey, *South Jersey's Oyster Industry* (Millville, NJ: South Jersey Publishing Co).

"Bayshore Center at Bivalve," BCB History, http://BayshoreCenter.org/about-us/bdp-history/.

"Delaware Bay Oyster Culture—Past, Present and Potential Future," W. J. Conzonier, NJ Aquaculture Association, 3/10/04; rev. 4/10/04, The Beginning of the Decline in Production, http://www.state.nj.us/seafood/DelawareBayOysters.pdf.

Chapter 5

"Fourteen Foot Bank, DE," Lighthouse Friends.com, http://www.lighthousefriends.com/light.asp?ID=386.

The descriptions and locations of the lighthouses found in this chapter are all cited from Lighthouse Friends.com, http://www.lighthousefriends.com/light.asp?ID=385.

Chapter 6

Betty Higbee and Clarence Higbee, *Around Fortescue*, 8; Margaret Louis Mints with Alex Ogden, *Man, the Sea and Industry, A History of Life on the Delaware Bay from 1492 to 1992*, 126–127.

"Sink Rum-Rummer and Arrest Three," Lewiston Evening Journal, Aug. 18, 1933, Google Archive, http://news.google.com/newspapers?nid=1913&dat=19330818&id=s9AoAAAAIBAJ&sjid=02YFAAAAIBAJ&pg=2647,3564467.

Betty Higbee and Clarence Higbee, *Around Fortescue* (Arcadia Publishing 2009), 7.

"History of the J. & E. Riggin," The Schooner J.& E. Riggin, http://www.mainewindjammer.com/history.

Margaret Louis Mints with Alex Ogden, *Man, the Sea and Industry, A History of Life on the Delaware Bay from 1492 to 1992* (Self-published 1992), 111.

"Philadelphia Sketch Club History," http://sketchclub.org/sample-page/history/.

Betty Higbee and Clarence Higbee, *Around Fortescue* (Arcadia Publishing 2009), 75.

Nick DiUlio, "The Other Shore," New Jersey Monthly, June 8, 2009, http://njmonthly.com/articles/lifestyle/the-other-shore.html.

Chapter 7

As told to me by Bill Bowen, long time resident of Money Island and former resident of Gandy's Beach.

"Cumberland County is Born," Cumberland County, NJ, County History, http://www.co.cumberland.nj.us/content/163/233/391/default.aspx; *Fortescue in 1883*, from an unnamed newspaper clipping of 1881, reprinted in *South Jersey Magazine*, Spring, 1995.

"Rufa Red Knot," US Fish & Wildlife Service, May 13, 2014, http://www.fws.gov/northeast/redknot/.

"Nearly empty now, Sea Breeze was a party town," Asbury Park Press, May 2, 2013, http://archive.app.com/article/20130502/NJNEWS/305020067/Nearly-empty-now-Sea-Breeze-party-town; "Sea Breeze, NJ is the 'Bees Knees' on the Delaware Bay," September 3, 2012, South Jersey History & Adventures, http://southjerseyexplorer.com/2012/09/03/sea-breeze-nj/.

Chapter 8

C. A. Weslager, *New Sweden on the Delaware, 1638–1655*. (Wilmington, DE: Middle Atlantic Press 1988), 6–8.

Encyclopedia of the North American Colonies, *Volume I, Dutch and Swedish Settlements*. (Charles Scribner's Sons, 1993), 142; C. A. Weslager, *New Sweden on the Delaware, 1638–1655*. (Wilmington, DE: Middle Atlantic Press, 1988) 11–29; "Delaware Living History," http://www.delawareliving.com/history.html.

Encyclopedia of the North American Colonies, Volume I. Charles T. Gehring, *Dutch and Swedish Settlements*. (Charles Scribner's Sons. 1993) 147–149; Benjamin Ferris, *A History of the Original Settlements on The Delaware* (Kennikat Press, 1846/1972). 28–31.

Russell Shorto, *The Island at the Center of the World*. (New York: Vintage Books 2005), 48–50.

Russell Shorto, *The Island at the Center of the World* (New York: Vintage Books 2005), 64–66.

Russell Shorto, *The Island at the Center of the World* (New York: Vintage Books, 2005), 75.

Quote was taken from the online source "History of the Kalmar Nyckel," http://colonialswedes.org/history/history.html.

C. A. Weslager, *New Sweden on the Delaware, 1638-1655* (Wilmington, DE: Middle Atlantic Press 1988), 35–36.

C. A. Weslager, *New Sweden on the Delaware, 1638-1655* (Wilmington, DE: Middle Atlantic Press 1988), 49.

C. A. Weslager, *New Sweden on the Delaware, 1638–1655*. (Wilmington, DE: Middle Atlantic Press 1988); Albert Cook Myers, *Narratives of Early Pennsylvania, West New Jersey and Delaware, 1630-1707*. (New York: Barnes & Noble, 1912). From the writing of Adrien van der Donck, 62 (Google digitized version).

C. A. Weslager, *New Sweden on the Delaware, 1638–1655*. (Wilmington, DE: Middle Atlantic Press 1988), 79–88.

Christopher Ward, *The Dutch & Swedes on the Delaware, 1609–64* (University of Pennsylvania Press, 1930), 31, 34; C. A. Weslager, *New Sweden on the Delaware, 1638-1655* (Wilmington, DE: Middle Atlantic Press 1988).

Chapter 9

Joseph S. Sickler, *Tea Burning Town* (Greenwich, NJ: The Greenwich Press. 1950), 7; "Cumberland County is Born," Cumberland County, NJ, County History, http://www.co.cumberland.nj.us/content/163/233/391/default.aspx.

Joseph S. Sickler, *Tea Burning Town* (Greenwich, NJ: The Greenwich Press. 1950), 1–8.

Joseph S. Sickler, *Tea Burning Town*. (Greenwich, NJ: The Greenwich Press. 1950), 38–42; "Greenwich Tea Burning: 1774," Cumberland County, NJ, County History, http://www.co.cumberland.nj.us/content/163/233/391/default.aspx.

Joseph S. Sickler, *Tea Burning Town* (Greenwich, NJ: The Greenwich Press, 1950).

Chapter 10

C. A. Weslager, *New Sweden on the Delaware, 1638–1655*. (Wilmington, DE: Middle Atlantic Press 1988), 132.

Christopher Ward, *The Dutch & Swedes on the Delaware, 1609–64* (University of Pennsylvania Press, 1930), 143, 152–153; C.

A. Weslager, *The English on the Delaware, 1610–1682.* (New Brunswick, NJ: Rutgers University Press, 1967), 111–112.

C. A. Weslager, *The English on the Delaware, 1610–1682.* (New Brunswick, NJ: Rutgers University Press, 1967), 76–88; Richard P. McCormick, *New Jersey from Colony to State 1609-1789.* (Newark, NJ: New Jersey Historical Society 1981), 14–15.

Richard P. McCormick, *New Jersey from Colony to State 1609–1789.* (Newark, NJ: New Jersey Historical Society 1981). 39–41; R. Craig Koedel, *South Jersey Heritage: A Social, Economic and Cultural History.* (Lanham, MD: University Press of America 1979. html version); "Brief History of Salem County, New Jersey", http://www.rootsweb.ancestry.com/~njsalem/documents/History-SalemCounty-NJ.txt

"A Brief and Partial History of the City of Salem," Preservation Salem, http://www.preservationsalem.org/PSIHIST.HTM; "Jersey Jottings: "The South Jersey Legend of Colonel Robert Gibbons Johnson and the Wolf Peach," *Jersey Man Magazine,* 4/09/2012.

"Chapter Eleven: New Interpretations at Valley Forge," National Park Service, updated 06/09/2014, http://www.nps.gov/vafo/historyculture/treese11.htm; "Tales from Salem County, NJ: The Great Cow Chase," Auburn Road Vineyard & Winery, 2014, http://www.auburnroadvineyards.com/real-south-jersey/.

The Hancock House, brochure prepared by NJ State Park Service.

"Abigail Goodwin, Quaker Abolitionist," 7 Steps to Freedom, 07/28/2011, Salem County Cultural & Heritage Commission, http://7stepstofreedom.wordpress.com/2011/07/28/abigail-goodwin/.

"The History of Mannington Mills," http://www.mannington.com/Corporate/OurCompany/History.aspx.

"Salem Nuclear Generating Station Facts," PSEG, http://www.pseg.com/family/power/nuclear/pdf/salem_factsheet.pdf.

CHAPTER 11

Fort Delaware, A Brief History, brochure prepared by the Fort Delaware Society.

"Rat call," notes written by Capt. John Sterling Swann, Co. A, 26th Battalion, Virginia Infantry, from the Library of Congress, Manuscript Division, Transcribed 1998.

"Fort Delaware, US Civil War," Fort Wiki Historic US and Canadian Forts, http://fortwiki.com/Fort_Delaware.

"Fort Delaware History," Ibid. President Monroe quoted from "Message to Congress on the Re-examination of Positions on Dauphin Island and Mobile Point for Fortifications," American State Papers: Military Affairs, vol. 2, 368. As taken from Willard Robinson, *American Forts, Architectural Form and Function* (Chicago: University of Illinois Press, Amon Carter Museum of Art, 1977), http://web.archive.org/web/20060915045103/http://www.visitthefort.com/historyx.html.

Fort Delaware, A Brief History, brochure prepared by the Fort Delaware Society; "Fort Delaware," Wikipedia, multiple citations, last modified 05/12/2014, http://en.wikipedia.org/wiki/Fort_Delaware.

Tracey Bryant, "Escape from Fort Delaware," University of Delaware Research Online Magazine, http://www.udel.edu/researchmagazine/issue/vol2_no2_security/escape_from_fort_delaware.html.

"James J. Archer," Wikipedia, last modified 5/3/2014, http://en.wikipedia.org/wiki/James_J._Archer; Larry Tagg, "The Generals of Gettysburg: The Leaders of America's Greatest Battle," http://www.rocemabra.com/~roger/tagg/generals/.

CHAPTER 12

William A. Mecum, "Friendly Fire - Delaware Style," *South Jersey Magazine*, Spring 1996.

"The History of Fort Mott," Terry Muse, last updated 10/8/2001, http://coastalheritagetrail.tripod.com/history.htm.

"Gershom Mott," last modified 9/17/2013, Wikipedia, multiple citations, http://en.wikipedia.org/wiki/Gershom_Mott.

CHAPTER 13

"Theodore O'Hara," Explore Kentucky History, Sanders, 6/16/2014, http://explorekyhistory.ky.gov/items/show/105#.U57oLChiF8Y.

Josephine Jaquett and Elmer VanName, "Finn's Point," Place Names of Salem County, NJ, Salem County Historical Society, vol. 2, no. 4, 1964, West Jersey History Project, http://www.westjerseyhistory.org/books/salemnames/.

"Finn's Point National Cemetery," Fort Delaware Sociey, updated 2/11/2012, http://www.fortdelaware.org/Finns%20Point%20National%20Cemetery.htm.

Maureen Orth, "The Killer's Trail," *Vanity Fair*, September 1997, http://www.vanityfair.com/magazine/1997/09/cunanan199709. "Andrew Cunanan," Wikipedia, updated 5/13/2014, multiple citations, http://en.wikipedia.org/wiki/Andrew_Cunanan.

"Finn's Point Range, NJ," Lighthouse Friends.com, http://www.lighthousefriends.com/light.asp?ID=374.

CHAPTER 14

Charles T. Gehring, *Encyclopedia of the North American Colonies, Dutch and Swedish Settlements*: 150; John A. Munroe, *Colonial Delaware, A History*, 31–33.

Christopher Ward, *The Dutch & Swedes on the Delaware, 1609-64*. (University of Pennsylvania Press 1930), 23–24.

Charles T. Gehring, *Encyclopedia of the North American Colonies, Volume I: Dutch and Swedish Settlements*. (Charles Scribner's Sons. 1993), 151.

Christopher Ward, *The Dutch & Swedes on the Delaware, 1609-64*. (University of Pennsylvania Press 1930), 251–255, 322–323; John A. Munroe, *Colonial Delaware, A History* (Millwood, NY: KTO Press. 1978), 41–46.

C. A. Weslager, *New Sweden on the Delaware, 1638-1655*. (Wilmington, DE: Middle Atlantic Press 1988). 144.

Christopher Ward, *The Dutch & Swedes on the Delaware, 1609-64*. (University of Pennsylvania Press 1930). 355-358.

Christopher Ward, *The Dutch & Swedes on the Delaware, 1609-64*. (University of Pennsylvania Press 1930). 361.

Christopher Ward, *The Dutch & Swedes on the Delaware, 1609-64* (University of Pennsylvania Press 1930), 371.

Henry Graham Ashmead, "*History of Delaware County, Pennsylvania*," (Philadelphia: L.H. Everts & Co., 1884), digital version, www.delcohistory.org/ashmead/, 158; John A. Munroe, *Colonial Delaware, A History*. (Millwood, NY: KTO Press, 1978), 68.

C. A. Weslager, *The English on the Delaware, 1610–1682*. (New Brunswick, NJ: Rutgers University Press 1967), 226.

CHAPTER 15

John A. Munroe, *Colonial Delaware, A History*. (Millwood, NY: KTO Press. 1978), chapter 1.

John A. Munroe, *Colonial Delaware, A History*. (Millwood, NY: KTO Press. 1978), 49–50.

John A. Munroe, *Colonial Delaware, A History*. (Millwood, NY: KTO Press. 1978). 153-158.

The Hagley Museum: A Story of Early Industry on the Brandywine, booklet produced by Eleutherian Mills-Hagley Foundation. 44–45.

CHAPTER 16

*Hessian is a convenient but inaccurate term when referring to German soldiers in the employ of the British government. Hesse-Cassel is merely one of the regions of Germany that contributed men who actually were working for their local princes. I had a chance to speak with a re-enactor at a Soldier's Weekend that took place at Fort Mott. When I mentioned the Red Bank battle, he admitted, "Yeah, we got slaughtered there," as if he had actually taken part. He was dressed in the uniform of a Jager, who were professional hunters in their homeland. Some of you will no doubt associate this with the popular cough-syrup-like swill served at bars known as Jagermeister. It means something like "Hunt Master."

Logan Pearsall Smith, "Two Generations of Quakers–An Old Diary (of Ann Whitall)," from the *Atlantic Monthly*, July, 1901, copy provided by Joyce Stevenson of Mullica Hill, NJ, to Gloucester County, NJ History & Genealogy, http://www.nj.searchroots.com/Gloucesterco/awhitall-diary.html.

"James and Ann Whitall House," Red Bank Battlefield Park, updated 6/16/2014, Gloucester County, NJ, http://www.gloucestercountynj.gov/depts/p/parks/parkgolf/redbank/default.asp.

Richard Patterson, Director of the Old Barracks Museum, Trenton, NJ, Washington Crossing Historic Park, "What Was a 'Hessian'?" http://www.ushistory.org/washingtoncrossing/history/hessian.htm.

"Battle of Red-Bank," Thrilling Incidents in American History, http://www.generalatomic.com/AmericanHistory/battle_of_red_bank.html; Wallace McGeorge, M.D., "The Battle of Red Bank: Resulting in the Defeat of the Hessians and the Destruction of the British Frigate Augusta, Oct. 22 and 23, 1777," 1905, Library of Congress, https://archive.org/details/battleofredbankroomcge.

"Jonas Cattell," Haddonfield, NJ chapter of DAR, http://www.rootsweb.ancestry.com/~njhcdar/jonas_cattell.html; Edward Collmore, Inquirer Staff Writier, "Haddonfield Statue to Honor Revolutionary Hero," 10/2/2013, http://articles.philly.com/2013-09-02/news/41665234_1_history-books-fort-mercer-jonas-cattell-run.

Benson J. Lossing, *Pictorial Field Book of the Revolution. Volume II, 1850*, Chapter III, http://freepages.history.rootsweb.ancestry.com/~wcarr1/Lossing1/Chap35.html.

Logan Pearsall Smith, "Two Generations of Quakers–An Old Diary (of Ann Whitall)," from the *Atlantic Monthly*, July, 1901, copy provided by Joyce Stevenson of Mullica Hill, NJ to Gloucester County, NJ History & Genealogy, http://www.nj.searchroots.com/Gloucesterco/awhitall-diary.html.

"Fort Mifflin on the Delaware: A National Monument and Historic Landmark," 11/17/2001, http://www.thebrandywine.com/photoop/fort_mifflin.html; "Fort Mifflin's Role in the American Revolution," http://fortmifflin.us/about-the-fort/.

"Fort Mifflin," Wikipedia, updated 4/4/2014, multiple citations, http://en.wikipedia.org/wiki/Fort_Mifflin.

CHAPTER 17

"Campbell's About Us, The Campbell Story, 1869–Present," http://www.campbellsoupcompany.com/about-campbell.

Matthew DeLuca, Staff Writer, NBC News, "What's the Matter with Camden?" 3/7/2013, http://www.nbcnews.com/feature/in-plain-sight/whats-matter-camden-v17226041.

Howard Gillette, Jr., *Camden: Historical Impressions, Evoking Camden's Rich Historical Heritage* (Private Printing, 2000).

Charles S. Boyer, "Annals of Camden, No. 3, Old Ferries," Privately Printed 1921, The Library of Congress, https://archive.org/details/oldferriescamden00boye.

"History, Early Settlement," City of Camden, http://www.ci.camden.nj.us/history/.

John T. Cunningham, *This is New Jersey.* (Rutgers University Press, 1953), 163; Ben Kragting Jr. and Harry Coster, "Victor's Church Studio, Camden (1918-1935): Lost and Found?" http://www.vjm.biz/new_page_25.htm; "Victor Talking Machine Company Recording Locations," http://www.stokowski.org/Camden%20Church%20Studio%20Recording%20Location.htm; "RCA," Wikipedia, multiple citations, last updated 6/14/2014, http://en.wikipedia.org/wiki/RCA.

"New York Ship Building," last updated 5/07/2014, http://www.globalsecurity.org/military/facility/camden.htm; Michael Kube-McDowell, "A Place Called Yorkship: The Ships of New York Shipbuilding Co.," http://yorkship.us/html/Yorkships.htm.

Mark M. Cleaver, "The Life, character, and public services of Commodore Jacob Jones," Published 1906 by The Historical Society of Delaware in Wilmington, online archive, https://openlibrary.org/books/OL7087183M/The_life_character_and_public_services_of_Commodore_Jacob_Jones.

"Reuben James", http://en.wikipedia.org/wiki/Reuben_James, Last updated 1/17/2015.

Jason Laday-South, "Demolition begins on historic Sears building in Camden; site will be office park," *Jersey Times*, 6/06/2013, http://www.nj.com/camden/index.ssf/2013/06/camden_sears_building_coming_d.html.

"Walt Whitman House," Wikipedia, multiple citations, last updated 8/01/2013, http://en.wikipedia.org/wiki/Walt_Whitman_House#cite_note-23.

CHAPTER 18

Catherine Owens Peare, *William Penn.* (Philadelphia, PA: J.B. Lippincott Company, 1957). 12–13. Hans Fantel, *William Penn: Apostle of Dissent* (New York: William Morrow & Co., 1974), 19.

Hans Fantel, *William Penn: Apostle of Dissent.* (New York: William Morrow & Co., 1974), 32.

Ibid., 23.

Catherine Owens Peare, *William Penn.* (Philadelphia, PA: J. B. Lippincott Company 1957), 36.

Catherine Owens Peare, *William Penn.* (Philadelphia, PA: J. B. Lippincott Company 1957). 13.

Hans Fantel, *William Penn: Apostle of Dissent.* (New York: William Morrow & Co., 1974), 97–98, 104.

Ibid., 149.

Ibid., 155.

CHAPTER 19

Hans Fantel, *William Penn: Apostle of Dissent*. (New York: William Morrow & Co., 1974), 185.

Ibid., 191; "Peace Treaty," Penn Treaty Museum.org, multiple citations.

Harry Kyriakodis, *Philadelphia's Lost Waterfront* (Mount Pleasant, SC: History Press, 2011) 38–43.

Ibid., 7.

Harry Emerson Wildes, *The Delaware*. (New York: Farrar & Rinehart, Inc. 1940). 76; Hans Fantel, *William Penn: Apostle of Dissent*, pg. 194.

Hans Fantel, *William Penn: Apostle of Dissent*. (New York: William Morrow & Co., 1974), 199.

Harry Emerson Wildes, *The Delaware* (New York: Farrar & Rinehart, Inc., 1940), 135.

Hans Fantel, *William Penn: Apostle of Dissent* (New York: William Morrow & Co., 1974), 217.

Ibid., 239–242.

Ibid., 195.

Christine Sismondo, *America Walks into a Bar*. (New York: Oxford University Press 2011), 70; "Taverns and Beer in Philadelphia's History," John Fischer, About.com/Philadelphia, http://philadelphia.about.com/od/barsandpubs/a/taverns.htm.

Catherine Owens Peare, *William Penn* (Philadelphia, PA: J.B. Lippincott Company 1957), 389–404.

CHAPTER 20

*The feeling of division continues to this day, although only as a dwindling number of business and organization names: West Jersey Air Conditioning and Heating, West Jersey Animal Shelter, West Jersey Chamber Music Society, and so on.

Samuel Smith, *The History of Nova Caesaria. The Colonial History of New Jersey, 1765*. (Online archive courtesy of West Jersey History Project. www.westjerseyhistory.org), 7–8.

William E. Schermerhorn, *The History of Burlington, New Jersey* (Burlington, NJ: Private Printing), 6–7.

Bob Barnett, "Where was the West Jersey/East Jersey Line?" last updated 9/15/2007, http://westjersey.org/wj_line.htm.

Catherine Owens Peare, *William Penn*. (Philadelphia, PA: J. B. Lippincott Company 1957), 171.

William E. Schermerhorn, *The History of Burlington, New Jersey* (Burlington, NJ: Private Printing), 15–20.

John T. Cunningham, *This is New Jersey 4th Edition*. (New Brunswick, NJ: Rutgers University Press 1953), 204; "Revell House," City of Burlington Historic District, http://www.tourburlington.org/SeeSites26-30.html#Revell.

"William Franklin Appointment, 1762," State of New Jersey Department of State, http://www.nj.gov/state/archives/docfranklin.html.

"Places to See," City of Burlington Historic District, http://www.tourburlington.org/See.html.

"Conspirators court-martialed for plotting to kill Lincoln, Grant and Andrew Johnson," This Day in History, http://www.history.com/this-day-in-history/conspirators-court-martialed-for-plotting-to-kill-lincoln-grant-and-andrew-johnson.

Michele P. Stricker, *The Historical Collections of the Library Company of Burlington*.

Lloyd E. Griscom, *The Historic County of Burlington*, 18; "John Fitch and Steamboats," About.com Inventors, http://inventors.about.com/library/inventors/bljohnfitch.htm; "John Fitch (inventor)," Wikipedia, multiple citations, http://en.wikipedia.org/wiki/John_Fitch_(inventor).

"Ancient Trust," Twelve Mile Circle, last updated 9/4/2012, http://www.howderfamily.com/blog/tag/matennecunk/; "Burlington Island and Jessup's Grove," NJPineBarrens, from a post dated 1/7/2009, http://forums.njpinebarrens.com/threads/burlington-island-and-jessups-grove.5151/

CHAPTER 21

"The Writings of Thomas Paine, Volume 4," Thomas Paine, 434, Google ebook, http://bit.ly/1dO8WDJ; Richard P. McCormick, *New Jersey from Colony to State*. (Newark, NJ: New Jersey Historical Society 1981). 35-36; Christine Sismondo, *America Walks into a Bar*. (New York: Oxford University Press 2011). 74; "Thomas Paine," Wikipedia, multiple citations, last updated 6/22/2014, http://en.wikipedia.org/wiki/Thomas_Paine.

"Bordentown City," Delaware River Heritage Trail, http://www.delrivgreenway.org/heritagetrail/Bordentown-City.html; W. Jay Mills, "The Hopkinson Mansion Bordentown," from Historic Houses of New Jersey 1902, edited by GET NJ, http://www.getnj.com/historichouses/bordentownhopkinsonmansion.shtml; "Bordentown Historic District," Living Places, http://www.livingplaces.com/NJ/Burlington_County/Bordentown_City/Bordentown_Historic_District.html.

3. David Hackett Fischer, *Washington's Crossing* (New York: Oxford University Press 2004), 173, 187; Richard P. McCormick, *New Jersey from Colony to State* (Newark, NJ: New Jersey Historical Society 1981), 137; Arthur D. Pierce, *Smuggler's Woods* (New Brunswick, NJ: Rutgers University 1960), 183.

4. "Patience Lovell Wright, America's First Sculptor and Revolutionary Spy," History of American Women, posted 1/05/2009, http://www.womenhistoryblog.com/2009/01/patience-lovell-wright.html.

5. Percy Harold Epler, *The Life of Clara Barton*, Macmillan, 1915, Google eBook, 20-23.

6. Miriam V. Studley, *Historic New Jersey Through Visitors' Eyes*. (New York: Van Nostrand Co., Inc., 1964), 65-74; Lloyd E. Griscom, *The Historic County of Burlington* (The Burlington County Cultural and Heritage Commission, 1973), 32.

Lloyd E. Griscom, *The Historic County of Burlington*. (The Burlington County Cultural and Heritage Commission, 1973), 18; John T. Cunningham, New Jersey, America's Main Road. (New York: Doubleday & Company, 1966), 135-137; "The Camden & Amboy Railroad," compiled from articles from the Camden & Amboy Railroad Historical Society, updated 12/26, 2011, http://www.jcrhs.org/camden&amboy.html.

John T. Cunningham, *New Jersey, America's Main Road* (New York: Doubleday & Company, Inc. 1966), 208; "Delaware and Raritan Canal," Living Places, multiple citatations, http://www.livingplaces.com/NJ/Delaware_and_Raritan_Canal.html.

CHAPTER 22

*The reason Von Donop wanted to stay was that he made the acquaintance of a beautiful young widow of a doctor. He spent the night of December 23 at her house, then Christmas Eve and Christmas Day as well. There is much speculation that the British may have lost Trenton because of Von Donop's indiscretions. It is also thought that the young widow may have been a clandestine colonial agent. Further speculation brings up the suspicion that the lady in question may have been someone General Washington was well acquainted with—the widow Betsy Ross.

David Hackett Fischer, *Washington's Crossing* (New York: Oxford University Press, 2004). The definitive source.

Bruce Stutz, *Natural Lives, Modern Times* (New York: Crown Publishers 1992), 150, 205–206; Miriam V. Studley, *Historic New Jersey Through Visitor's Eyes* (New York: Van Nostrand Co., 1964), 19, 49, 59; L. A. Parker, "City celebrating role as U.S. capital in 1784," for *The Trentonian*, 11/06/2009; "Trenton, New Jersey," Wikipedia, multiple citations, last updated 06/11/2014, http://en.wikipedia.org/wiki/Trenton,_New_Jersey.

Bruce Stutz, *Natural Lives, Modern Times* (New York: Crown Publishers 1992), 148–149.

John T. Cunningham, *This is New Jersey* (New Brunswick, NJ: Rutgers University Press, 1953), 148.

John T. Cunningham, *This is New Jersey* (New Brunswick, NJ: Rutgers University Press, 1953), 151; Bruce Stutz, *Natural Live, Modern Times* (New York: Crown Publishers, 1992), 209–215; Kathy Pelta, Bridging the Golden Gate (Minneapolis, MN: Lerner Publications Company, 1987), 53; *Roebling New Jersey*, from a brochure produced by the Roebling Historical Society.

6. John T. Cunningham, *This is New Jersey* (New Brunswick, NJ: Rutgers University Press, 1953), 150–151; "Thomas Maddock's Sons' Pottery is Famous the World Over After 50 Golden Years," from a newspaper article facsimile given to me by Thomas Maddock, a descendant of the founder, newspaper and author not known.

"1911: Trenton Makes History," John Blackwell, the Trentonian, http://www.capitalcentury.com/1911.html.

CHAPTER 23

*Another river connection: the vice-president of Union Mills Paper was Ferdinand Roebling White, nephew of Ferdinand Roebling, Jr., president of John A. Roebling's Sons, the steel manufacturing giant of Trenton.

Bruce Stutz, *Natural Live, Modern Times*. (New York: Crown Publishers 1992), 174–175.

John T. Cunningham, *New Jersey, America's Main Road* (New York: Doubleday & Company, 1966). 136–138; Bruce Stutz, *Natural Live, Modern Times* (New York: Crown Publishers, 1992), 177–178; "Delaware and Raritan Canal," from a report issued for the Federal Highway Administration and New Jersey Department of Transportation, June 1983, Living Places, http://www.livingplaces.com/NJ/Delaware_and_Raritan_Canal.html.

"Canal Lore: Delaware & Lehigh Canal History," Friends of the Delaware Canal, http://www.fodc.org/mission.html.

"U.S. Canals 1825–1860," Perry-Castañeda Library Map Collection, University of Texas at Austin, http://www.lib.utexas.edu/maps/map_sites/hist_sites.html.

"Delaware Canal State Park," Delaware River Recreation Page, http://www.delawareriver.net/DelCan.php.

"Bowman's Hill Tower," Washington Crossing Historic Park, Pennsylvania Historical and Museum Commission, http://www.ushistory.org/washingtoncrossing/visit/bowman.htm.

Terry A. McNealy, a Director of the New Hope Historical Society, "A Brief History of New Hope, Pennsylvania," Borough of New Hope, PA, http://www.newhopeborough.org/; "Historic New Hope, PA," http://www.visitnewhope.com/history/; "New Hope, PA, Information & History, http://www.newhopepa.com/history.htm.

Dennis Gaffney, "Pennsylvania Impressionists: Valued at Last," posted 4/7/2003, Antiques Roadshow, http://www.pbs.org/wgbh/roadshow/tips/impressionists.html; An American Tradition: The Pennsylvania Impressionists, Westmoreland Museum of American Art, last updated 12/08/2010, http://www.tfaoi.com/newsmu/nmus16a.htm.

"History," Bucks County Playhouse, http://www.bcptheater.org/about-us/history/.

"Our History, J & Ps Greatest Hits - Live Since 1972," http://www.johnandpeters.com/our-history.html.

John T. Cunningham, *This is New Jersey* (New Brunswick, NJ: Rutgers University Press 1953), 35; Sarah Gallagher "Early History of Lambertville 1703–1903," Lambertville, NJ, http://www.newhopepa.com/Lambertville/lam_hist_Gallagher_2.htm.

Chapter 24

Bruce Stutz, *Natural Lives, Modern Times*. (New York: Crown Publishers 1992), 227–229.

Harry Emerson Wildes. *The Delaware*. (New York: Farrar & Rinehart, Inc. 1940), 24.

Bruce Stutz, *Natural Lives, Modern Times*. (New York: Crown Publishers 1992), 230–231.

American Shad, printed handout produced by Delaware River Basin Commission.

5. "Atlantic Sturgeon," NOAA Fisheries, Office of Protected Resources, last updated 6/02/2014, http://www.nmfs.noaa.gov/pr/species/fish/atlanticsturgeon.htm; "Ongoing Issues: Atlantic Sturgeon," Delaware Riverkeeper Network, http://www.delawareriverkeeper.org/riveraction/ongoing-issue-detail.aspx?Id=29.

"History of Relevant Flood Studies and Related Actions," US Army Corps of Engineers, http://www.nap.usace.army.mil/Missions/CivilWorks/DelawareRiverBasinComprehensiveStudy/HistoryofDelawareRiverFlooding.aspx; "Delaware River Flooding History," Vinessa Erminio/The Star Ledger, updated 10/30/2008, http://blog.nj.com/ledgerarchives/2006/09/delaware_river_flooding_histor.html.

From a personal interview with Robert Rando.

Lynn H. Miller "Frenchtown, New Jersey," posted 1/2009, USA Revisted, http://usarevisited.com/2009/01/frenchtown-new-jersey/; John T. Cunningham, *This is New Jersey*. (New Brunswick, NJ: Rutgers University Press 1953), 35.

"Frenchtown Historic District," Living Places, http://www.livingplaces.com/NJ/Hunterdon_County/Frenchtown_Borough/Frenchtown_Historic_District.html.

Chapter 25

Arline Zatz, *New Jersey's Special Places*. (Woodstock, VT: The Countryman Press, 1994), 181–184.

"Ringing Rocks," David's Photographic Tour of Bucks County, Pennsylvania, http://www.davidhanauer.com/buckscounty/ringingrocks/; "Weird Geology: Ringing Rocks," Museum of Unnatural Mystery, http://www.unmuseum.org/ringrock.htm.

"Riegelsville Toll Supported Bridge," Delaware River Joint Toll Bridge Commission, http://www.drjtbc.org/default.aspx?pageid=76; "Riegelsville Bridge," Wikipedia, multiple citations, http://en.wikipedia.org/wiki/Riegelsville_Bridge.

"Benjamin Riegel House," Living Places, http://www.livingplaces.com/PA/Bucks_County/Riegelsville_Borough/Benjamin_Riegel_House.html.

Renée Kiriluk-Hill/Hunterdon Democrat, "Milford citizens group meets tonight to discuss Riegel Paper Mill site needs, once cleanup ends," 1/30/2012, NJ.com, http://www.nj.com/hunterdon-county-democrat/index.ssf/2012/01/milford_citizens_group_meets_t.html.

"LORES—Riegelsville Ghosts," Ima Gohner, posted 9/30/2013, Geochaching, http://www.geocaching.com/geocache/GC4N9XY_lores-riegelsville-ghosts.

"History of Durham," Durham Historical Society, http://durhamhistoricalsociety.org/history1.html; Ruth Fassman, "Crossing into Freedom: The Durham Boat," Spring, 2010, http://pabook.libraries.psu.edu/palitmap/DurhamBoat.html; Jack E. Boucher, Of Batsto and Bog Iron, Published by The Batsto Citizens Committee, online archive courtesy of Stockton College, https://blogs.stockton.edu/hist2177/files/2011/01/Jack-Boucher-Of-Batsto-and-Bog-Iron.pdf.

CHAPTER 26

*Crayola, inchworm, mango tango, wild blue yonder and jazzberry jam are registered trademarks of Crayola, used with permission.

"History," Crayola, http://www.crayola.com/about-us/company/history.aspx.

Richard F. Hope, *Easton PA: A History*. (Bloomington, IN: AuthorHouse 2006). 21, 23; Daniel Gilbert, "What Ye Indians Call 'Ye Hurry Walk,'" Fall 2009, http://pabook.libraries.psu.edu/palitmap/WalkingPurchase.html.

Richard F. Hope, *Easton PA: A History* (Bloomington, IN: AuthorHouse 2006), 3–7, 9–13.

Ibid., 21-29.

Ibid., 38-40.

Frank Dale, *Delaware Diary: Episodes in the Life of a River*. (New Brunswick, NJ: Rutgers University Press 1996). 29; Richard F. Hope, *Easton PA: A History*. (Bloomington, IN: AuthorHouse 2006), 56–57.

7. C. P. Yoder, *Delaware Canal Journal: A Definitive History* (Bethlehem, PA: Canal Press Incorporated, 1972), 176, 143; signage text from restored locktenders house, New Hope, Pennsylvania.

C. P. Yoder, *Delaware Canal Journal: A Definitive History*. (Bethlehem, PA: Canal Press Incorporated 1972), 205–207.

9. Richard F. Hope, *Easton PA: A History* (Bloomington, IN: AuthorHouse 2006), 46.

CHAPTER 27

Bruce Stutz, *Natural Lives, Modern Times*. (New York: Crown Publishers 1992), 243–245.

John T. Cunningham, *This is New Jersey*, 11, 21; Bruce Stutz, *Natural Lives, Modern Times* (New York: Crown Publishers, 1992), 250–252; C.G. Hine, *The Old Mine Road* (New Brunswick, NJ: Rutgers University Press, 1909, 1963), 1–5.

"Old Mine Road," Robert Koppenhaver, Updated Jan. 2014, Skylands Visitor, http://www.njskylands.com/hsoldmine072.

Lawrence Squeri, *Better in the Poconos*. (Philadelphia, PA: University of Pennsylvania Press 2002), 2–3; Bruce Stutz, *Natural Lives, Modern Times*, (New York: Crown Publishers 1992), 254–255.

Lawrence Squeri, *Better in the Poconos* (Philadelphia, PA: University of Pennsylvania Press, 2002), 22, 25, 41, 63, 69.

Martin W. Wilson, "Delaware Water Gap," http://www.dutotmuseum.com/history.htm.

CHAPTER 28

Bruce Stutz, *Natural Lives, Modern Times*. (New York: Crown Publishers 1992). 278-279.

Lawrence Squeri, *Better in the Poconos*. (Philadelphia, PA: University of Pennsylvania Press, 2002), 195; Michael E. Ruane, Inquirer Staff Writer, "Bitterness Lives Where Dam is Dead. A Delaware River Project Lived Too Long for Some. In 30 Years, Many Lost Their Land." Posted 7/19/1992, http://articles.philly.com/1992-07-19/news/26028023_1_tocks-island-dam-project-delaware-river-project-delaware-water-gap

Bruce Stutz, *Natural Lives, Modern Times*. (New York: Crown Publishers 1992), 282; Frank Dale, *Delaware Diary*, 154–155.

Bruce Stutz, *Natural Lives, Modern Times* (New York: Crown Publishers, 1992), 294–296.

"Tocks Island Dam Project," Delaware WaterGap.org, http://delawarewatergap.org/TOCKS_ISLAND_DAM_PROJECT.html.

Robert Williams and Mary Christman, *Over the Mountain: A Place Called Walpack*, 4.

Millbrook Village, from a brochure produced by the National Park Service.

Robert Williams and Mary Christman, *Over the Mountain: A Place Called Walpack* (Walpack, NJ: The Walpack Historical Society 1988), 25.

Jennie Sweetman "History of Delaware River bridges span many years," the New Jersey Sunday Herald, 9/22/2013.

CHAPTER 29

Bruce Stutz, *Natural Lives, Modern Times* (New York: Crown Publishers, 1992), 281, 340–342.

Alfred Mathews, "History of Pike County, Chapter V, Borough of Milford," online archive 854–898, History of Wayne, Pike and Monroe Counties, originally published by R.T. Peck & Co., 1886, http://www.pa-roots.com/pike/history/chapter5.html

"Gifford Pinchot," Wikipedia, last updated 6/30/2014, http://en.wikipedia.org/wiki/Gifford_Pinchot.

"Charles Sanders Peirce," revised 8/03/2010, Stanford Encyclopedia of Philosophy, http://plato.stanford.edu/entries/peirce/.

C. G. Hine, *The Old Mine Road* (New Brunswick, NJ: Rutgers University Press, 1909, 1963), 133; "New York-New Jersey Line War," Wikipedia, last updated 4/23/2014, multiple citations, http://en.wikipedia.org/wiki/New_York_-_New_Jersey_Line_War.

CHAPTER 30

*The earliest Dutch colonists and explorers called the Hudson River the North River and called the Delaware the South River. Little did they know that the Delaware's headwaters are probably no more than twenty-five miles from the Hudson.

"Port Jervis, New York 12771," PortJervisNY.com, http://portjervisny.com/.

"The Railroads of Port Jervis," Raymond Pinglora, Minisink Valley Historical Society, http://portjervisny.com/fr-pj.pics.htm.

"Erie Railroad Turntable," Port Jervis, New York, http://www.portjervisny.org/.

Frank Dale, Delaware Diary: Episodes in the Life of a River. (New Brunswick, NJ: Rutgers University Press, 1996), 50–56.

"Roebling's Delaware Aqueduct," Wikipedia, multiple citations, last updated 5/13/2014, http://en.wikipedia.org/wiki/Roebling's_Delaware_Aqueduct#cite_note-1.

"Zane Grey," Upper Delaware Scenic & Recreational River, NY, PA, National Park Service, http://www.nps.gov/upde/historyculture/zanegrey.htm; "Biography of Zane Grey," Marian Kester Coombs, http://www.zgws.org/zgbio.php.

"History," Hancock, New York, http://www.hancockny.org/hancockny4.htm.

Bibliography

Bailey, Shirley R. *South Jersey's Oyster Industry*. Millville, NJ: South Jersey Publishing Co. (defunct).

Bailey, Shirley R. *Yesteryear on The Maurice River*. South Jersey Publishing Co., 1977.

Christensen, Gardell Dano & Burney, Eugenia. *Colonial Histories: Delaware*. Nashville, TN: Thomas Nelson, 1974.

Cunningham, John T. *Colonial Histories New Jersey*. Nashville, TN: Thomas Nelson & Sons, 1971.

Cunningham, John T. *New Jersey: America's Main Road*. New York: Doubleday & Company, 1966.

Cunningham, John T. *This is New Jersey*. New Brunswick, NJ: Rutgers University Press, 1953.

Dale, Frank. *Delaware Diary: Episodes in the Life of a River*. New Brunswick, NJ: Rutgers University Press, 1996.

Di Ionno, Mark. *A Guide to New Jersey's Revolutionary War Trail*. (New Brunswick, NJ: Rutgers University Press, 2000).

Dorwart, Jeffrey M. *Cape May County, New Jersey. The Making of an American Resort Community*. New Brunswick, NJ: Rutgers University Press, 1992.

Elmer, Lucius Q. C. *Early History of Cumberland County, NJ*. Bridgeton, NJ: George F. Nixon, 1869.

Encyclopedia of the North American Colonies. Volume I. New York: Charles Scribner's Sons, 1993.

Fantel, Hans. *William Penn: Apostle of Dissent*. New York: William Morrow & Co. 1974.

Ferris, Benjamin. *A History of the Original Settlements on The Delaware*. Port Washington, NY: Kennikat Press. 1846/1972.

Fischer, David Hackett. *Washington's Crossing*. New York: Oxford University Press 2004.

Griscom, Lloyd E. *The Historic County of Burlington*. The Burlington County Cultural and Heritage Commission, 1973.

Higbee, Betty & Clarence Jr. *Around Fortescue*. Mount Pleasant, SC: Arcadia Publishing, 2009.

Hine, C.G. *The Old Mine Road*. (New Brunswick, NJ: Rutgers University Press, 1909, 1963.

Hughes, Howard L. *History of the Burlington Library*. Librarian of the Trenton Public Library.

Hoffecker, Dr. Carol E. *Delaware, The First State*. Wilmington, DE: Middle Atlantic Press, 1988.

Hope, Richard F. *Easton, PA: A History*. Bloomington, IN: AuthorHouse, 2006.

Koedel, R. Craig. *South Jersey Heritage: A Social, Economic and Cultural History*. Lanham, MD: University Press of America 1979. html version.

Kyriakodis, Harry. *Philadelphia's Lost Waterfront*. Mount Pleasant, SC: History Press, 2011.

Leiby, Adrian C. *The Early Dutch and Swedish Settlers of New Jersey*. New York: D. Van Nostrand Company. 1964.

McCormick, Richard P. *New Jersey from Colony to State 1609-1789*. Newark, NJ: New Jersey Historical Society, 1981.

McMahon, William. *South Jersey Towns: History and Legend*. New Brunswick, NJ: Rutgers University Press, 1973.

Miller, Ben. *The First Resort. Fun, Sun, Fire and War in Cape May, America's Original Seaside Town.* Cape May, NJ: Exit Zero Publishing, 2009.

Mints, Margaret Louise with Ogden, Alex. *Man, the Sea and Industry.* Self-published, 1992.

Munroe, John A. *Colonial Delaware: A History.* Millwood, NY: KTO Press, 1978.

Myers, Albert Cook, *Original Narratives of Early American History.* New York: Barnes & Noble, 1912.

Peare, Catherine Owens. *William Penn.* Philadelphia, PA: J. B. Lippincott Company, 1957.

Pelta, Kathy. *Bridging the Golden Gate.* Minneapolis, MN: Lerner Publications Company. 1987.

Pierce, Arthur D. *Smugglers' Woods.* New Brunswick, NJ: Rutgers University, 1960.

Salvini, Emil R. *The Summer City by the Sea. Cape May, New Jersey: An Illustrated History.* Belleville, NJ: Wheal-Grace Publications, 1995.

Schermerhorn, William E. *The History of Burlington.* Burlington NJ: Enterprise Publishin, 1927.

Shorto, Russell. *The Island at the Center of the World.* New York: Vintage Books, 2005.

Sickler, Joseph S. *Tea Burning Town.* Greenwich, NJ: The Greenwich Press, 1950.

Sismondo, Christine. *America Walks into a Bar.* New York: Oxford University Press, 2011.

Smith, Samuel. *History of Nova Caesarea. The Colonial HIstory of New Jersey. 1765.* Online archive courtesy of West Jersey History Project. www.westjerseyhistory.org)

South Jersey Magazine (defunct). Millville, NJ: South Jersey Publishing Co.

Squeri, Lawrence. *Better in the Poconos.* Philadelphia, PA: University of Pennsylvania Press, 2002.

Studley, Miriam V. *Historic New Jersey Through Visitor's Eyes.* New York: Van Nostrand Co., 1964.

Stutz, Bruce. *Natural Lives, Modern Times.* New York: Crown Publishers, 1992.

"The Historical Collections of the Library Company of Burlington," Michele P. Stricker, Director.

Ward, Christopher. *The Dutch & Swedes on the Delaware, 1609-64.* Philadelphia, PA: University of Pennsylvania Press, 1930.

Weslager, C. A. *Dutch Explorers, Traders and Settlers in the Delaware Valley 1609-1664.* Philadelphia: University of Pennsylvania Press, 1961.

Weslager, C. A. *New Sweden on The Delaware: 1638–1655.* Wilmington, DE: Middle Atlantic Press, 1988.

Weslager, C. A. *The English on the Delaware, 1610-1682.* New Brunswick, NJ: Rutgers University Press 1967.

Wildes, Harry Emerson. *The Delaware.* New York: Farrar & Rinehart, 1940.

Williams, Robert and Christman, Mary. *Over the Mountain: A Place Called Walpack.* Walpack, NJ: The Walpack Historical Society, 1988.

Yoder, C. P. *Delaware Canal Journal. A Definitive History.* Bethlehem, PA: Canal Press, 1972.

Zatz, Arline. *New Jersey's Special Places.* Woodstock, VT: The Countryman Press, 1994.

Index

abatis 125
Abbott, Charles Conrad 170
Abbott Marshlands 170
Absecon Light 49
Ada C. Lore 35
Adams, John 223
Adams, John Quincy 175
"Admiral Dewey's Flagship" 158
Adventure Aquarium 139
African Americans 162
African slaves 9
A .J. Meerwald 33
Albany, NY 161
Alcohol Beverage Control 50
Alexander Grant Mansion 92
Alexandria, NJ 204
Algonquian 13
Allegheny 15
Allen, J. 78
Alloway Creek 88
Alricks, Peter 162
Altena 117
American Kestrels 30
American Nickel Works 132
American Philosophical Society 214
Amundsen, Roald 23
American colonies 10
American Red Cross 174
American Revolution 184
American shad 198
American Weekly Mercury, The 10
Amstel House 114

Amstel, New 110, 112–114
Amsterdam 111
Andersonville 93
André, Major John 166, 167
Andross, Edmund 87
Anglicans 143
Anglo-Powhatan War 12
Annapolis, Maryland 80
Anshutz, Thomas P. 54
anthracite coal 177, 217
"Antiques Roadshow" 175, 197
Apache helicopter 101
Appalachian Mountains 216, 221
Appalachian Mountain Club 211
Appalachian Trail 227, 245
Appomattox Court House 102
Archer, General James J. 95, 96
Argall, Captain Samuel 11, 24
Arkansas 14
Army Corps of Engineers, US 28, 108, 201, 229, 230
Army of Northern Virginia 95
Army of the Potomac 94
Arnold, General Benedict 167, 193
Asamo Hackingskijl 85
Assunpink Creek 183, 184
Astaire, Fred 226
"Athens of America" 157
Atkins, Chet 138
Atlantic sturgeon 200, 201
Atlantus 30
Audubon, John James 168

Index

Augusta 125
Azores 12

Babe Ruth 251
Babylon 125
Bachman Publick House 213
Bald Eagles 250
Baltimore, Lord 19, 117, 118, 152, 153
Bank of America 121
Barbados 113
Barbary Pirates 137, 165
Barclays 121
barges 10, 190
Barnegat Lighthouse 49
Barnum, P. T. 21
Baron De La Warr (Warre) 11, 24
Barry, Commodore John 137
Barton, Clarissa Harlowe (Clara) 174
Batsto, New Jersey 211
Battery Harker 101
Battle of Manila 158
Battle of Seven Pines 102
Battle of the Crater 102
Battle of Minisink 247
Battleship New Jersey 139
Bayshore Center at Bivalve 33
Becuna, USS 157
Beatty, Elizabeth 80
beer 154, 155, 156
Belgium 161
Belleview House 226
Benjamin Cooper House 133
Berkeley, John Lord 87
Biddis, John 236
"Big Belly" 72
Big Timber Creek 126
Billingsport, New Jersey 125
Binney, Edwin 213
Bivalve 33
Bivalve Packing Company 34

Bivouac of the Dead 105
Bix Beiderbecke 134
black powder 121
Black River & Western Railroad 197
Blommaert's Kill 17
Blommaert, Samuel 69
Book Garden 202
Bloomfield, Joseph 79
"Blue Rocks" 115, 122
"Bohemians" 53
Bonaparte, Joseph 174, 175
Bonny Prince Charlie 76
Borden, Joseph 172
Bordentown 171, 172, 190
Boston 36, 88
Boston Symphony with Karl Muck 134
Boston Tea Party 88
Boudinot, Elias 164
Bowen, Bill 59
Bowen, Daniel 78
Bowers Beach 32
Bowman, Dr. John 192
Bowman, Thomas 192
Bowman's Hill Tower and Wildflower Preserve 191, 192
Boyle, Pete 54
Brandywine, Battle of 125
Brandywine Blue Gneiss granite 115
Brandywine Light 39
Brandywine River 120
Brandywine Shoal 45
Brant, Joseph 247, 248
Brewerytown 155
Bristol, PA 181, 191, 217
British Lieutenant Colonel Abercrombie 133
British titling system 10
Brooklyn Bridge 185
Brotherly Love 149
Buchanan, James 27
Buckinghamshire, England 156

273

Bucks County Playhouse 194
Buckwood Inn 226, 227
Bull, John 176
Burlington County Historical Society 164
Burlington Island 9, 169
Burlington, NJ, City of 33, 163, 164
Burns, Ken 195
Bushkill Falls 234
Byllynge, Edward 87, 163,

Cabot, John 161
Callowhill, Hannah Margaret 153
Camden 131, 166
Camden & Amboy Railroad 176
Camden River Sharks 139
Camden Ship Repair Company 133
"Campbell Kids" 131
Campbell, Joseph A. 131
Campbell Soup Company 131, 137, 138
canals 177, 189, 217, 218, 219
Cape Cod 67
Cape Island 26
Cape May 24
Cape May County 24
Cape May County Museum 49
Cape May Diamond 29
Cape May Lighthouse 30, 48
Cape May Point State Park 30
Cape May Real Estate Company 28
Cape May Salts 36
Cape May-Lewes Ferry 21, 47
Cape Henlopen 17, 24, 161
Cape Henlopen State Park 20
Captain Horatio Hornblower 60
Captain Kidd 19, 64
Caribbean 12, 90
Carter Family, The 134
Caruso, Enrico 134
Carteret, Sir George 87, 162
Cashier 33

Castle Inn 226
Catskills 10, 251
Cattell Jonas 126
Catskill Mountains 10, 221
Chancellorsville 102
Charles I 85, 142
Charles II 111, 117, 144, 162
Carr, Sir Robert 112
cave dwellers 151
Centre Square 214
Centennial Exhibition in Philadelphia, 1876 40
Charlesworth, Ruella 53
Chase 121
cheveaux-de-fries 125
Christina 69,
Christinahamn 117
Christina River 115, 118
Christy, Howard Chandler 54
Chygoes Island 163
Cedarville 33
Chesapeake Bay 21
Chesapeake and Delaware Canal 22
City of Brotherly Love 214
Civil War 32, 51, 93, 94, 102, 107, 121, 127, 223
Clay, Henry 27
Cleveland, President Grover 99
Cohansey 75
Cohansey Cove 64
Cohansey River 64, 76
College of New Jersey 79
"Colony of the City" 111
"Colony of The Company" 111
Colonel Cadwalader 181
Columbiad cannon 97
Commandant's House 127
Commercial Township 32
Commodore Barry Bridge 137
Common Sense 171
Compton, Spencer, Earl of Wilmington 120

Index

Conestoga Wagons 121
Confederate 93, 105
Congress Hall 27, 28
"Congress Hall March" 27
Connecticut River 18
Consolidated Fisheries Company 19
Constellation, USS 137
container ships 10
Continental Army 180
Continental Congress 7, 223
Coolidge, Calvin 239
Cooper, Daniel 132
Cooper, Dr. 7
Cooper Hospital 7, 133
Cooper's Ferry 133
Cooper's Ferry Partnership 139
Cooper's Landing 7
Cooper River 7
Cooper, James Fenimore 164
Cooper, John 7
Cooper, Ann 7, 124
Cornwallis, Lord 184
Coryell's Ferry 193
Coryell's Inn 193
Coryell, John, Cornelius, Emanuel 195, 196
Count Axel Oxenstierna 69
"Count Survillier" 174
Crayola Crayons, Crayola Experience 213
Crisis Papers 171
Croghan, George 216
Cromwell, Oliver 142
Crosswicks Creek 174
Cullington, England 51
Cumberland County 76
Cumberland County Historical Society 80
Cumberland County Prehistorical Museum 76, 80
Cunanan, Andrew 107
Custis 80

Daniel S. Frawley Stadium 122
Dartmouth College 247
Davis, Jefferson 96
"deathbed edition" 139
de Verenigde Oostindische Compagnie 23
DeBraak, His Majesty's Sloop of War 20
Decatur, Lieutenant Stephen 137
Declaration of Independence 216
Delaware
    and Bay Lighthouse Foundation 47
    & Hudson Canal 248
    and Raritan Canal 177
    Aqueduct 248
    Bay 4, 17, 24, 67
    Bay and River Pilots Association 22
    Bay Lighthouse Keepers & Friends Association, 38
    Bay Oyster Restoration Project 38
    bay oysters 61
        Bay Schooner Project 34
    Breakwater East End 47
    Canal 191
    City 22
    D&R Canal 189
    Front Street 152
    House 226
    Lackawanna and Western Railroad 226
    Memorial Bridge 21
    River 9, 12, 99, 111
    River & Bay Authority 47
    River Basin 235
    Deepening project 201
    East Branch 10, 250
    Riverkeeper 201
    Master, Deputy 235
    West Branch 10, 250
    State of 97, 116, 121
    Upper 242, 247
    Water Gap 202, 220, 221
    Water Gap National Recreation Area

275

222, 231
River watershed 8
Delhi, New York 252
DeMarco, Rich 75, 80
de Nemours, Eleuthère Irénée du Pont 121
de Vries, David Pietersz 17
Dermo 36
Dingman Andrew, Andrew III 233
Dingman's Falls 234
Dingman's Ferry 233
"disappearing guns" 98, 99
Dividing Creek 34
"Dixie" 118
Dixon, Jeremiah 19, 118
Dock Street 154
Dorchester, NJ 34
Dorrance, John T. 131
Doubleday, Maj. General Abner 96
Douglas, William O. 230
Downe Township 33, 58
Dripps, Isaac 176
Duffield, John 79
Duke Ellington 134
Duke of York 87, 111, 152, 162
dugout canoes 10
Durham boats, John Durham, Durham, PA 211
Dutch 9, 67, 68, 85, 116, 192, 221, 233, 245
Dutch East India Company 24
Dutch explorers 10
Dutch West India Company 9, 67, 86
Dutot, Antoine, Dutotsburg, Dutot School & Museum 225
DWIC 69
Dylan, Bob 138

Eakins, Thomas 54
East Branch Delaware 10, 250
East Fenwick 91
East Jersey 146, 162

Easton Flag 217
Easton, PA 191, 213
Easton, Treaty of 216
East Point Light 43
egrets 93
Elbow of Cross Ledge 41
Elfreth's Alley 157
Elizabethtown, NJ 222
Ellis Island 157
Elmer, Ebenezer 79
Elmer, Jonathan 79
Elmer, Timothy 79
Eloise Moore 52
Elsinboro Township 85, 101
Empire State Building 251
Endicott Period, Endicott, William C. 99
England 51, 85, 111, 151, 156
England, King of 111
English 111
English Civil War 142
English dandies 11
English Quakers 163
Episcopalian 77
Erie Canal 189
Erie Railroad 246
Erwinna 202
Esopus 221
Esterbrook Pen Company 132
Europe 14
Europeans 9
Ewing, Thomas 79

factorij 161
Fairview 17
"falles, the" 85
Farnsworth Avenue 171
Farnsworth, Thomas, 172
"father of Pragmatism" 240
Federal Water Pollution Control Act 199
Fenwick Grove 87

Index

Fenwick, Major John 86, 163
Fiji Mermaid 21
Fillmore, President Millard 246
Financial Center Development Act 121
Finland 68
Finns 72
Finn's Point 105, 107
Fisherman's Wharf 29
Fishtown 14, 150
Fitch, John 168
Fithian, Philip Vickers 79
Flemish bond 89, 124
Flying Stag 71
Fogel Grip 69, 115
Ford, Bridget 156
Ford, Gerald 27
Ford, Henry 231
Ford, Philip 153, 156
Forks, The 213,
Fort DuPont 100
Fortescue 50
Fortescue Creek 51
Fortescue House 51
Fort Casimir 66, 110, 117
Fort Christina 71, 84, 117
Fort Christina Park 115
Fort Decker 245
Fort Delaware, Fort Delaware State Park 93, 97, 106
Fort Dix, New Jersey 107
Fort Depuy, Nicholas 227
Fort DuPont 28, 100
Fort Elfsborg 67, 73, 84
Fort Hancock 100
Fort Mercer 124, 125, 129
Fort Mifflin 125, 127, 128, 129
Fort Miles 28,
Fort Mosquito 84
Fort Mott 99-101
Fort Nassau 70, 161

Fort New Gothenborg 73
Fort Orange 161
Fort Saulsbury 100,
Fort Trinity (Fort Trefaldighet) 73
Fort Wilhelmus 161
Fourteen Foot Bank 39, 44
Foster, Herbert and Preston 53
Fox, George 143, 163
Frampton, William 154
Franklin, Benjamin 127, 133, 151, 157, 164, 168, 214
Franklin, William 79, 164, 168
Fredericksburg 102
French 9
French & Indian Wars 215, 222, 247
Frenchtown 202, 240
Fresnel lens 45
Frick, Henry 135
Front Street 152
Fulton Fish Market 198
Fulton, Robert 169

Garden State 131
Garrison House, Garrison Lodge 53
Gale, Dr. Henry 94
Gandy's Beach 57
Gandy, Miles 57
"General of the Sea" 142
George II 168
George III 247
German POWs 107
German U-boats 28
Gettyburg 93, 95, 106
Gibbon House 80
Gilbert, Elizabeth 202
Gilbert, Linus 170
Gilligan, Painter John 60
Godyn's Bay 17
Godyn, Samuel 17
Gorey, Edward 167

277

Gothenburg, Sweden 85
"Governor-for-Life" 12
Goose, 50
Glassboro 90
Glenwood, The 226
Gloucester, NJ 67
Golden Gate Bridge 186
Goodwin, Abigail 89
Governor William Franklin 164
GPS 39
"Grand Fairs" 114
"Grandpop Gilligan" 60
Grant, U.S. 27, 166
Gray Goose 50
Great Britain 179
Greeley, Horace 27
Green Bank 164
Greene, Colonel Christopher 125
Green Door 50
greenhead flies 84
Greenwich Boat Works 81
Greenwich, New Jersey 75
Grey, Zane, Museum 249
Greyhound 78
Grey Towers, Heritage Association 239
Gulielma, (Guli), Penn 152
Gustavus Adolphus II 68
Guthrie, Woody 137

Haddonfield 7, 125
Hagley Museum 121
Halve Maen, Half Moon 23
Hamburg, Germany 40
Hamilton, Alexander 114
Hamilton, George 81
Hancock, Judge William 88, 89
Hancock, New York 251
Harbor of Refuge Breakwater, Lighthouse 46
Harrison, Burton H. 97
Harrison, William Henry 27

Harvard 240
Hart, Moss 194
Harvey Wallbanger 81
Hawk's Nest 247
Haynes, Frederick 245
headboats 55
Heislerville 43
Hendrix, Jimi 138
Henry VII 161
Hepburn, Stacy 79
Hereford Inlet Light 49
"Heroine of Red Bank" 7
Heritage of the Desert 249
herons 93
Hessian 129, 173, 179
Hessian Grenadier guards 125
Heyes, Peter 17
Hicks, Edward 14
Higbee, Betty 53
Higbee. Jim 56
Higbee's Marina, Restaurant 53
"High Mightinesses" 70
High Point monument 245
Hindloopen 24
"His Master's Voice" 133
Hobart Book Village 253
Hoerenkill 19
Holland 18, 24, 85, 145, 207
Holme, Thomas 149
Hoorn 17
"Holy Experiment" 156
Hope Creek Generating Station 92
Hopkinson, Francis 172
Horowitz, Vladimir 134
Hossitt, Gillis 17
Hotel Cape May 28
Hotel Charlesworth 53
Howard, Lt. McHenry 96
Howe, General William 125
Howell, Richard 79

278

Index

Hudson, Henry 12, 23, 76
Hudson River 13, 198, 221
Huguenot 222
Hunter, Andrew, Jr. 79
Hunterdon County, NJ 207
Hurricane Connie, Diane 201

ibis 93
Independence Hall 157
Independence Seaport Museum 157
Indians 10, 18, 25, 215, 225
Interstate I-95 157
Ireland 142, 144
Irish 157
Island Beach Park 169
"Island of Pines" 161

Jacob Jones 137
Jacob's Creek 181
Jacobite Rebellion 76
Jacobson, Marcus 112
Jäger 183
James, Reuben 137
James II 153
J & E Riggin 52
Jackson, Andrew 27
Jackson Street 28
Jamestown 12, 24
Jelly Roll Morton 134
Jennings, Samuel 168
Jervis, John Bloomfield 246
Jessup's Tavern 114
Jimmy Rodgers 134
Jockey Hollow 184
Joe Flogger Shoal 44
Joe Sixpack 156
John A. Warner 65
John & Peter's 194
Johnson, Colonel Robert Gibbon 88
Johnson, Eldrige 133

Johnson, Sir William 216
Jones, Jacob 137
Jorgenson, Poul 207
Joseph, Chester P. 39
Josephine Jaquette Memorial Research Library 92
Judy Johnson Field 122
Jus Gentium, Law of Nations 161
Justison, Andrew 118

Kaigns Point 133
Kalmar Nyckel 69, 71
Kansas 14
Kashagawigamog 50
Kechemeche 29
Kellogg Bridge Company 107
Kemper, Virginia Governor James L. 106
Kent, The 163
Kentucky 27
Kernstown, VA 95
Key, Francis Scott 96
Key, John 151
King of Sweden 68
King Nummy Trail 25
Kingston, New York 221
King William County Courthouse 87
Kittatinny 15
Kittatinny House 226
Kitty Hawk, USS 136
knotty pine 58
Kyriakodis, Harry 57

Lackawaxen, PA 248
Lafayette College 219
Lambert, Capt. John 196
Lamberton, NJ 102
Lambertville, NJ, Lambertville House 195–197
Lanson, Snooky 134
Lathrop, William L. 194

279

Laurie, Gawen 163
Lawrence, James 165
Lazy K Bar Ranch 233
Leaves of Grass 7, 139
Lee 80
Lehigh Valley 217
Lehigh River 207, 213, 214
Leipsic 32
Leesburg 33
Leeward Islands 71
Lena Blackburne Baseball Rubbing Mud 10
Lenape 13, 198
Lenape Wihittuck 13
Lend-Lease program 101
L'Enfant, Pierre 127
Lenni Lenape 13, 76, 149, 161, 204
Lennox 187
Levers, Robert 216
Lewes Creek 17
Lewes, Delaware 17, 72
Liberty Bell 217
Lighthouse Challenge 49
Lighthouse Road 107
Lindestrom, Peter 199
Lincoln, Abe 166
Lincoln, Mary Todd 166
Liston Rear Range Light 108
Little Creek 32
"livery of seisin" 113
Liverpool 125
Lobster House 29
lock keepers 190
Loe, Thomas 143
Logan, James 214
log cabin 71
London 78, 149
London Virginia Company 11
Lord Baltimore 19, 117, 118, 152, 153
Lord John Fortescue 51
Lore, Ada C. 34

Lumberville 24
Louis Armstrong 17
Louisiana 1
"Lough Erne" 19
"love apples" 10
Lumberville, PA 202
Lubbock, F. R. 96
Lucas, Nicholas 163
"Lunch With Uncle Pete" 54

Macroom Castle 142
Mad Batter, The 28
Maddock, Thomas, Thomas Maddock's Sons 187
Mahackamack 45
Maillard, Louis 175
Manayunk 15
Manhattan 69, 87, 113, 162
Mannington Mills 91
Mannington, Township of 91
Maneto 91
"manor lots" 77
Marine Corps Band 27
Market Square 79
Market Street 89
Marquis de Lafayette 219
Martin, David 214
Maryland 19, 118
Mason, Charles 118
Mason-Dixon line 19, 119
Massachusetts 85, 150,
Master and Commander 21
Matamoras 238
Matennecunk Island 9, 161
Mauch Chunk 14, 219
Maull, Nehemiah 42
Maurice River 32, 35, 43
Maurice River Historical Society 43
Maurice River Lighthouse 43
Mauricetown 75

Index

Mawhood, General Charles 88
Mayflower 25
McClellan, George B. 94
McConkey's Ferry, Inn 180, 181
Meade, George 49
Mellon, Andrew 135
Mencken, H. L. 143
menhaden 19, 20
Mercer, General Hugh 124
Merlin 125
Mexican-American War 102
Mey, Captain Cornelius Jacobsen 9, 24, 161
Miah Maull Light 43
Miah Maull Shoal 42
Michaelius, Reverend Jonas 70
Mickle Street 139
Middle Colonies 10
Mifflin, Thomas 127
Milford, NJ, PA, DE; Knob 202, 207, 235, 240, 242
Millbrook Village, Days 27, 28
"Millionaire's Row" 219
Millville 27, 57, 91
Minisink Ford 247
Minisink Valley Historical Society 246
Minor League 9, 115
Minuit, Peter 69, 76, 116
Minquas 70
Minquas Kill 70,
Miss Fortescue 55
Mississippi 10
Missouri 14
Mohawk Nation 247
Molasses 60
Molly-Polly Chunker 219
Money Island 59, 61
Montague, NJ 235
Moorestown Mall 137
Morris Canal 217
Morristown, NJ 184, 222

Morse, Henry G. 135
Mott, Captain John 102
Mott, Major General Gershom 102
Mount Jefferson 250, 251
Mount Vernon 184
MSX 36
Mt. Holly, NJ 180
Mud Island 127
Muddy Waters 138
Muir, John 239
multinucleated sphere X 36
Munsi 13
muskrats 52, 53
Myggenborg 84
Nantuxent Creek 61
Narrowsburg, NY 248
National Guard 54
National Lampoon's Christmas Vacation 62
National Park Service 224, 229, 240
Navasink 15
Navy destroyer 136
Netherlands, The 13, 221
Neversink River 245
New Albion 85
New Amstel 111, 113
New Amsterdam 110, 150
New Brunswick 190
New Buccaneer 81
New Castle 110, 117
New Castle upon Tyne 112
Newgate Prison 145, 146
New Gothenburg 73
New Haven, Colony, Puritans 25, 85
New Hope, Pennsylvania 192–194, 240
New Hope Mills 193)
New Jersey 9, 32, 86, 126, 131, 136, 161, 170, 173, 176, 178, 180, 188, 217, 235
New Jersey Gazette 168
New Jersey Lighthouse Society (www.njlhs.org) 49

281

New Netherland(s) 67, 69, 74, 150, 221
New Sweden 70, 72, 74 84, 110, 116
New Wales 146
New World 71
New York (City) 36, 87, 111, 150, 189, 198, 225, 229, 230, 235
New York & Erie Railroad 246
New York Harbor, Bay 67, 172
New York Ship Building Corporation 135
New York State 229, 245, 248, 250, 251, 252
New Netherland 67, 69, 111, 116, 161
Nicolls, Colonel Richard 111
Nieu Nederlandt 9
"Nipper" 133
"No Cross, No Crown" 146
Nomini Hall 80
Noort Rivier 67
North America 146
North Delaware Avenue 150
"Northhampton County Liberty Bell" 217
Northern Harriers 30
Northwest Passage 13, 23
North Wildwood 49
Norway 68
"no-see-ems" 84

O'Hara, Theodore 106
Ohio, Valley 14, 215, 216
oil tankers 10
Oklahoma 14
Oklahoma, USS 136
Old Dominion 80
Old Dutch House 112
Old Mine Road 221, 245
"Old Stone Jug" 133
Olympia, USS 158
Omega-3 20
Ontario 14
"open discourse" 147
Ordnance Building 100

Original People 13
Örn 84
Osenosisakak 50
Osius, Frederick Jacob 228
Owen, John 144
Oxenstierna, Count Axel 69
Oxford 143
oyster 32
oyster dredges (dredging) 33, 52
oyster saloons 32
oyster schooner(s) 33, 52

"Painted Ladies" 28
Paine, Thomas 171
Painter John 57, 60
Paleo-Indians 221
palisades 73
Palmer, Harry H. 48
Paris 144
Parry, Benjamin 193
Parsons, William 214
Pastorius, Francis Daniel 151
patroons 17
Paulsboro, New Jersey 49, 125
Pea Patch Island 93
Pearl 125
Peggy Stewart 80
Peirce, Charles Sanders 240
Penn, Admiral Sir William 143
Penn, John 214
Penn, Thomas 14, 214
Penn Treaty Park 150
Penn, William 14, 19, 113, 117, 141, 149, 193
Penn, William, Jr. 156
Penn's Landing 157
Pennel, Joseph 54
Pennsbury Manor 153
Pennsville, Township 99
Pennsylvania 14, 117, 146, 149, 170, 180, 215, 234, 249

Index

Pennsylvania Academy of the Fine Arts 53
Pennsylvania Highlands Trail 211
Pennsylvania, Royal Charter for 149
Pentagon 97
peregrine Falcons 30
Perrault, Suzanne 197
Perth Amboy 164
pesos de ocho 216
Petersburg 102
PGA Championships 227
Pidcock, Jonathan 192
Philadelphia 76er's 139
Philadelphia 32, 40, 88, 125, 149, 150 166, 168, 174, 217, 225, 236
Philadelphia City Hall 150
Philadelphia Electric Company 136
Philadelphia's Lost Waterfront 157
Philadelphia Naval Shipyard 139
Philadelphia Orchestra with Leopold Stokowski 134
Philadelphia, Old City 157
Philadelphia Sketch Club 53
Philco 54
Phillipsburg 207, 217
Phillips Mill 194
Picketts' charge, General George 96, 106
Pierce, Franklin 27
Pike's Peak 102
Pike, Zebulon 102
Pilgrims 81
Pinchot, Gifford 239
Pitt, William (Lord Chattam) 173
Pitz, Henry 54
Plaza Hotel 36
pneumatic-caisson 44
Pohatcong Township, NJ 209
Point Breeze 174
Point Pleasant 202
Polly 78
Popeye 39

Port Jervis, NY 229, 245
Port Norris 32
Port Penn, Delaware 108
Portuguese 68
Plowden, Sir Edmund 85
Plymouth 25
Post HQ 100
Powhatan 11
Pratt, Charles, 1st Earl of Camden 133
Presbyterian 77
Prevost. Paul Henri-Mallet 204
Prime Hope Mills 193
Princeton University 79
Princeton, Battle of 183
Printz, Johan Bjornsson 72, 84
Printzhoff 73
privateers 26
Pumpkin Flood 209
Puritan(s) 143, 146

Quaker(s) 9, 16, 143, 145–147, 149, 150, 151, 154, 156, 163, 192
Quaker Oats 141
Quick, Thomas 236–238
Quinton's Bridge 88

Raccoon Creek 163
Radio Corporation of America 133
rafts, timber 189, 217
Rago Arts, David Rago 197
Rall, Colonel Johann 182, 183
Rando, Robert 202
Rapid Stream of the Lenape 13
Raritan River 190
"Rat call! Rat call!" 93
RCA Camden 134
Read House & Gardens 114
Reagan, Ronald 27
Rear Range lights 38, 49, 107
"recording laboratories: 134

Red Bank 124, 173
Red Bank Battlefield 126
Red Cross, American 174
Redfield, Edward 194
Reese, William R. 107
Religious Society of Friends 77, 143
re-enactors 97
Rensselaerswyck Manor 17
Reuben James 137
Revell House 164
Revolutionary War 75, 124, 166, 173, 245
Rhode Island 14
Rick 9, 49, 61, 240, 251
Ridder, Peter Hollander 72
Riders of the Purple Sage 249
Riegel, Benjamin 209
Riegelsville, Pennsylvania 211
Rights of Man 172
Ringing Rocks County Park 208
Ringoes, New Jersey 197
Rising, Johan 73, 84
river pilot(s) 21
Robbi, 50
Robbins 33
Roebling Company, Museum, Town of 186
Roebling, John Augustus 185, 186
Roebuck 125
Roosevelt, Theodore 226
Rosenkrans House 232
"Round John" 72
Royden, William 132
rufa red knot 63
"Rum Row" 50
Rutgers University 35

Second Battle of Bull Run 102
Salem County Historical Society 92
Salem Courthouse 87
Salem Creek, 85
Salem, NJ 84, 85, 86, 87, 89, 90, 91

Salem Nuclear Generating Station 92
Salem Oak 86
Salem River 101
Salem Standard and *Jerseyman* 101
Salem-Woodstown Road 87
Samuel Jacoby 52
Samuels, Christian 162
"Sandy Foundation Shaken" 145
Sandy Hook, Lighthouse 49, 100
San Francisco 28
Santhoeck 73
Santo Domingo (Dominican Republic) 225
Saratoga Springs 225
Savage, Annette 175
Savannah, NS 136
Scots 111, 222
Schmidt's 155
Schuylkill River 73, 127, 149
screw-pile technology 45
Sea Breeze 64
Sea Breeze Hotel 65
Sea Breeze Tavern 64
Sea Girt 49
Seahorse Cottage 53
Sears, Roebuck & Company 137
Sears Silvertone 137
Seaside Heights, NJ 170
Settlers Monument 238
Seven Years War 215
Shackamaxon 14, 149
shad, American 198–200
Sharp, John 101
sharp-shinned hawks 30
Shawnee Inn 27
Shawnee-Minisink 227
Sheffield Farms 253
Shellenger's Landing 29
Shield of Stockton 163
Ship Inn 208
Ship John Inn 81

Index

Ship John Lighthouse 40, 82
Ship John Shoal 40, 81
Shipley, William 119
Shippen, Judge Edward 166
Shippen, Peggy 166
"shoebee" 27
Shukaitis, Nancy 230
Siconese 18
Simcoe, John Graves 88
Sinnickson's Landing 101
Skute, Sven 74, 84
"Sleeping with the Ghosts" 128
slow food movement 36
smallpox 93, 144
Smith, C. Harold 213
Smithsonian Institute 177
Smith, William 51
Smyrna, Delaware 137
Sockwell 33
Spanish-American War 99
Spruance, Benton 54
Society of Friends 77, 143
Sousa, John Philip 27
South River 67
Spanish 11
Spotsylvania 102
Stacy, Mahlon 184
Stauber, Dr. L.A. 35
Stevens, John 176
Stephens, Adam 182
Stockton, NJ 202
Stoker, Bram 138
Stonewall Jackson's army 95
Stowman's Shipyard 52
Stuart, Gilbert 173
Studebaker 59
Stuyvesant, Peter 73, 110, 116
submarine (power) cables 38, 41
Summer White House 27
Sunset Beach 29

Sunset Boulevard 30
Superstorm Sandy 55, 170
"surplus site" 97
Sussex 19
Suyd Rivier 67
Swedes, Swedish, Sweden 68, 70, 71, 74, 110, 115, 150, 192
Swedish Granary 81

Tamamend 14
Tashiowycan 162
Taylor, George (Easton) 216
Taylor, Capt. Samuel 96
Taylor, President Zachary 96
"tea party" 79
Tea Party, Boston 88
Teedyuscung (Chief) 215–216
ten-inch 100
Texas 14, 96
Thayer, Major Simeon 127
The Albion Knights for the Conversion of the Twenty-Three Kings 85
The Affable 14
"the great cow chase" 88
The King's Highway 7, 126
"The Long Finn" 112
The Peaceable Kingdom 14
"The Ripps" 29
the rocks 115
The Society of Friends 77, 143
"the starving time" 11
These Thirty Years 231
Thirty Years War 68
Three Forts Ferry 12
Three Lower Counties 117
Tifffany, Louis Comfort 219
Tinicum 38
Tinicum Island 73
Tinicum Rear Range light 49
tobacco 85)

Tocks Island. Dam 229, 231
Tower Hill 143
Trenton Makes . . . 185
Trenton, New Jersey 168, 184
Trent-towne 184
Trent, William 184
Tropical Storm Allison 202
Tripoli 137, 165
Trinity Baptist Church 134
tri-states monument 242
"Truth Exalted" 145
Tuckahoe 24
Tucker's Beach Lighthouse 49
Tuckerton Seaport 49
tugboats 10
Tusten, Lt. Colonel Benjamin 247
Twin Lights of Navasink 49
Twain, Mark 22
twelve-inch guns 100

U-858 28
U-Boat 28
Unami 13
Unilachtigo 13
Union Guard Monument 106
Union, guards, forces 93, 95
Union Mills Paper Manufacturing Company 193, 198
Union Street 167
University of Delaware's College of Marine Studies 44
University of Pennsylvania 170, 172
Upper Delaware Scenic Byway 246-47
Upperville, VA 32
US Coast Guard 29
US Coast and Geodetic Survey (USCG) 240
US National Park Service 224, 229, 231, 232
Usselinx, Willem 68
Utah, USS 136

Utrecht 69

Valley Forge 88, 125
Valley of the Swans, The 17
Van Campen's Inn, Issac 223
van Rensselaer, Kiliaen 17
Varken's Kill 85
Veltscheeder. Peter 162
Verhulsten 161
Verrazano, Giovanni da 13
Versace, Gianni 107
Vicksburg, battle of 95
Victor Talking Machine Company 133
Victrola 133
Victorian 23, 28
Volendam Windmill Museum 208
Virginia 12, 19, 87, 118
Virgin Queen 15
Virginia colonies 11
VOC 23, 24
Voltaire 14, 149
von Dunop, Colonel Count Carl Emil Kurt 125, 182
von Wiederholdt, Lieutenant Andreas 179

Walking Purchase, "Ye Hurry Walk" 14, 214
Waller, Fats 134
Walloons 9
Walpack Center, New Jersey 231, 233
Walpack Historical Society 232
Walvis 17
Wanamaker, John 27
Warhol, Andy 132
Waring, Fred 227
Waring Blendor 228
War of 1812 19, 165
Warner House 65
Washington 22, 23, 29
Washington's Crossing 179
Washington's Crossing Bridge 233

Washington's Crossing State Park 191
Washington, General George 9, 180–184, 193, 195, 211
Washington Street Wharf 157
Waters, Mudddy 138
Wayne, General "Mad" Anthony 88
weakfish 52
Weakfish Capitol of the World 50
Webster, Daniel 175
Wedding of the Waters 251
Weir, Peter 21
Welcome 113
West, Benjamin 14
West Delaware 10
West Jersey 146, 151, 163
West India Company 18, 24, 67
West Point 20
West, Thomas 10, 24
Westville 60
West Virginia 29
whaling station, industry 17, 25
Wheaton Glass 91
Whitall, Ann Cooper 7, 124, 126
Whitall, James 124
White, Josiah 191
Whitman, Walt 7, 138
Wilde, Oscar 138
William Augustus, Duke of Cumberland 76
Williamsburg 76
William of Orange 161
Willing, Thomas 118
Willingtown 119
Wilmington 120, 122
Wilmington, Delaware 115, 120
Wilmington Riverfront project 122
Wilson, Woodrow 187
Windward House, The 28
Winterthur Museum 81
wire rope 185

Wisconsin 14
Wisconsin Glacier 10
Wistarburgh 90
Wistarburgh Glass 90
Wistar, Casper 90
Witness Monument 242
Woodstock 59
Wood Street 166
World War I 28, 30 100, 107, 207
World War II 28-29, 33, 107, 135, 137, 239
Worthington, C. C. 227
Wren, Megan 33
Wright, Patience Lovell 173
Wyanamettamo 162
Wyeth, N. C. 54
Wissahickon 15

Yardship 136
Yaugh House 223
Ye Greate Street 77
Young Frankenstein 54
Zuydt 13
Zwaanendael 17
Zwaanendael Museum 20

About the Author

In a career in graphic arts that has spanned more than thirty years, Hal Taylor has worked as a typographer, logo designer, type designer, and illustrator. He has provided hand-lettering services for award-winning designer John Langdon and has also taught graphic design at the college level. His illustrations have been featured in various gallery exhibits at the Philadelphia Sketch Club, the oldest artist's club in the Western Hemisphere. In addition, Taylor continues to work on a freelance basis for Townsend Press, a publisher of scholastic works and classic and contemporary literature. He has also developed numerous type designs that are available at many online font resources. Writing is a relatively new venture, but one he hopes to continue in the future. He makes his home in historic New Jersey.